Federal Benefits for Veterans,

Dependents, and Survivors

A Comprehensive Guide to the Process & Benefits
Available for U.S. Military Veterans,
their Dependents, & Survivors

D1418154

Federal Benefits for Veterans,

Dependents, and Survivors

A Comprehensive Guide to the Process & Benefits Available for U.S. Military Veterans, their Dependents, & Survivors

Judge Hal Moroz

Washington, D.C.   Atlanta   New York

Federal Benefits for Veterans,
Dependents, and Survivors

A Comprehensive Guide to the Process & Benefits
Available for U.S. Military Veterans, their Dependents, & Survivors

Judge Hal Moroz

The "Federal Benefits for Veterans, Dependents and Survivors" section in this book is a reprinted copy of the official U.S. government 2013 edition of this publication and is herein identified with a new ISBN. It is a reprinted copy made in accordance with the directives of the U.S. government on that publication.

"Defending America's Defenders: Advocating on Behalf of Georgia's Military Veterans" is reprinted with permission from the Georgia Bar Journal, Volume 7, Number 4, February 2002. Copyright State Bar of Georgia.
Statements expressed within this article should not be considered endorsements of products or procedures by the State Bar of Georgia.

Unless otherwise noted, Scripture quotations are from
The King James Version of the Bible.

Hal Moroz presents the information in this book as an informational service to its readers. **While this book and the information in this book may concern legal issues, it is not legal advice.** Moreover, due to the rapidly changing nature of the law, Hal Moroz and any other entity mentioned herein makes no warranty or guarantee concerning the accuracy or reliability of the content.
If you have specific questions related to information available in this book, you are encouraged to consult an attorney who can investigate the particular circumstances of your situation.

The opinions expressed in this book are solely the opinions of the author and do not necessarily reflect the opinions of any individual, groups, organizations or business or government entities mentioned herein.
The quotes, selected writings, and articles contained in this book
are reprinted with permission or
are permissible for use under existing law.

Printed in the United States of America

4

"With malice toward none, with charity for all,
with firmness in the right as God gives us to see the right,
let us strive on to finish the work we are in,
to bind up the nation's wounds,
**to care for him who shall have borne the battle
and for his widow and his orphan,**
to do all which may achieve and cherish a just and lasting peace
among ourselves and with all nations."

~~~ President Abraham Lincoln
Second Inaugural Address, March 4, 1865

Federal Benefits for Veterans, Dependents, and Survivors

A Comprehensive Guide to the Process & Benefits
Available for U.S. Military Veterans,
their Dependents, & Survivors

Contents

Preface
Duty, Honor, Country

~ ~ ~ ~ ~

"We see these soldiers in our mind as old and wise.
We see them as something like the Founding Fathers, grave and gray haired. But
most of them were boys when they died, and they gave up two lives –
the one they were living and the one they would have lived. When they died,
they gave up their chance to be husbands and fathers and grandfathers.
They gave up their chance to be revered old men.
They gave up everything for our country, for us."

~~~ *President Ronald Reagan*
Veterans Day National Ceremony, November 11, 1985

~ ~ ~ ~ ~

This is a book for, by, and about veterans. It is a comprehensive guide for navigating through the Department of Veterans Affairs (VA) and the myriad of benefits and services available to our nation's veterans, their dependents, and their survivors. It is an important work!

As a veteran and an attorney and counselor at law, both as an advocate and judge, I have witnessed the plight of military veterans and their families in understanding how the VA works, and what assistance is available to them. Many of these veterans and their families have suffered hardships directly connected to their military service. These veterans -- soldiers, sailors, airmen, and marines -- served 24 hours a day, 7 days a week, 365 days a year as the watchmen on the walls of this *"Bright Shining City,"* as President Reagan called it. These patriots provided the very blanket of freedom and security that allows us to live our lives as God intended!

The first part of this book contains a legal article I wrote years ago for the *Georgia Bar Journal* entitled, "Defending America's Defenders: Advocating on behalf of Georgia's Military Veterans." Although it was originally written for

Georgia lawyers, so they could assist veterans, it was written in plain English for all veterans, and is readable and understandable by all veterans and their families. It was an instant success, winning praise from the Chief Justice of Georgia's Supreme Court at the time, along with hundreds of attorneys and thousands of veterans advocates. It was also the basis for a decade of Veterans Law seminars for the Institute of Continuing Legal Education in Georgia, culminating in my address to the Annual Convention of the State Bar of Georgia at Amelia Island, Florida, on June 5th, 2008.

Not a week goes by without someone asking for a reprint of this article. And while the law changes regularly with new precedent by our courts, new regulations by the executive branch, and new laws from our Congress, this work provides a general framework and rare insight to the whole process, followed by up-to-date information, contacts, and resources. Well, here it is, with the gracious consent of the *Georgia Bar Journal*.

The second major portion of this book, the "Federal Benefits for Veterans, Dependents and Survivors" section, is a reprinted copy of the official U.S. government 2013 edition of this publication, identified with a new ISBN. It is a reprinted copy published in accordance with the directives of the U.S. government for the reprinting of the publication. This is the authority on legislated benefits from the federal government, with a wide array of resources and contact information.

Combined, this book's sections form a comprehensive guide to the process and benefits available for U.S. military veterans, their dependents, and their survivors.

Federal Benefits ...

VA Claims ...

Federal Tort Claims ...

And more! This book covers them all!

And the beauty of this book is that it is a compact, portable reference for veterans and/or their family members when the need to know something about Veterans Law or VA benefits arises. More often than not, people contact me or other attorneys or veterans advocates for help on such matters, but many times those services incur costs. This book is a low-cost, simple guide to understanding the process and the bureaucracy. It does not eliminate the need for competent counsel in such matters, as this is not the purpose of this work. This book is designed to educate laymen in veterans matters, and better prepare them to ask questions of the VA or legal counsel, should the need arise. In the words of Sir Francis Bacon, *"Knowledge is power."* This book is powerful!

This book is a resource for veterans and their families, including the legions of veterans who email and call me for help, or the pastors and friends of veterans who contact me with urgent questions from survivors about the final matters of loved ones who have passed away, or those who seek action regarding the more than 611,000 backlogged claims at the VA as of this writing. Making the complex as simple as possible is the least we can do for those who, as President Ronald Reagan said, *"gave up everything for our country, for us."*

And there exists today an overwhelming need for assistance in the veterans' community. The sad fact is that the federal government has not focused the resources necessary to adequately support our military veterans in a timely manner. It is one of the reasons why I represent veterans and wrote and edited this work, and it was the driving force behind my founding of the Veterans Law Center, Inc. (VLC), in 2008. The VLC, located on the internet at VeteransLawCenter.org, is a non-profit, 501(c)(3) charitable organization that serves the interests of America's 24 million military veterans. It does so by fielding questions from veterans, their family members, and others interested in assisting veterans. And as resources permit, the VLC provides additional support and counsel to America's honorably discharged veterans, wherever they may be, and does this free of charge to the veteran. It is a labor of love, steeped in the officer's creed of *"Duty, Honor, Country."*

Thank you for reading this book ... It is my hope and prayer it will be a great blessing to you!

Thank you for your service! Welcome home!

With every best wish, I remain,

At your service,

Judge Hal Moroz
U.S. Army Retired
Attorney & Counselor at Law

~ ~ ~ ~ ~

"The willingness with which our young people are likely to serve in any war, no matter how justified, shall be directly proportional to how they perceive the Veterans of earlier wars were treated and appreciated by their nation."

~~~ President George Washington

"Experience is the teacher of all things."

~~~ Julius Caesar

Defending America's Defenders:

Advocating on Behalf of Georgia's Military Veterans

By Harold Ronald Moroz

With some 769,000 veterans residing in the state of Georgia, the prospect that your practice will encounter a veterans law issue is great. Fort Benning, Fort Stewart and Kings Bay Naval Submarine Base are but a few of the military bases located throughout the state, and Georgia also hosts a large veterans' support structure that includes Veterans' Administration hospitals, clinics and assistance centers. Based on this large military presence, Georgia attorneys have a good chance of being called upon to represent a client who has a claim based on his or her status as a veteran.

Veterans law issues manifest themselves in a myriad of ways. They may be embedded in a civil or criminal law matter, or arise as an ancillary issue in the form of a veteran's claim or a federal tort claim involving injury, death or damage to property. The underlying cause of the event that gives rise to the claim may be rooted in a known or unknown service-connected disability (e.g., post-traumatic stress disorder) or in a negligent act of an agent of the federal government. Regardless of how they arise, attorneys must be attuned to the unique issues and complex, time-sensitive procedures that veterans law issues bring in to play.

This article examines the procedures that need to be followed in pursuing two of the most common types of claims involving veterans: (a) a claim before the Department of Veterans Affairs (VA); and (b) a claim brought under the Federal Tort Claims Act.[3] With regard to the first type of claim, this article presents an overview and analysis of both a typical claim before the VA and of an appeal to the U.S. Court of Appeals for Veterans Claims. The article then goes on to provide an overview and analysis of a claim prosecuted under the Federal Tort Claims Act.

ADJUDICATION OF A CLAIM BEFORE THE VA

A claim brought by a veteran before the VA traverses a myriad of gauntlets. (*See chart at right titled Veteran's Adjudication Process.*) After a claim is filed, the VA has a duty to assist the veteran in developing and establishing his or her claim,[4] and the relationship is non-adversarial. In addition, the VA has a duty to

February 2002

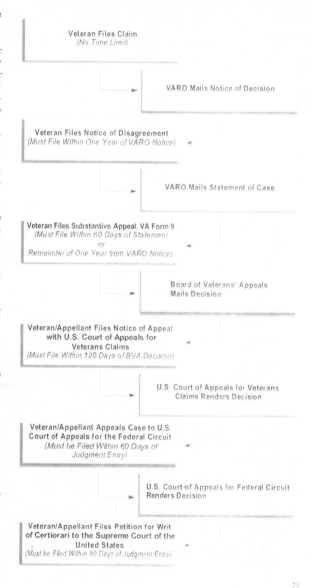

VETERAN'S ADJUDICATION PROCESS

Veteran Files Claim
(No Time Limit)

VARO Mails Notice of Decision

Veteran Files Notice of Disagreement
(Must File Within One Year of VARO Notice)

VARO Mails Statement of Case

Veteran Files Substantive Appeal, VA Form 9
(Must File Within 60 Days of Statement
or
Remainder of One Year from VARO Notice)

Board of Veterans' Appeals
Mails Decision

Veteran/Appellant Files Notice of Appeal
with U.S. Court of Appeals for
Veterans Claims
(Must File Within 120 Days of BVA Decision)

U.S. Court of Appeals for Veterans
Claims Renders Decision

Veteran/Appellant Appeals Case to U.S.
Court of Appeals for the Federal Circuit
(Must be Filed Within 60 Days of
Judgment Entry)

U.S. Court of Appeals for Federal Circuit
Renders Decision

Veteran/Appellant Files Petition for Writ
of Certiorari to the Supreme Court of the
United States
(Must be Filed Within 90 Days of Judgment Entry)

infer issues or claims not expressly raised by the veteran.[5] Recent legislation placed an even greater burden on the VA when it comes to assisting veterans at this juncture.[6]

Suffice it to say, the often long road traveled by a veteran's claim presented to the VA frequently begins rather innocently. A claim may be presented at any one of 58 VA Regional Offices (VARO) either informally[7] or formally on a VA Form 21-526. A typical claim can involve a hearing loss originating from the firing of weapons during military service, wherein the veteran seeks hearing aids, medical attention and/or monthly monetary compensation based on the severity of the disability. Once the claim is received, a threshold review is conducted to verify that the claimant is an eligible veteran. Character and dates of service are of particular concern.

Following this review of the claim and gathering of information, the claim, in most cases, will be referred to a VARO rating board. The board usually consists of three members, one of whom is a medical specialist. The board makes a determination of the claim on a "Rating Decision" which is a judgment as to whether the disability is service-connected. If it is determined to be service-connected, the VA will address that particular disability, including such options as further medical evaluation, the authorization of medical treatment at government expense and/or monthly monetary compensation. The veteran then is notified of the determination through an Award Letter or a Denial Letter.[8] When the latter is issued, the letter must include a statement of the reasons for the decision and a summary of the evidence considered by the VA.[9]

22

UNIQUE STANDARD OF PROOF: BENEFIT-OF-THE-DOUBT DOCTRINE

Peculiar to veterans law is the standard of proof used to decide a claim. When all material issues of record are considered and the evidence is in equipoise, the veteran will be given the benefit of the doubt. This Benefit-of-the-Doubt Doctrine, also called the Doctrine of Reasonable Doubt, has been codified.[10] In construing this doctrine, the U.S. Court of Appeals for Veterans Claims held that the veteran "need only demonstrate that there is an 'approximate balance of positive and negative evidence' in order to prevail. . . [and] the preponderance of the evidence must be against the claim for benefits to be denied."[11] In other words, the veteran is given the benefit of the doubt.

Should the veteran's claim be denied at the VARO level, the veteran has the right to appeal that decision. An appeal is perfected by a Notice of Disagreement (NOD) to the VARO. This notice consists of "a written communication from a claimant or his or her representative expressing dissatisfaction or disagreement with an adjudicative determination."[12] There is no formal language or particular VA form required in order to establish a NOD.

Once the NOD is received, the VARO must again review the file and either grant the claim or continue the denial. At this point, the VA may issue a decision in the form of a Statement of the Case, but it is has no statutory or regulatory deadline by which it must do so.[13]

Should the VARO continue the denial and issue a Statement of the Case, the veteran has the right to appeal the decision to the final arbiter of the administrative appellate process, the Board of Veterans' Appeals (BVA). Such an appeal is perfected on a VA Form 9, and must be filed by no later than 60 days from the mailing of the Statement of the Case or the end of the one-year period following the date of the mailing of the VA Letter of Denial, whichever is longer.[14]

Appeals to the BVA are considered *de novo*. The BVA will have the full record created by the VARO, and new documentary evidence and witnesses may be presented.[15]

BVA decisions are required to contain "a written statement of the Board's findings and conclusions, and the reasons or bases for those findings and conclusions, on all material issues of fact and law presented on the record."[16]

ADJUDICATION OF THE CLAIM BEFORE THE U.S. COURT OF APPEALS FOR VETERANS CLAIMS

Should the claim still be denied by the BVA, the veteran has the right to judicial appeal before the U.S. Court of Appeals for Veterans Claims. This court was established in November , pursuant to the Veterans' Judicial Review Act (VJRA),[17] and was previously called the U.S. Court of Veterans Appeals.[18] The court is located in Washington, D.C., and has exclusive jurisdiction to review VA BVA decisions.[19]

The immediate impact of the establishment of this new court,

VETERAN'S COURT PROCESS*

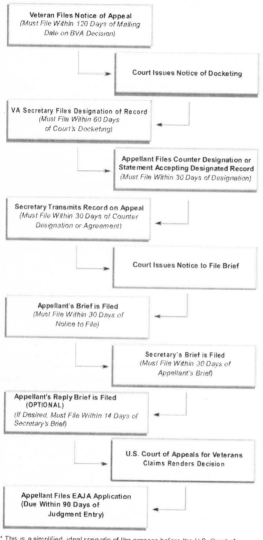

Veteran Files Notice of Appeal
(Must File Within 120 Days of Mailing Date on BVA Decision)

Court Issues Notice of Docketing

VA Secretary Files Designation of Record
(Must File Within 60 Days of Court's Docketing)

Appellant Files Counter Designation or Statement Accepting Designated Record
(Must File Within 30 Days of Designation)

Secretary Transmits Record on Appeal
(Must File Within 30 Days of Counter Designation or Agreement)

Court Issues Notice to File Brief

Appellant's Brief is Filed
(Must File Within 30 Days of Notice to File)

Secretary's Brief is Filed
(Must File Within 30 Days of Appellant's Brief)

Appellant's Reply Brief is Filed (OPTIONAL)
(If Desired, Must File Within 14 Days of Secretary's Brief)

U.S. Court of Appeals for Veterans Claims Renders Decision

Appellant Files EAJA Application
(Due Within 90 Days of Judgment Entry)

* This is a simplified, ideal scenario of the process before the U.S. Court of Appeals for Veterans Claims and does not include the court-ordered tele-conference following the Designation of Record.

championed by the Reagan administration, was twofold. First, it provided a legal remedy to the federal government's longstanding practice of barring the adjudication of claims beyond the VA level. Specifically, prior to the court's creation, if the VA decided to deny a veteran's claim, then the claim expired and the veteran had no judicial recourse.[20] Since the court's establishment, however, veterans have the right to appeal their claim beyond the VA level, and have their "day in court." Secondly, at the court-level, attorneys representing veterans before the U.S. Court of Appeals for Veterans Claims are entitled to reasonable fees and expenses.[21] In contrast, in a proceeding regarding benefits brought before the VA, a fee may not be charged, allowed or paid for the services of agents and attorneys before the date on which the BVA first makes a final decision on the claim.[22]

When a veteran files a Notice of Appeal with the court, the veteran, identified as the "appellant" by the court, effectively files suit against the federal government through the Secretary of Veterans Affairs, who is identified by the court as the "Secretary" or the "Appellee." Such appeals must be filed in a timely manner, that is, within 120 days following the mailing date of the BVA decision. (*See chart at left titled Veteran's Court Process.*)

Appeals to the court are argued primarily by legal brief, and the veteran and his or her counsel are not required to travel to Washington, D.C. Oral arguments are the exception to the rule, and are conducted by order of the court if requested by the appellant, or if the court deems such argument necessary. The court renders its ultimate decision based upon the record, the facts, the argu-

23

ments presented and the law. Attorneys representing veterans before the U.S. Court of Appeals for Veterans Claims are entitled to reasonable fees and expenses.23

A veteran prevailing in an action before the court also may be entitled to attorney's fees and expenses from the government under the Equal Access to Justice Act (EAJA).24 The EAJA provides:

> Except as otherwise specifically provided by statute, a court shall award to a prevailing party other than the United States fees and other expenses, . . . incurred by that party in any civil action (other than a case sounding in tort), including proceedings for judicial review of agency action, brought by or against the United States in any court having jurisdiction of that action, unless the court finds that the position of the United States was substantially justified or that special circumstances make an award unjust.25

To be awarded attorney fees and expenses under the EAJA, the appellant must file a complete, non-defective EAJA application that complies with the statutory guidelines of 28 U.S.C. § 2412, which, *inter alia*, require that the application be filed within 30 days of "final judgment" in the action. A U.S. Court of Appeals for Veterans Claims judgment becomes final, and is not appealable, 60 days after it is entered.26 Accordingly, the EAJA application is due within 90 days after judgment is entered. However, if the Secretary of Veterans Affairs and the veteran/appellant agree to a joint remand, and it is approved by the court, then such an order is considered an order of settlement that is "final and not appealable."27 Therefore, in the case of an order approving a joint remand, the EAJA application is due within 30 days of the date on which that order is entered.

It is an absolute necessity that the EAJA Application be filed in a timely manner. The filing deadline is jurisdictional, and the consequence of a late filing is its dismissal from court, no exceptions.28 Additional statutory requirements for the EAJA Application are as follows:

a. The appellant must show prevailing party status. This is done by both asserting such status and demonstrating how such status was attained.29

b. The appellant must show that his or her net worth at the time the appeal was filed did not exceed $2 million dollars.30

c. The appellant must allege that the government's position was not substantially justified.31

d. The appellant must file an itemized statement of the fees and expenses sought.32

Both the veteran/appellant and the VA can appeal a final decision by the U.S. Court of Appeals for Veterans Claims to the U.S. Court of Appeals for the Federal Circuit within 60 days after the former court's entry of judgment, provided that grounds for appeal exist.33 The Federal Circuit has exclusive jurisdiction to review any challenge to the validity of any statute or regulation or any interpretation thereof, and to interpret constitutional and statutory provisions to the extent presented and necessary to a decision in the matter under consideration.34 In turn, Federal Circuit decisions are appealable by either party to the Supreme Court of the United States by Writ of Certiorari. Petitions for Writ of Certiorari must be filed within 90 days of the Federal Circuit's entry of judgment.35

FEDERAL TORT CLAIMS ACT

Since the birth of our republic, and through most of our history, Americans could not sue the United States for property damage, personal injury or wrongful death caused by employees of the federal government. This was particularly true for veterans and retirees who historically maintained close proximity to government installations and availed themselves of government healthcare entitlements. Americans injured by the federal government relied exclusively on members of Congress to pass individual bills of relief to recover for injuries or property losses caused by federal employees. This procedure afforded most Americans inadequate remedies that resulted in little or no compensation at all for their losses.

Following several years of debate, most of which occurred during the Second World War, Congress passed the Federal Tort Claims Act (FTCA)36 in 1946. The FTCA allows individuals37 to recover from the United States for property damage, personal injury, and wrongful death caused by the negligence of a federal employee.38 Since the enactment of the FTCA, veterans and fellow Americans of all walks have recovered millions of dollars annually from the United States for the negligent acts of its employees.39

Under the FTCA, individuals may recover for numerous types of injuries, including, but not limited to, those suffered in traffic accidents, slips and falls in government facilities, medical treatment, etc.40 In the area of medical treatment, individuals may recover for injuries caused by surgical errors, failure to diagnose cancer, or any other negligent diagnosis or treatment.[41]

The FTCA is limited by a number of exceptions per which the government is not subject to suit, even if a private employer could be liable under the same circumstances. These exceptions include the Discretionary Function Exception, which bars a claim "based upon the exercise or performance or the failure to exercise or perform a discretionary function or duty on the part of a federal agency or an employee of the Government, whether or not the discretion involved be abused."[42] Another such exception involves purely constitutional issues. Specifically, an FTCA claim cannot be brought against the government based solely on conduct that violates the Constitution, because such conduct may have violated only federal law, not state law.[43]

STATE SUBSTANTIVE LAW APPLIES

Federal law governs the procedure for processing claims against the United States;[44] however, the FTCA specifies that the liability of the United States is to be determined "in accordance with the law of the place where the [allegedly tortious] act or omission occurred."[45] In an action under the FTCA in the state of Georgia, a claim must be based on state substantive law, and the federal court must apply the law Georgia state courts would apply in the analogous tort action.[46]

It is critical that claims be brought against the United States in a timely manner. Specifically, individuals must file their claim with the appropriate federal agency within two

years of discovery of the their injury.[47] The claim is a prerequisite to bringing a lawsuit against the United States, and its filing tolls the mandated two-year statute of limitations.[48] Accordingly, an individual who believes that he or she has been injured by the negligence of a federal employee[49] should not delay in making a claim against the federal agency.[50]

PROCEDURAL REQUIREMENTS

The first step beyond an initial investigation into the facts and the law underlying a potential FTCA claim is the filing of that claim against the United States on a Standard Form 95, Claim for Damage, Injury or Death. This form can be obtained from any military base legal office, VA hospital or via the Internet from the Government Printing Office. The claim may be filed with the Office of General Counsel for any Veterans Administration hospital or the Judge Advocate General office on any U.S. military installation. The claim may be filed in person or through the mail. The claimant must demand a "sum certain" on the face of his or her claim, and the failure to

state an amount may result in the dismissal of the claim.[51]

A claimant cannot recover any sum in excess of the amount of the face of the administrative claim, unless "the increased amount is based on newly discovered evidence" or he alleges and proves "intervening facts."[52] In *Reilly v. United States*,[53] the government appealed an FTCA damages award of $11 million dollars on the grounds that the claimant's sum certain amount was listed as $11 million dollars on the face of the Standard Form 95. The appellate court ruled all damages in excess of the $10 million dollar claim were awarded in error because the claimant failed to state an amount in excess of $10 million dollars on the original Standard Form 95.[54]

Once the claim is filed, the government has six months to resolve the claim before a lawsuit can be filed. In the event the government does not deny the claim, the statute of limitations is indefinitely tolled.[55] The claimant, however, has the right to sue following the six-month period because the government's failure to act within this time period constitutes a denial.[56] If the government denies the claim, the claimant has a mandatory six months in which to file a civil action in the appropriate federal district court from the mailing of a written denial.[57]

Other provisions unique to the FTCA include, but are not limited to, limitations on attorney fees, no punitive damages, no jury trials and the inability to collect interest prior to judgment.[58] Finally, with regard to attorney fees, the FTCA provides a maximum recovery of 20 percent of the sum certain amount in settlement and 25 percent once the case is in litigation.[59]

CONCLUSION

The profound impact of the September 11th terrorist attacks and ensuing global conflicts may very well precipitate a vast expansion of the military establishment with a resulting increase in the veteran population. In such event, Georgia's already sizeable veteran population would no doubt experience a corresponding increase.

As a consequence of this high, and likely growing, veteran population, Georgia attorneys have a good chance of being called upon to advocate on behalf of former military personnel who have claims based on their status as veterans. As noted, veterans law issues and procedures are numerous, time-sensitive and complex. Accordingly, all Georgia attorneys should ensure that they are well-armed with a working knowledge of the veterans law issues and procedures described in this article if they are called upon to defend one of America's defenders. ●

Harold (Hal) Ronald Moroz is judge of the Magistrate Court of Camden County, Ga., and a private practitioner who represents veterans

before the Supreme Court and the U.S. Court of Appeals for Veterans Claims in Washington, D.C. The latter lists him as one of only eight Georgia appellate attorneys for veterans appeals on its Public List of Practitioners. He received his J.D. from the District of Columbia School of Law and a graduate certificate in International Law and Diplomacy from St. John's University, New York. Moroz is a veteran, having served 20 years as a U.S. Army airborne infantry officer. He is also an adjunct professor at Florida Coastal School of Law, Jacksonville, Fla., and Brenau University, Gainesville, Ga.

ENDNOTES

1. U.S. DEP'TOFVETERANS AFFAIRS, VETERAN DATA & INFORMATION. VETPOP2000, SUPPLEMENTAL TABLES (September 30, 2000), *available at* http://www.va.gov/vetdata/Dem ographics/VPwelcome.htm (last visited Jan. 8, 2002).
2. A veteran is a "person who served in the active military, naval, or air service, and who was discharged or released therefrom under conditions other than dishonorable." 38 U.S.C. § 101(2) (1994); 38 C.F.R. § 3.1(d) (2001).
3. 28 U.S.C. §§ 1346(b), 2671 - 2680 (1994).
4. 38 U.S.C. § 5107(a) (1994).
5. Akles v. Derwinski, 1 Vet.App. 118, 121 (1991).
6. For instance, the Veterans Claims Assistance Act of 2000, Pub. L. No. 106-475, 114 Stat. 2096 (2000) (codified at 38 U.S.C.A. §§ 5100 – 5103A, 5106 – 5107 (West Supp. 2001) (the "VCAA"), clarified the claimant's and VA's duties with respect to obtaining evidence in support of claims for veterans' benefits. Specifically, the Act requires the VA to obtain any relevant records in the VA's possession, or within the possession of any other federal agency, at no cost to the veteran. 38 U.S.C.A. §§ 5103A(b) & (c). The VCAA mandates that the VA Secretary make several efforts to obtain relevant evidence identified by the claimant and notify the claimant and his or her representative of those efforts. *Id.* at § 5103(a)(b)(2). The VA is also required to provide a medical examination if warranted. *Id.* at § 5103A(d). In addition, the VCAA eliminated the requirement that the claimant first submit a well-grounded claim before receiving assistance from the VA. *Compare* 38 U.S.C. § 5107(a) (1994) *with* 38 U.S.C.A. 5107(a) (West Supp. 2001).
7. 38 C.F.R. § 3.155 (2001).
8. 38 U.S.C. § 5104 (1994).
9. The VA is obligated under 38 U.S.C. § 7104(a) (1994) to base its decisions on the "entire record in the proceeding and upon consideration of all evidence and material of record and applicable provisions of law and regulation."
10. 38 U.S.C. § 5107(b) (1994).
11. Gilbert v. Derwinski, 1 Vet.App. 49, 54 (1990).
12. 38 C.F.R. § 20.201 (1994).
13. 38 U.S.C. § 7105(d) (1994); 38 C.F.R. § 19.29 (2001).
14. 38 C.F.R. § 20.302(b) (2001).
15. 38 U.S.C. § 7104(a) (1994). *See also* Litke v. Derwinski, 1 Vet. App. 90, 93 (1990) (remand is appropriate where the BVA has based its decision upon an inadequate record); Obert v. Brown, 5 Vet.App. 30, 33 (1993) (remand ordered for additional development of the record).
16. 38 U.S.C. § 7104(d)(1) (1994).
17. Pub.L. No.100-687, 102 Stat. 4105 (1988) (codified at 38 U.S.C. §7251 (1994)).
18. *Compare* 38 U.S.C. § 7252(a) (1994) *with* 38 U.S.C.A. §7252(a) (West Supp. 2001).
19. 38 U.S.C.A. § 7252(a) (West Supp. 2001).
20. *See generally* Spencer v. Brown, 4 Vet.App. 283 (1993), *aff'd*, 17 F.3d 368 (Fed Cir.), *cert. denied*, 513 U.S. 810 (1994).
21. 28 U.S.C. § 2412(d)(1)(A) (1994).
22. 38 U.S.C. § 5904(c)(1) (1994).
23. *Id.* The limitation on fee for services rendered before the VA does not apply to services provided with respect to proceedings before a court.
24. 28 U.S.C. § 2412 (1994).
25. 28 U.S.C. § 2412(d)(1)(A) (1994).
26. U.S. CT. APP. VET. CL. R. 36.
27. U.S. CT. APP. VET. CL. R. 41(b).
28. Grivois v. Brown, 7 Vet.App. 100, 101 (1994).
29. 28 U.S.C. § 2412(d)(2)(B) (1994).
30. *Id.* at § 2412(d)(1)(C)(2)(B), *cf.* Bazalo v. West, 150 F.3d. 1380 (Fed. Cir. 1998)(court held that veteran was permitted to amend his timely-filed EAJA application in order to show that he met the EAJA net worth requirements, provided that government was not prejudiced by the filing of amendment).
31. 28 U.S.C. at § 2412(d)(1)(B).
32. *Id.*
33. 38 U.S.C. § 7292 (West Supp. 2001); FED. R. APP. P. 4(a)(1)(B).

34. 38 U.S.C. § 7292(c) (1994); see also Collette v. Brown, 82 F.3d 389, 392 (Fed. Cir. 1996).

35. Sup. Ct. R. 13.

36. Federal Tort Claims Act, 28 U.S.C. §§ 1346(b), 2671 - 2680 (1994).

37. FTCA claims by military personnel are barred, but claims by family members and veterans injured at military hospitals are not. The Feres Doctrine, first articulated by the Court in Feres v. United States, acts as a bar to civil claims of medical malpractice by all military personnel incurred "incident to service." 340 U.S. 135, 147 (1950). However, the courts permit certain veterans' claims under the FTCA. For example, the Supreme Court in the case of United States v. Brown held that a claim brought by a veteran under the FCTA for medical malpractice at a veterans hospital is not barred. 348 U.S. 110, 111 (1954). In Brown, the Court considered a claim for malpractice where the veteran's original injury involved a wound incurred on active duty six years prior to the negligent treatment at the veterans' hospital. The Court concluded that although a veteran's access to a veteran's hospital was incident to service, the claim was not barred under Feres. 348 U.S. at 113. (last visited Jan. 8, 2002).

38. The FTCA provides a limited waiver of the federal government's sovereign immunity when its employees are negligent within the scope of their employment. Under the FTCA, the government can only be sued "under circumstances where the United States, if a private person, would be liable to the claimant in accordance with the law of the place where the act or omission occurred." 28 U.S.C. § 1346(b) (1994). Thus, the FTCA does not apply to conduct that is uniquely governmental, that is, incapable of performance by a private individual. Note that 28 U.S.C. § 2680(h) (1994) provides that the government is not liable when any of its agents commits the torts of assault, battery, false imprisonment, false arrest, malicious prosecution, abuse of process, libel, slander, misrepresentation, deceit, or interference with contract rights. However, the statute also provides an exception: the government is liable if a law enforcement officer commits assault, battery, false imprisonment, false arrest, abuse of process, or malicious prosecution, but not if he commits libel, slander, misrepresentation, deceit, or interferes with contract rights. Id.

39. ANDREW H. PRESS, CAROL H. DEFRANCES, U.S. DEP'T OF JUSTICE, February 2002

FEDERAL TORT TRIALS AND VERDICTS, 1994-95, BJS SPECIAL REPORT, NCJ-165810 (December 1997), 4-5, available at http://www.ojp.usdoj.gov/bjs/pub/pdf/fttv95.pdf.

40. Id. at 4, 7, 9

41. Id.

42. 28 U.S.C. § 2680(a). In order to determine if conduct meets the Discretionary Function Exception, the courts must apply a two-part test established in Berkovitz v. United States 486 U.S. 531, 536 (1988); see also, Kennewick Irrigation Dist. v. United States. 880 F.2d 1018, 1025 (9th Cir.1989). First, the court must determine if the conduct involved "an element of judgment or choice." United States v. Gaubert, 499 U.S. 315, 322 (1991)(quoting Berkovitz, 486 U.S at 536). This requirement is not satisfied if a "federal statute, regulation, or policy specifically prescribes a course of action for an employee to follow." Berkovitz, 486 U.S. at 536. Once the element of judgment is established, the next inquiry must be "whether that judgment is of the kind that the discretionary function exception was designed to shield" in that it involves considerations of "social, economic, and political policy." Gaubert, 499 U.S. at 322-23 (quoting Berkovitz, 486 U.S. at 536). Absent specific statutes or regulations, where the particular conduct is discretionary, the failure of the government properly to train its employees who engage in that conduct is also discretionary. Flynn v. U.S., 902 F.2d 1524 (10th Cir. 1990) (failure of National Park Service to train its employees as to proper use of emergency equipment was covered by discretionary function exception to FTCA).

43. FDIC v. Meyer, 510 U.S. 471, 478 (1994)(a federal tort claim alleging only a deprivation of a federal constitutional right is not "cognizable" under the FTCA because the FTCA's reference to the "place of the law where the act or omission occurred" means the law of the state where it occurred, and, therefore, in the case of a claim alleging violation of a federal constitutional right, federal law, not state law, provides the source of liability for such a claim).

44. United States v. Yellow Cab Co., 340 U.S. 543, 553 (1951); Warden v. United States, 861 F. Supp. 400, 402 (E.D.N.C. 1993), aff'd, 25 F.3d 1042 (4th Cir. 1994)

45. 28 U.S.C. § 1346(b) (1994).

46. See Caban v. United States, 728 F.2d 68, 72 (2d Cir. 1984); see also

Richards v. United States, 369 U.S. 1, 11-13 (1962).

47. 28 U.S.C. § 2401(b) (1994). Although federal courts apply state law to substantive legal issues, it is important to recognize that the statute of limitations begins to run when the plaintiff learns of an injury's existence and cause, as opposed to when the plaintiff learns the injury was negligently inflicted. See United States v. Kubrick, 444 U.S. 111, 124-125 1979) (the Court held that there was nothing in the language or legislative history of the FTCA that provided for an extension of the statute of limitations beyond the time the plaintiff learns of an injury's existence and cause).

48. 28 U.S.C. § 2675(a)(1994).

49. Under the FTCA, the United States is liable for the negligence of an independent contractor only if it can be shown that the government had authority to control the detailed physical performance of the contractor and exercised substantial supervision over its day-to-day activities. See United States v. Orleans, 425 U.S. 807, 814-15 (1976); Letnes v. United States, 820 F.2d 1517, 1519 (9th Cir.1987)

50. The substitution provision of the Federal Employees Liability Reform and Tort Compensation Act (FELRTCA) provides that "[u]pon certification by the Attorney General that the defendant employee was acting within the scope of his office or employment at the time of the incident out of which the claim arose ... the United States shall be substituted as the party defendant." 28 U.S.C. § 2679(d)(1) (1994). The purpose of this amendment to the FTCA was to "remove the potential personal liability of Federal employees for common law torts committed within the scope of their employment, and ... instead provide that the exclusive remedy for such torts is through an action against the United States under the FTCA." H.R. REP. NO. 700. (1988).

51. Erickson v. United States, 668 F.2d 268, 271 (7th Cir. 1981).

52. Id. at 273 (quoting 28 U.S.C. § 2675(b) (1994)).

53. 863 F.2d 149, 172-73 (1st Cir. 1988).

54. Id.

55. " The failure of an agency to make final disposition of a claim within six months after it is filed shall, at the option of the claimant any time thereafter, be deemed a final denial of the claim for purposes of this section." 28 U.S.C. § 2675(a) (1994)

56. Id.

57. Id.

58. 28 U.S.C. § 2674 (1994).

59. 28 U.S.C. § 2678 (1994).

Phone Numbers

Bereavement Counseling...1-202-461-6530
Civilian Health and Medical Program (CHAMPVA)...........1-800-733-8387
Caregiver Support 1-855-260-3274
Debt Management Center..1-800-827-0648
Education...1-888-442-4551
Federal Recovery Coordination Program 1-877-732-4456
Foreign Medical Program..1-888-820-1756
Headstones and Markers...1-800-697-6947
Health Care...1-877-222-8387
Homeless Veterans...1-877-424-3838
Home Loans...1-888-827-3702
Life Insurance...1-800-669-8477
National Cemetery Scheduling Offce..............................1-800-535-1117
Pension Management Center...1-877-294-6380
Presidential Memorial Certifcate Program......................1-202-565-4964
Special Health Issues...1-800-749-8387
Telecommunication Device for the Deaf (TDD)...............1-800-829-4833
VA Benefits...1-800-827-1000
VA Combat Call Center 1-877-927-8387
Veterans Crisis Line..1-800-273-8255
Women Veterans...1-877-222-8387

Web Sites

Burial and Memorial Benefts ....www.cem.va.gov
Caregiver Support .... www.caregiver.va.gov
CHAMPVA...........www.va.gov/hac/forbenefciaries/forbenefciaries.asp
eBenefits...www.ebenefits.va.gov
Education Benefts...www.gibill.va.gov
Environmental Exposures...............www.publichealth.va.gov/exposures
Health Care Eligibility....................................www.va.gov/healthbenefts
Homeless Veterans................................... www.va.gov/homeless
Home Loan Guaranty.......................................www.homeloans.va.gov
Life Insurance.. www.insurance.va.gov
Memorial Certifcate .Program........................www.cem.va.gov/pmc.asp
Mental Health...www.mentalhealth.va.gov
My HealtheVet...www.myhealth.va.gov
National Resource Directory ....www.nrd.gov
Prosthetics... www.prosthetics.va.gov
Records.......................www.archives.gov/st-louis/military-personnel
Returning Servicemembers...................................www.oefoif.va.gov
State Departments of Veterans Affairs......www.va.gov/statedva.htm
Women Veterans..www.womenshealth.va.gov
VA Vet Centers..www.vetcenter.va.gov
VA Home Page..www.va.gov
VA Benefit Payment Rates.........................www.vba.va.gov/bln/21/rates
VA Forms..www.va.gov/vaform
Vocational Rehabilitation and Employment............www.vetsuccess.gov

21

Federal Benefits for Veterans, Dependents and Survivors

This is a reprinted copy of the official U.S. government edition of this publication and is herein identified with a new ISBN.

Department of Veterans Affairs

810 Vermont Ave., N.W.
Washington, DC 20420

Contents

Introduction

Veterans of the United States armed forces may be eligible for a broad range of benefts and services provided by the U.S. Department of Veterans Affairs (VA). Some of these benefts may be utilized while on active duty. These benefts are codifed in Title 38 of the United States Code. This booklet contains a summary of these benefts effective Jan. 1, 2013. For additional information, visit www. va.gov/.

La versión en español de este folleto se encuentra disponible en formato Adobe Acrobat a través de el link: http://www.va.gov/opa/publications/benefts_book/federal_benefts_spanish.pdf

General Eligibility: Eligibility for most VA benefts is based upon discharge from active military service under other than dishonorable conditions. Active service means full-time service, other than active duty for training, as a member of the Army, Navy, Air Force, Marine Corps, Coast Guard, or as a commissioned offcer of the Public Health Service, Environmental Science Services Administration or National Oceanic and Atmospheric Administration, or its predecessor, the Coast and Geodetic Survey.

Dishonorable and bad conduct discharges issued by general courts-martial may bar VA benefits. Veterans in prison must contact VA to determine eligibility. VA benefits will not be provided to any Veteran or dependent wanted for an outstanding felony warrant.

Certain VA Benefits Require Wartime Service: under the law, VA recognizes these periods of war:

Mexican Border Period: May 9, 1916, through April 5, 1917, for Veterans who served in Mexico, on its borders or in adjacent waters.

World War I: April 6, 1917, through Nov. 11, 1918; for Veterans who served in Russia, April 6, 1917, through April 1, 1920; extended through July 1, 1921, for Veterans who had at least one day of service between April 6, 1917, and Nov. 11, 1918.

World War II: Dec. 7, 1941, through Dec. 31, 1946.

Korean War: June 27, 1950, through Jan. 31, 1955.

Vietnam War: Aug. 5, 1964 (Feb. 28, 1961, for Veterans who served "in country" before Aug. 5, 1964), through May 7, 1975.

Gulf War: Aug. 2, 1990, through a date to be set.

Important Documents

In order to expedite benefts delivery, Veterans seeking a VA beneft for the frst time must submit a copy of their service discharge form (DD-214, DD-215, or for World War II Veterans, a WD form), which documents service dates and type of discharge, or provides full name, military service number, and branch and dates of service.

The Veteran's service discharge form should be kept in a safe location accessible to the Veteran and next of kin or designated representative.

The following documents will be needed for claims processing related to a Veteran's death:

1. Veteran's marriage certifcate for claims of a surviving spouse or children.
2. Veteran's death certifcate if the Veteran did not die in a VA health care facility.
3. Children's birth certifcates or adoption papers to determine children's benefts.
4. Veteran's birth certifcate to determine parents' benefts.

eBenefts

eBenefts is a joint VA/Department of Defense (DoD) Web portal that provides resources and self-service capabilities to Servicemembers, Veterans, and their families to apply, research, access, and manage their VA and military benefts and personal information through a secure Internet connection.

Through eBenefts Veterans can: apply for benefts, view their disability compensation claim status, access offcial military personnel documents (e.g., DD Form 214, Certifcate of Release or Discharge from Active Duty), transfer entitlement of Post-9/11 GI Bill to eligible dependents (Servicemembers only), obtain a VA-guaranteed home loan Certifcate of Eligibility, and register for and update direct depos-

28

it information for certain benefts. New features are added regularly.

Accessing eBenefts: The portal is located at www.ebenefts. va.gov. Servicemembers or Veterans must register for an eBenefts account at one of two levels: Basic or Premium. A Premium account allows the user to access personal data in VA and DoD systems, as well as apply for benefts online, check the status of claims, update address records, and more. The Basic account allows access to information entered into eBenefts by the Servicemember or Veteran only. Basic accounts cannot access VA or DoD systems.

Servicemembers can obtain immediate Premium level access by following step-by-step instructions using their Common Access Card (CAC).

In order to register for an eBenefts account, Veterans must be listed in the Defense Enrollment Eligibility Reporting System (DEERS) and frst obtain a DoD Self Service (DS) Logon. Note: For those without a DEERS record, VA will frst need to verify military service and add the information to DEERS. This is most likely for Veterans who served prior to 1982. Individuals should contact a VA regional offce for assistance in being added to DEERS.

A DS Logon is an identity (user name and password) that is used by various DoD and VA Websites, including eBenefts. Those registered in DEERS are eligible for a DS Logon. A DS Logon is valid for the rest of your life.

Identity verifcation: Many people will be able to verify their identity online by answering a few security questions. A few may need to visit a VA regional offce or TRICARE Service Center to have their identities verifed. Servicemembers may verify their identity online by using their Common Access Card.

Military retirees may verify their identity online using their Defense Finance and Accounting Service (DFAS) Logon. Veterans in receipt of VA benefts via direct deposit may have their identity verifed by calling 1-800-827-1000 and selecting option 7. eBenefts users with Premium access with appropriate My HealtheVet access can login to their My HealtheVet account using the single sign on feature.

Abbreviations

ALS – Amyotrophic Lateral Sclerosis
CHAMPVA – Civilian Health and Medical Program of VA
CLC – Community Living Center
C&P – Compensation and Pension
COE – Certifcate of Eligibility
CRDP – Concurrent Retirement and Disability Payments
CRSC – Combat-Related Special Compensation
CWT – Compensated Work Therapy
CZTE – Combat Zone Tax Exclusion
DIC – Dependency and Indemnity Compensation
DoD -- Department of Defense
FHA – Federal Housing Administration
FSGLI – Family Servicemembers' Group Life Insurance
HUD – Department of Housing and Urban Development
IRR – Individual Ready Reserve
MGIB – Montgomery GI Bill
MIA – Missing in Action
NPRC – National Personnel Records Center
NSLI – National Service Life Insurance
OEF – Operation Enduring Freedom
OIF – Operation Iraqi Freedom
OND – Operation New Dawn
OPM – Offce of Personnel Management
POW -- Prisoner of War
PTSD – Post-Traumatic Stress Disorder
SAH – Specially Adapted Housing
SBA – Small Business Administration
S-DVI – Service-Disabled Veterans' Insurance
SGLI – Servicemembers' Group Life Insurance
SSB – Special Separation Benefts
TAP – Transition Assistance Program
TSGLI – Servicemembers' Group Life Insurance Traumatic Injury Protection
USCIS – U.S. Citizenship and Immigration Services
USDA – U.S. Department of Agriculture
VA – Department of Veterans Affairs
VEAP – Veterans Educational Assistance Program
VEOA – Veterans' Employment Opportunities Act
VGLI – Veterans' Group Life Insurance
VHA – Veterans Health Administration
VMET – Verifcation of Military Experience and Training
VMLI – Veterans' Mortgage Life Insurance
VR&E – Vocational Rehabilitation and Employment
VSI – Voluntary Separation Incentive
WAAC – Women's Army Auxiliary Corps
WASPs – Women Air Force Service Pilots

Chapter 1

Health Care Benefts

VA operates the nation's largest integrated health care system with more than 1,500 sites of care, including hospitals, community clinics, community living centers, domiciliaries, readjustment counseling centers, and various other facilities. For additional information on VA health care, visit: www.va.gov/health.

Basic Eligibility

A person who served in the active military, naval, or air service and who was discharged or released under conditions other than dishonorable may qualify for VA health care benefts. Reservists and National Guard members may also qualify for VA health care benefts if they were called to active duty (other than for training only) by a Federal order and completed the full period for which they were called or ordered to active duty.

Minimum Duty Requirements: Veterans who enlisted after Sept. 7, 1980, or who entered active duty after Oct. 16, 1981, must have served 24 continuous months or the full period for which they were called to active duty in order to be eligible. This minimum duty requirement may not apply to Veterans discharged for hardship, early out or a disability incurred or aggravated in the line of duty.

Enrollment

For most Veterans, entry into the VA health care system begins by applying for enrollment. Veterans can now apply and submit their application for enrollment (VA Form 1010EZ), online at www.1010ez. med.va.gov/sec/vha/1010ez/. If assistance is needed while completing the on-line enrollment form, an online chat representative is available to answer questions Monday - Friday between 8 a.m. and 8 pm EST. Veterans can also enroll by calling 1-877-222-VETS (8387) Monday through Friday, 8 a.m. to 8 p.m. Eastern time, or at any VA health care facility or VA regional benefts offce. Once enrolled, Veterans can receive health care at VA health care facilities anywhere in the country.

Veterans enrolled in the VA health care system are afforded privacy rights under federal law. VA's Notice of Privacy Practices, which describes how VA may use and disclose Veterans' medical information, is also available on line at www.va.gov/vhapublications/viewpublication.asp?pub_ID=1089

The following four categories of Veterans are not required to enroll, but are urged to do so to permit better planning of health resources:

1. Veterans with a service-connected disability of 50 percent or more.
2. Veterans seeking care for a disability the military determined was incurred or aggravated in the line of duty, but which VA has not yet rated, within 12 months of discharge.
3. Veterans seeking care for a service-connected disability only.
4. Veterans seeking registry examinations (Ionizing Radiation, Agent Orange, Gulf War/Operation Iraqi Freedom/Operation New Dawn and Depleted Uranium).

Priority Groups

During enrollment, each Veteran is assigned to a priority group. VA uses priority groups to balance demand for VA health care enrollment with resources. Changes in available resources may reduce the number of priority groups VA can enroll. If this occurs, VA will publicize the changes and notify affected enrollees. A description of priority groups follows:

Group 1: Veterans with service-connected disabilities rated 50 percent or more and/or Veterans determined by VA to be unemployable due to service-connected conditions.

Group 2: Veterans with service-connected disabilities rated 30 or 40 percent.

Group 3:
Veterans who are former POWs.
Veterans awarded the Purple Heart Medal.
Veterans awarded the Medal of Honor.
Veterans whose discharge was for a disability incurred or aggravated in the line of duty.
Veterans with VA service-connected disabilities rated 10 percent or
20 percent.
Veterans awarded special eligibility classifcation under Title 38, U.S.C., § 1151, "benefts for individuals disabled by treatment or vocational rehabilitation."

Group 4:
Veterans receiving increased compensation or pension based on their need for regular aid and attendance or by reason of being permanently housebound.
Veterans determined by VA to be catastrophically disabled.

Group 5:
Nonservice-connected Veterans and noncompensable service-connected Veterans rated 0 percent, whose annual income and/or net worth are not greater than the VA fnancial thresholds.
Veterans receiving VA Pension benefts.
Veterans eligible for Medicaid benefts.

Group 6:
Compensable 0 percent Service-connected Veterans.
Veterans exposed to ionizing radiation during atmospheric testing or during the occupation of Hiroshima and Nagasaki.
Project 112/SHAD participants.
Veterans who served in the Republic of Vietnam between Jan. 9, 1962 and May 7, 1975.
Veterans who served in the Southwest Asia theater of operations from Aug. 2, 1990, through Nov. 11, 1998.
Veterans who served in a theater of combat operations after Nov.11, 1998, as follows:
Veterans discharged from active duty on or after Jan. 28, 2003, for fve years post discharge;
Veterans who served on active duty at Camp Lejeune for not fewer than 30 days beginning Jan. 1, 1957 and ending Dec. 31, 1987.

Group 7:
Veterans with incomes below the geographic means test income thresholds and who agree to pay the applicable copayment.

Group 8:
Veterans with gross household incomes above the VA national income threshold and the geographically-adjusted income threshold for their resident location and who agrees to pay copayments. Veterans eligible for enrollment: Noncompensable 0-percent service-connected and:

Subpriority a: Enrolled as of Jan. 16, 2003, and who have remained enrolled since that date and/ or placed in this subpriority due to changed eligibility status.

Subpriority b: Enrolled on or after June 15, 2009 whose income exceeds the current VA National Income Thresholds or VA National Geographic Income Thresholds by 10 percent or less

Veterans eligible for enrollment: Nonservice-connected and Subpriority c: Enrolled as of Jan. 16, 2003, and who remained enrolled since that date and/ or placed in this subpriority due to changed eligibility status

Subpriority d: Enrolled on or after June 15, 2009 whose income exceeds the current VA National Income Thresholds or VA National Geographic Income Thresholds by 10 percent or less

Veterans NOT eligible for enrollment: Veterans not meeting the criteria above:
Subpriority e: Noncompensable 0 percent service-connected
Subpriority f: Nonservice-connected

VA's current income thresholds can be located at: www.va.gov/healtheligibility/Library/AnnualThresholds.asp

Recently Discharged Combat Veterans

Veterans, including activated reservists and members of the National Guard, are eligible for the enhanced Combat Veteran benefts if they served on active duty in a theater of combat operations after Nov. 11, 1998, and have been discharged under other than dishonorable conditions.

Effective Jan. 28, 2008, combat Veterans discharged from active duty on or after Jan. 28, 2003, are eligible for enhanced enrollment placement into Priority Group 6 (unless eligible for higher enrollment Priority Group placement) for fve-years post discharge.

Veterans receive VA care and medication at no cost for any condition that may be related to their combat service.

Veterans who enroll with VA under this Combat Veteran authority will remain enrolled even after their fve-year post discharge period ends. At the end of their post discharge period, VA will reassess the Veteran's information (including all applicable eligibility factors) and make a new enrollment decision. For additional information, call 1-877-222-VETS (8387), Monday through Friday between 8:00 a.m. and 8:00 p.m. Eastern time.

Special Access to Care
Service-Disabled Veterans: who are 50 percent or more disabled from service-connected conditions, unemployable due to service-connected conditions, or receiving care for a service-connected disability receive priority in scheduling of hospital or outpatient medical appointments.

Women Veterans
Women Veterans are eligible for the same VA benefts as male Veterans. Comprehensive health services are available to women Veterans including primary care, specialty care, mental health care, residential treatment and reproductive health care services

VA provides management of acute and chronic illnesses, preventive care, contraceptive and gynecology services, menopause management, and cancer screenings, including pap smears and mammograms. Maternity care is covered in the Medical Benefts package. Women Veterans can receive maternity care from an OB/GYN, family practitioner, or certifed nurse midwife who provides pregnancy care.

VA covers the costs of care for newborn children of women Veterans for seven days after birth. Infertility evaluation and limited treatments are also available. Women Veterans Program Managers are available at all VA facilities to assist women Veterans in their health care and benefts. For more information, visit http://www.womenshealth.va.gov/.

Military Sexual Trauma
Military sexual trauma (MST) is the term that the Department of Veterans Affairs uses to refer to sexual assault or repeated, threatening sexual harassment that occurred while the Veteran was serving on active duty (or active duty for training if the service was in the National Guard or Reserves). VA health care professionals provide counseling and treatment to help Veterans overcome health issues related to MST. Veterans who are not otherwise eligible for VA health care may still receive these services. Appropriate services are pro-

vided for any injury, illness or psychological condition related to such trauma. For additional information visit: http://www.mentalhealth. va.gov/msthome.asp

Veterans with Spinal Cord Injury/Disorders

There are 24 VA medical centers in the United States with special- ized centers (called Spinal Cord Injury Centers) for Veterans with spinal cord injuries and disorders (SCI/D). Comprehensive rehabili- tation, SCI/D specialty care, medical, surgical, primary, preventive, psychological, respite, and home care are provided at these centers by interdisciplinary teams which include physicians, nurses, thera- pists (physical, occupational, kinesiotherapists, therapeutic recre- ation), psychologists, social workers, vocational counselors, dieti- cians, respiratory therapy, and other specialists as needed.

There are fve Spinal Cord Injury (SCI) Centers that provide long term care for Veterans with SCI/D. In VA facilities that do not have SCI Centers, there is a designated team that consists of a physician, nurse, and social worker to address primary care needs for Veterans with SCI/D and to make referrals to SCI Centers. These SCI Centers and the teams in facilities that do not have centers, comprise the VA SCI System of Care. Some of the services provided in this system of care include rehabilitation, prosthetics and durable medical equip- ment, orthotics, sensory aids, assistive technology, environmental modifcations, telehealth, ventilator weaning and care, chronic pain management, mental health treatment, drivers training, peer coun- seling, substance abuse treatment, vocational counseling, and care- giver training and support.

There is a long-standing Memorandum of Agreement between VA and the Department of Defense (DoD) to provide specialized care at VA medical facilities for Active Duty Servicemembers who have sustained a spinal cord injury. Ongoing collaboration and education between VA and DoD ensures continuity of care and services. For more information about SCI/D care and the eligibility require- ments for the above benefts and services, contact your local VA SCI/D Center and/or visit http://www.sci.va.gov.

OEF/OIF/OND Care Management

Each VA medical center has an OEF/OIF/OND Care Management team in place to coordinate patient care activities and ensure that

Servicemembers and Veterans are receiving patient-centered, integrated care and benefts. OEF/OIF/OND clinical case managers screen all returning combat Veterans for the need for case management services to identify Veterans who may be at risk so VA can intervene early and provide assistance. Severely ill or injured Servicemembers/Veterans are provided with a case manager and other OEF/OIF/OND Servicemembers/Veterans are assigned a case manager as indicated by a positive screening assessment or upon request. OEF/OIF/OND case managers are experts at identifying and accessing resources within their health care system as well as in the local community to help Veterans recover from their injuries and readjust to civilian life.

Financial Assessment

Most Veterans not receiving VA disability compensation or pension payments must provide a fnancial assessment to determine whether they are below VA income thresholds. VA is currently not enrolling new applicants who decline to provide fnancial information unless they have a special eligibility factor exempting them from disclosure. VA's income thresholds are located at: www.va.gov/healtheligibility/Library/AnnualThresholds.asp

The fnancial assessment includes all household income and net worth, including Social Security, retirement pay, unemployment insurance, interest and dividends, workers' compensation, black lung benefts and any other income. Also considered are assets such as the market value of property that is not the primary residence, stocks, bonds, notes, individual retirement accounts, bank deposits, savings accounts and cash.

Medical Services and Medication Copayments

Some Veterans are required to make copayments (copays) to receive VA health care and/or medications.

Inpatient Care: Priority Group 7 and certain other Veterans are responsible for paying 20 percent of VA's inpatient copay or $236.80 for the frst 90 days of inpatient hospital care during any 365-day period. For each additional 90 days, the charge is $118.40. In addition, there is a $2 per diem charge.

Priority Group 8 and certain other Veterans are responsible for VA's inpatient copay of $1,184 for the frst 90 days of care during any 365-day period. For each additional 90 days, the charge is $592. In addition, there is a $10 per diem charge.

Extended Care: Veterans may be subject to a copay for extended care services. The copay is determined by a calculation using information from completion of VA Form 10-10EC, Application for Extended Care Services.

VA social workers or case managers will counsel Veterans or their family representatives on their eligibility and copay requirements. The copay amount is based on the Veteran's fnancial situation determined upon application for extended care services and can range from $0 to a maximum copayment amount of $97 a day.

NOTE: Veterans determined to be catastrophically disabled are exempt from copays applicable to the receipt of noninstitutional respite care, noninstitutional geriatric evaluation, noninstitutional adult day health care, homemaker/home health aide, purchase skilled home care, home-based primary care, hospice services and any other noninstitutional alternative extended care services.

Outpatient Care: While many Veterans qualify for free healthcare services based on a VA compensable service-connected condition or other qualifying factor, most Veterans are asked to complete an annual fnancial assessment, to determine if they qualify for free services. Veterans whose income exceeds the established VA Income Thresholds as well as those who choose not to complete the fnancial assessment must agree to pay required copays to become eligible for VA healthcare services.

   Primary Care Services: $15
   Specialty Care Services: $50

NOTE: Copay amount is limited to a single charge per visit regardless of the number of health care providers seen in a single day. The copay amount is based on the highest level of service received.

Outpatient Visits Not Requiring Copays: Certain services are not charged a copay. Copays do not apply to publicly announced VA health fairs or outpatient visits solely for preventive screening and/or vaccinations, such as vaccinations for infuenza and pneumococcal, or screening for hypertension, hepatitis B, tobacco, alcohol, hyperlipidemia, breast cancer, cervical cancer, Human papillomavirus (HPV), colorectal cancer by fecal occult blood testing, education about the risks and benefts of prostate cancer screening, HIV testing and prevention counseling (including the distribution of condoms), and weight reduction or smoking cessation counseling (individual and group). Laboratory, plaim flm radiology, electrocardiograms, and hospice care and in-home video telehealth are also exempt from copays. While hepatitis C screening and HIV testing and counseling are exempt, medical care for HIV and hepatitis C are NOT exempt from copays.

Medication: While many Veterans are exempt for medication copays, nonservice-connected Veterans in Priority Groups 7 and 8 are charged $9 for each 30-day or less supply of medication provided on an outpatient basis for the treatment of a nonservice-connected condition. Veterans enrolled in Priority Groups 2 through 6 are charged $8 for each 30-day or less supply of medication; the maximum copay for medications that will be charged in calendar year 2013 is $960 for nonservice-connected medications.

NOTE: Copays apply to prescription and over-the-counter medications, such as aspirin, cough syrup or vitamins, dispensed by a VA pharmacy. Copays are not charged for medical supplies, such as syringes or alcohol wipes. Copays do not apply to condoms.

Health Savings Accounts (HSA) can be utilized to make VA copayments. HSAs are usually linked to High Deductible Health Plans (HDHPs).

Private Health Insurance Billing
VA is required to bill private health insurance providers for medical care, supplies and medications provided for treatment of Veterans' non-service connected conditions. Generally, VA cannot bill Medicare, but can bill Medicare supplemental health insurance for covered services. VA is authorized to bill and accept reimbursement from High Deductible Health Plans (HDHPs) as well as employer-sponsored Health Reimbursement Arrangements (HRAs) for care provided for non-service connected conditions.

All Veterans applying for VA medical care are required to provide information on their health insurance coverage, including coverage provided under policies of their spouses. Veterans are not responsible for paying any remaining balance of VA's insurance claim not paid or covered by their health insurance, and any payment received by VA may be used to offset "dollar for dollar" a Veteran's VA copayment responsibility.

Release of Information (ROI) for Sensitive Diagnosis

An ROI authorization form VAF 10-5345 is a VA standard form used to obtain authorization to release sensitive (protected) health information to an insurance company for purposes of reimbursement.. Veterans/patients who were treated or offered treatment for a sensitive condition of drug abuse, alcohol abuse or alcoholism, HIV testing or treatment, and Sickle Cell Anemia or Trait must provide written authorization to allow VA to release their sensitive information to a third party (insurance company).

NOTE: Please note that if the ROI authorization form is not completed and signed, the VA cannot bill the insurance company for non-service connected care. Thus if the Veteran is required to pay a copayment for health visits, the Veteran will be responsible for the entire copayment amount as VA will not be able to credit account dollar for dollar based on what the insurance company has reimbursed.

Reimbursement of Travel Costs

Eligible Veterans may be provided mileage reimbursement or, when medically indicated, special mode transport (e.g. wheelchair van, ambulance) when traveling for approved VA medical care.

Mileage reimbursement is 41.5 cents per mile and is subject to a deductible of $3 for each one-way trip and $6 for a round trip; with a maximum deductible of $18 or the amount after six one-way trips (whichever occurs frst) per calendar month.

The deductible may be waived when travel is in relation to a VA compensation or pension examination; travel is by special mode; or when imposition would cause a severe fnancial hardship.

Eligibility: The following are eligible for VA travel reimbursement:
  Veterans rated 30 percent or more service-connected .
  Veterans traveling for treatment of service-connected conditions.
  Veterans who receive a VA pension.
  Veterans traveling for scheduled compensation or pension

examinations.
Veterans whose income does not exceed the maximum
annual VA pension rate.
Veterans in certain emergency situations.
Veterans whose medical condition requires a special mode of
transportation and travel is pre-authorized. (Advanced
authorization is not required in an emergency and a delay
would be hazardous to life or health).
Certain non-Veterans when related to care of a Veteran
(Caregivers, attendants & donors).

Benefciary travel fraud can take money out of the pockets of de-
serving Veterans. Inappropriate uses of benefciary travel benefts
include: incorrect addresses provided resulting in increased mileage; driving/riding together and making separate claims; and taking
no cost transportation, such as DAV, and making claims. Veterans
making false statements for benefciary travel reimbursement may be
prosecuted under applicable laws.

Reporting Fraud: Help VA's Secretary ensure integrity by reporting
suspected fraud, waste or abuse in VA programs or operations.

VA Inspector General Hotline
P.O. Box 50410
Washington, DC 20091-0410
E-mail: vaoighotline@va.gov
VAOIG hotline 1-800-488-8244
Fax: (202) 565-7936

VA Medical Programs

Veteran Health Registries
Certain Veterans can participate in a VA health registry and receive
free evaluations. These evaluations include a medical history, physical exam, and if deemed necessary by the clinician, laboratory tests
or other studies. VA maintains health registries to provide special
health evaluations and health-related information. To participate,
contact the Environmental Health Coordinator at the nearest VA
health care facility or visit www.publichealth.va.gov/exposures to see
a directory which lists Environmental Health Coordinators by state
and U.S. territory.

Veterans should be aware that a health registry evaluation is not a disability compensation exam. A registry evaluation does not start a claim for compensation and is not required for any VA benefts.

Gulf War Registry: For Veterans who served on active military duty in Southwest Asia during the Gulf War, which began in 1990 and continues to the present, and includes Operation Iraqi Freedom (OIF) and Operation New Dawn (OND). The Gulf War registry was designed to identify possible health effects resulting from U.S. military personnel service in certain areas of Southwest Asia. Potential exposures include endemic infectious diseases and hazardous occupational or environmental exposures, including heavy metals, air pollutants (particulate matter and gases such as nitrogen oxides, carbon monoxide sulfur oxides, hydrocarbons).

Depleted Uranium Registries: Depleted uranium (DU) is uranium left over after most of the more radioactive U-235 isotope has been removed. DU possesses about 60 percent of the radioactivity of naturally occurring uranium; it is a radiation hazard only in very large exposures for prolonged time. DU has some chemical toxicity related to being a heavy metal (similar to lead) which occurs at lower doses and is the main concern for Veterans with embedded DU fragments.

Veterans who are identifed by the Department of Defense (DoD) or have concerns about possible depleted uranium exposure are eligible for a DU evaluation at their local facility.

Agent Orange Registry: Agent Orange is an herbicide the U.S. military used between 1962 and 1971 during the Vietnam War to remove jungle that provided enemy cover. Veterans serving in Vietnam were possibly exposed to Agent Orange or its dioxin contaminant. Veterans eligible for this registry evaluation are those who served on the ground in Vietnam between Jan. 9,1962, and May 7,1975, regardless of the length of service; this includes Veterans who served aboard boats that operated on inland waterways ("Brown Water Navy") or who made brief visits ashore.

Other Veterans with possible exposure who are eligible include those who served: along the demilitarized zone in Korea (between April 1, 1968 and Aug. 31, 1971), on certain bases or in certain units in Thailand (between Feb. 28, 1961 and May 7, 1975), or on certain U.S. bases or locations in other countries where Agent Orange or other herbicides were tested or stored.

VA maintains a DoD-provided list of locations and dates where Agent Orange or other herbicides were tested or stored at military bases in the U.S. or locations in other countries at www.publichealth.va.gov/exposures. For sites not listed, the Veteran should provide some proof of exposure to obtain a registry examination. Information is also available through VA's Special Issues Helpline at 1-800-749-8387.

Ionizing Radiation Registry: For Veterans in receipt of nasopharyngeal (nose and throat) radium irradiation treatments while in the active military, naval, or air service and Veterans possibly exposed to, and who are concerned about, possible adverse effects of their atomic exposure during the following "radiation-risk activities" –

On-site participation in:
an atmospheric detonation of a nuclear device, whether or not the testing nation was the United States;
occupation of Hiroshima or Nagasaki from Aug. 6, 1945, through July 1, 1946; or
internment as a POW in Japan during World War II, which the Secretary of Veterans Affairs determines resulted in an opportunity for exposure to ionizing radiation comparable to that of Veterans involved in the occupation of Hiroshima or Nagasaki, or

Service at (VA regulations provide that "radiation-risk activity" refers to):
Department of Energy gaseous diffusion plants at Paducah, Kentucky, Portsmouth, Ohio, or the K-25 area at Oak Ridge, Tennessee, for at least 250 days before Feb. 1, 1992, if the Veteran was monitored for each of the 250 days using dosimetry badges to monitor radiation to external body parts; or
Amchitka Island, Alaska, before Jan. 1, 1974, if the Veteran served for at least 250 days in a position that had exposures comparable to a job that was monitored using dosimetry badges in proximity to Longshot, Milrow, or Cannikin underground nuclear tests.

Readjustment Counseling Services
VA provides outreach and readjustment counseling services through

300 community-based Vet Centers located in all 50 states, the District of Columbia, Guam, Puerto Rico, and America Samoa.

Eligibility: Veterans are eligible if they served on active duty in a combat theater or area of hostility during World War II, the Korean War, the Vietnam War, the Gulf War, or the campaigns in Lebanon, Grenada, Panama, Somalia, Bosnia, Kosovo, Afghanistan, Iraq and the Global War on Terror. Veterans, who served in the active military during the Vietnam-era, but not in the Republic of Vietnam, must have requested services at a Vet Center before Jan. 1, 2004. Vet Centers do not require enrollment in the VHA Health Care System.

Services Offered: Vet Center counselors provide individual, group, and family readjustment counseling to combat Veterans to assist them in making a successful transition from military to civilian life; to include treatment for post-traumatic stress disorder (PTSD) and help with any other military related problems that affect functioning within the family, work, school or other areas of everyday life. Other psycho-social services include outreach, education, medical referral, homeless Veteran services, employment, VA beneft referral, and the brokering of non-VA services. The Vet Centers also provide military sexual trauma counseling to Veterans of both genders and of any era of military service.

Bereavement Counseling related to Servicemembers: Bereavement counseling is available through VA's Vet Centers to all immediate family members (including spouses, children, parents, and siblings) of Servicemembers who die while serving on active service. This includes federally-activated members of the National Guard and reserve components. Vet Center bereavement services for surviving family members of Servicemembers may be accessed by calling (202) 461-6530.Vet Center Combat Call Center (1-877-WAR-VETS) is an around the clock confdential call center where combat Veterans and their families can call to talk about their military experience or any other issue they are facing in their readjustment to civilian life. The staff is comprised of combat Veterans from several eras as well as family members of combat Veterans. For additional information, contact the nearest Vet Center, listed in the back of this book, or visit www.vetcenter.va.gov/.

Vet Center Combat Call Center: (1-877-WAR-VETS) is an around the clock confdential call center where combat Veterans and their families can call to talk about their military experience or any other issue they are facing in their readjustment to civilian life. The staff is comprised of combat Veterans from several eras as well as family members of combat Veterans.

Prosthetic and Sensory Aids

Veterans receiving VA care for any condition may receive VA prosthetic appliances, equipment and services, such as home respiratory therapy, artifcial limbs, orthopedic braces and therapeutic shoes, wheelchairs, powered mobility, crutches, canes, walkers, special aids, appliances, optical and electronic devices for visual impairment and other durable medical equipment and supplies. Veterans who are approved for a guide or service dog may also receive service dog benefts including veterinary care and equipment.

VA medical services include diagnostic audiology and diagnostic and preventive eye care services. VA will provide hearing aids and eyeglasses to the following Veterans:

(a) Those with any compensable service-connected disability.

(b) Those who are former Prisoners of War (POWs).

(c) Those who were awarded a Purple Heart.

(d) Those in receipt of benefts under Title 38 United States Code (U.S.C.) 1151.

(e) Those in receipt of an increased pension based on being rated permanently housebound or in need of regular aid and attendance.

(f) Those with vision or hearing impairment resulting from diseases or the existence of another medical condition for which the Veteran is receiving care or services from VHA, or which resulted from treatment of that medical condition, e.g., stroke, polytrauma, traumatic brain injury, diabetes, multiple sclerosis, vascular disease, geriatric chronic illnesses, toxicity from drugs, ocular photosensitivity from drugs, cataract surgery, and/or other surgeries performed on the eye, ear, or brain resulting in vision or hearing impairment.

(g) Those with signifcant functional or cognitive impairment evidenced by defciencies in the ability to perform activities of daily living. but not including normally occurring visual or hearing impairments. Note: Veterans with normally occurring visual and/or hearing impairments that interfere with their medical care are eligible for eyeglasses and hearing aids.

(h) Those who have vision or hearing impairment or combined visual and hearing impairments severe enough that it interferes with their ability to participate actively in their own medical treatment. **Note:** The term "severe" is to be interpreted as a vision and/or hearing loss that interferes with or restricts access to, involvement in, or active participation in health care services (e.g., communication or reading medication labels). The term is not to be interpreted to mean that a severe hearing or vision loss must exist to be eligible for hearing aids or eyeglasses.

(i) Those Veterans who have service-connected which contribute to a loss of communication ability; however, hearing aids are to be provided only as needed for the service-connected hearing disability.

Nonservice-connected (NSC) Veterans are eligible for hearing aids or eyeglasses on the basis of medical need. All such Veterans (including Medal of Honor recipients who do not have entitling conditions or circumstances and catastrophically disabled Veterans) must receive a hearing evaluation by a state-licensed audiologist prior to determining eligibility for hearing aids or an appropriate evaluation by an optometrist or ophthalmologist prior to determining eligibility for eyeglasses to establish medical justifcation for provision of these devices. These Veterans must meet the following criteria for eligibility based on medical need:

(a) Be enrolled at the VA medical facility where they receive their health care; and

(b) Have hearing or vision loss that interferes with or restricts communication to the extent that it affects their active participation in the provision of health care services as determined by an audiologist or an eye care practitioner or provider.

For additional information, contact the prosthetic chief or representative at the nearest VA medical center or go to www.prosthetics. va.gov.

Home Improvements and Structural Alterations

VA provides up to $6,800 lifetime benefts for service-connected Veterans/Servicemembers and up to $2,000 lifetime beneft for or nonservice-connected Veterans to make home improvements and/or structural changes necessary for the continuation of treatment or for disability access to the Veterans/Servicemembers home and essential lavatory and sanitary facilities.

Modifcations can include but are not limited to:
Ramps allowing entrance to, or exit from, the Veterans/Service-

members primary residence; Widening of doorways to allow access to essential lavatory and sanitary facilities; Raising or lowering kitchen or bathroom sinks and/or counters; Improving entrance paths or driveways in immediate area of the home to facilitate access to the home by the Veteran/Servicemember;   Improving plumbing or electrical systems made necessary due to installation of dialysis equipment or other medically sustaining equipment in the home. For application information, contact the Prosthetic Representative at the nearest VA medical center.

Special Eligibility Programs

Special Eligibility for Children with Spina Bifda: VA provides comprehensive health care benefts, including outpatient, inpatient, pharmacy, prosthetics, medical equipment, and supplies for certain Korea and Vietnam Veterans' birth children diagnosed with Spina Bifda (except spina bifda occulta).

Special Eligibility for Veterans Participating in Vocational Rehabilitation: Veterans participating in VA's vocational rehabilitation program may receive VA health care benefts including prosthetics, medical equipment, and supplies.

Limitations on Benefts Available to Veterans outside the U.S.: Veterans outside the U.S. are eligible for prosthetics, medical equipment, and supplies only for a service-connected disability.

Services for Blind and Visually Impaired Veterans

Severely disabled blind Veterans may be eligible for case management services at a VA medical center and for admission to an inpatient or outpatient VA blind or vision rehabilitation program. In addition, blind Veterans enrolled in the VA health care system may receive:

1. A total health and benefts review as well as counseling on obtaining benefts that may be due to the Veteran but have not been received.
2. Adjustment to blindness training and counseling.
3. Home improvements and structural alterations.
4. Specially adapted housing and adaptations.
5. Automobile grant.
6. Rehabilitation assessment and training to improve independence and quality of life.
7. Low-vision devices and training in their use.

8. Electronic and mechanical aids for the blind, including adaptive computers and computer-assisted devices such as reading machines and electronic travel aids.
9. Facilitation and recommendation for guide dogs and support in the use of guide dogs.
10. Costs for veterinary care and equipment for guide dogs.
11. Talking books, tapes and Braille literature.
12. Family education and support.

Eligible visually impaired Veterans (who are not severely visually disabled) enrolled in the VA health care system may be eligible for services at a VA medical center or for admission to an outpatient VA blind rehabilitation program and may also receive:

1. A total health and benefts review.
2. Adjustment to vision loss counseling.
3. Rehabilitation assessment and training to improve independence and quality of life.
4. Low-vision devices and training in their use.
5. Electronic and mechanical aids for the visually impaired, including adaptive computers and computer-assisted devices, such as reading machines and electronic travel aids, and training in their use.
6. Family education and support.

Mental Health Care Treatment

Veterans eligible for VA medical care may receive general and specialty mental health treatment as needed. Mental health services are available in primary care clinics (including Home Based Primary Care), general and specialty mental health outpatient clinics, inpatient mental health units, residential rehabilitation and treatment programs, specialty medical clinics, and Community Living Centers. Mental Health services are also available in medical settings in which patients are receiving treatment, such as inpatient medicine and outpatient specialty medical clinics. In addition to general mental health care, this may include specialized PTSD services, treatment for Veterans with psychological conditions related to a history of military sexual trauma, psychosocial rehabilitation and recovery services, treatment for substance use disorders, suicide prevention programs, geriatric mental health problems, violence prevention, evidence-based psychotherapy programs, treatment with psychiatric medications consistent with VA Clinical Practice Guidelines , integrated care services, and mental health disaster response/post deployment

activities.
Specialized programs, such as mental health intensive case management, psychosocial rehabilitation and recovery centers, and work programs are provided for Veterans with serious mental health problems. VA's Program of Comprehensive Assistance for Family Caregivers entitles the designated primary and secondary Family Caregiver(s) access to mental health. These services may be offered at the VA and/or contracted agencies. General Caregivers (of all era Veterans) can receive counseling and other services when necessary if the treatment supports the Veteran's treatment plan. For more information on VA Mental Health services visit http://www. mentalhealth.va.gov/VAMentalHealthGroup.asp

*Veterans Crisis Line:*Veterans experiencing an emotional distress/ crisis or who need to talk to a trained mental health professional may call the Veterans Crisis Line 1-800-273-TALK (8255). The hotline is available 24 hours a day, seven days a week. When callers press "1", they are immediately connected with a qualifed and caring provider who can help.

Chat feature: Veterans Chat is located at the Veterans Crisis Line and enables Veterans, their families and friends to go online where they can anonymously chat with a trained VA counselor. Veterans Chat can be accessed through the suicide prevention Website www. Veterancrisisline.net by clicking on the Veterans Chat tab on the right side of the Webpage.

Text feature: Those in crisis may text 83-8255 free of charge to receive confdential, personal and immediate support.

European access: Veterans and members of the military community in Europe may now receive free, confdential support from the European Military Crisis Line, a new initiative recently launched by VA. Callers in Europe may dial 0800-1273-8255 or DSN 118 to receive confdential support from responders at the Veterans Crisis Line in the U.S. For more information about VA's suicide prevention program, visit: http://www.mentalhealth.va.gov/suicide_prevention/ or www.veteranscrisisline.net.

Make the Connection Resources: help Veterans and their family members connect with information and services to improve their lives. Visitors to MakeTheConnection.net will fnd a one-stop resource where Veterans and their family and friends can privately explore information, watch stories similar to their own, research content on mental health issues and treatment, and easily access support and information that will help them live more fulfilling lives.

At the heart of Make the Connection are powerful personal testimonials, which illustrate true stories of Veterans who faced life events, experiences, physical injuries or psychological symptoms; reached out for support; and found ways to overcome their challenges. Veterans and their families are encouraged to "make the connection" - with strength and resilience of Veterans like themselves, with other people who care, and with information and available resources for getting their lives on a better track. For more information, go to www. MakeTheConnection.net

Coaching Into Care: works with family members or friends who become aware of the Veteran's post-deployment diffculties, and supports their efFt.s to fnd help for the Veteran. This national clinical service provides information and help to Veterans and the loved ones who are concerned about them. More information about the service can be found at http://www.mirecc.va.gov/coaching/contact.asp

VA's National Center for PTSD serves as a resource for healthcare professionals, Veterans and families. Information, self-help resources, and other helpful information can be found at www.ptsd.va.gov.

The PTSD Coach is a mobile application that provides information about PTSD, self assessment and symptom management tools and provides information about to connect with resources that are available for those who might be dealing with post trauma effects. The PTSD Coach is available as a free download for iPhone or Android devices.

Mental Health Residential Rehabilitation

Mental Health Residential Rehabilitation Treatment Programs (MH RRTP) (including domiciliaries) provide residential rehabilitative and clinical care to Veterans who have a wide range of problems, illnesses, or rehabilitative care needs which can be medical, psychiatric, substance use, homelessness, vocational, educational, or social. The MH RRTP provides a 24-hour therapeutic setting utilizing a peer and professional support environment. The programs provide a strong emphasis on psychosocial rehabilitation and recovery services that instill personal responsibility to achieve optimal levels of

independence upon discharge to independent or supportive community living. MH RRTP also provides rehabilitative care for homeless
Veterans.

Eligibility: VA may provide domiciliary care to Veterans whose annual gross household income does not exceed the maximum annual
rate of VA pension or to Veterans the Secretary of Veterans Affairs
determines have no adequate means of support. The copays for
extended care services apply to domiciliary care. Call the nearest
benefts or health care facility to obtain the latest information.

Outpatient Dental Treatment
Dental benefts are provided by VA according to law. In some instances, VA is authorized to provide extensive dental care, while in
other cases treatment may be limited by law. This Fact Sheet table
describes dental eligibility criteria and contains information to assist
Veterans in understanding their eligibility for VA dental care.

By law, the eligibility for Outpatient Dental Care is not the same as for
most other VA medical benefts. It is categorized in classes. Those
eligible for VA dental care under Class I, IIC, or IV are eligible for any
necessary dental care to maintain or restore oral health and mastica-
tory function, including repeat care. Other classes have time and/or
service limitations.

*Note: Public Law 83 enacted June 16, 1955, amended Veterans'
eligibility for outpatient dental services. As a result, any Veteran who
received a dental award letter from VBA dated before 1955 in which
VBA determined the dental conditions to be noncompensable are no
longer eligible for Class II outpatient dental treatment.

Veterans receiving hospital, nursing home, or domiciliary care will be
provided dental services that are professionally determined by a VA
dentist, in consultation with the referring physician, to be essential to
the management of the patient's medical condition under active treatment. For more information about eligibility for VA medical and dental
benefts, contact VA at 1-877-222-8387 8387, Monday through Friday
between 8:00am and 8:00pm Eastern time or www.va.gov/healthben-
efts

Vocational and Work Assistance Programs
VHA provides vocational assistance and therapeutic work opportunities through three primary **Therapeutic & Supported Employment**

If you:	You are eligible for:	Through
Have a service-connected compensable dental disability or condition.	Any needed dental care.	Class I
Are a former prisoner of war.	Any needed dental care.	Class IIC
Have service-connected disabilities rated 100 percent disabling, or are unemployable and paid at the 100 percent rate due to service-connected conditions.	Any needed dental care. [note: Veterans paid at the 100 percent rate based on a temporary rating, are not eligible for comprehensive outpatient dental services.	Class IV
Apply for dental care within 180 days of discharge or release from active duty (under conditions other than dishonorable) of 90 days or more during the Gulf War era.	One-time dental care if a DD214 certifcate of discharge does not indicate that a complete dental examination and all appropriate dental treatment had been rendered prior to discharge.(NOTE)	Class II
Have a service-connected noncompensable dental condition or disability resulting from combat wounds or service trauma.	Any dental care necessary to provide and maintain a functioning dentition. A Dental Trauma Rating (VA Form 10-564-D) or VA Regional Offce Rating Decision letter (VA Form 10-7131) identifes the tooth/teeth that are trauma rated.	Class IIA
Have a dental condition clinically determined by VA to be associated with and aggravating a service-connected medical condition.	Dental care to treat the oral conditions that are determined by a VA dental professional to have a direct and material detrimental effect to a service-connected medical condition.	Class III
Are actively engaged in a 38 USC Chapter 31 vocational rehabilitation program.	Dental care to the extent necessary to: to enter, achieve goals, and prevent interruption of a rehab program; hasten the return to a rehab program because of a dental condition; or to secure and adjust to employment during employment assistance, or enable to achieve maximum independence in daily living.	Class V
Are receiving VA care or are scheduled for inpatient care and require dental care for a condition complicating a medical condition currently	Dental care to treat the oral conditions that are determined by a VA dental professional to complicate a medical condition currently under treatment.	Class VI
Are an enrolled Veteran who may be homeless and receiving care under VHA Directive 2007-039.	A one-time course of dental care that is determined medically necessary to relieve pain, assist in gaining employment, or treat moderate to severe gingival and periodontal conditions.	Class IIB

Services (TSES) programs for Veterans enrolled in the VA system of care. These programs are designed to assist Veterans to live and work as independently as possible in their respective communities. Participation in TSES vocational services cannot be used to deny or discontinue VA disability benefts. Payments received from Incentive Therapy and Compensated Work Therapy Sheltered Workshop and Transitional Work cannot be used to deny or discontinue SSI and/or SSDI payments and they are not subject to IRS taxes.

CWT/Transitional Work (CWT/TW) is vocational assessment program that operates in VA medical centers and/or local community business and industry. CWT/TW participants are matched to real life work assignments for a time-limited basis. Veterans are supervised by personnel of the sponsoring site, under the same job expectations experienced by non-CWT workers. Veterans participating in the CWT/TW program are not employees of either the Federal government or a host company and, as such, receive no traditional employee benefits. CWT/TW participants receive, at a minimum, the greater of Federal or state minimum wage for all hours worked. Approximately 40 percent of participants secure competitive employment at the time of discharge.

CWT/Supported Employment (CWT/SE) is a recovery-based intervention provided through an integrated partnership with the primary Mental Health treatment team. The employment is intended to be an extension of treatment to manage symptoms and advance recovery. CWT/SE consists of full or part-time competitive employment with extensive clinical supports to Veterans, and accommodations/supervision guidance to employers.

Other Initiatives include the adaption of SE evidence-based principles for specialty Therapeutic and Supported Employment Services programs for Veterans diagnosed with Spinal Cord Injury, Polytrauma, Traumatic Brain Injury, and/or Post Traumatic Stress Disorder. A list of CWT program sites can be found on the Location Page at http://www.cwt.va.gov.

Vocational Assistance is a set of assessment, guidance, counseling, or other related services that may be offered to groups or individuals. These services are designed to enable Veterans to realize skills, resources, attitudes and expectations needed to prepare for searching for employment, succeeding in the employment interview

process, and succeeding in employment.
Compensated Work Therapy/Sheltered Workshop operates
sheltered workshops at approximately 25 VA medical centers. CWT
Sheltered Workshop is a pre-employment vocational activity that provides an opportunity for work hardening and assessment in a simu-
lated work environment. Participating Veterans are paid the greater
of Federal or state minimum wage on a piece rate basis.

Incentive Therapy (IT) is a pre-employment program that provides
a limited work experience at VA medical centers for Veterans who
are not actively seeking competitive employment and exhibit severe
mental illness and/or physical impairments. IT services may consist
of full- or part-time work with nominal remuneration limited to the
maximum of one half of the Federal minimum wage.

Nursing Home Care
VA provides nursing home services to Veterans through three
national programs: VA owned and operated Community Living
Centers (CLC), State Veterans' Homes owned and operated by the
states, and the community nursing home program. Each program
has admission and eligibility criteria specifc to the program. Nursing
home care is available for enrolled Veterans who need nursing home
care for a service-connected disability, or Veterans or who have a
70 percent or greater service-connected disability and Veterans with
a rating of total disability based on individual unemployability. VA provided nursing home care for all other Veterans is based on available
resources.

VA Community Living Centers: Community Living Centers (CLC)
provide a dynamic array of short stay (less than 90 days) and long
stay (91 days or more) services. Short stay services include but are
not limited to skilled nursing, respite care, rehabilitation, hospice, and
continuing care for Veterans awaiting placement in the community.
Long stay services include but are not limited to dementia care and
continuing care to maintain the Veteran's level of functioning. Short
stay and long stay services are available for Veterans who are enrolled in VA health care and require CLC services.

State Veterans' Home Program: State Veterans homes are owned
and operated by the states. The states petition VA for grant dollars
for a portion of the construction costs followed by a request for rec-
ognition as a state home. Once recognized, VA pays a portion of the

per diem if the state meets VA standards. States establish eligibility criteria and determine services offered for short and long-term care. Specialized services offered are dependent upon the capability of the home to render them.

Community Nursing Home Program: VA health care facilities establish contracts with community nursing homes. The purpose of this program is to meet the nursing home needs of Veterans who require long-term nursing home care in their own community, close to their families and meet the enrollment and eligibility requirements.

Admission Criteria: The general criteria for nursing home placement in each of the three programs requires that a resident must be medically stable, i.e. not acutely ill, have suffcient functional defcits to require inpatient nursing home care, and be determined by an appropriate medical provider to need institutional nursing home care. Furthermore, the Veteran must meet the specifc eligibility criteria for community living center care or the contract nursing home program and the eligibility criteria for the specifc state Veterans home.

Home and Community Based Services: In addition to nursing home care, VA offers a variety of other long-term care services either directly or by contract with community-based agencies. Such services include adult day health care, respite care, geriatric evaluation and management, hospice and palliative care, skilled nursing and other skilled professional services at home, home health aide services, and home based primary care. Veterans receiving these services may be subject to a copay.

Emergency Medical Care in U.S. Non-VA Facilities
In the case of medical emergencies, VA may reimburse or pay for emergency non-VA medical care not previously authorized that is provided to certain eligible Veterans when VA or other federal facilities are not feasibly available. This beneft may be dependent upon other conditions, such as notifcation to VA, the nature of treatment sought, the status of the Veteran, the presence of other health care insurance, and third party liability.

Because there are different regulatory requirements that may affect VA payment and Veteran liability for the cost of care, it is very important that the nearest VA medical facility to where emergency services are furnished be notifed as soon as possible after emergency

treatment is sought. If emergency inpatient services are required, VA
will assist in transferring the Veteran to a Department facility, if available. Timely fling claim limitations apply. For additional information,
contact the nearest VA medical facility. Please note that reimbursement criteria for Veterans living or traveling outside the United States
fall under VA's Foreign Medical Program (FMP), and differ from the
criteria for payment of emergency treatment received in the United
States.

Foreign Medical Program

VA will provide reimbursement for medical services for service-connected disabilities or any disability associated with and found to be
aggravating a service-connected disability for those Veterans living
or traveling outside the United States. This program will also reimburse for the treatment of foreign medical services needed as part of
an approved VA vocational rehabilitation program. Veterans living in
the Philippines should register with the U.S. Veterans Affairs offce
in Pasay City, telephone 011-632-838-4566 or by email at manlopc.
inqry@vba.va.gov. All other Veterans living or planning to travel
outside the U.S. should register with the Denver Foreign Medical
Program offce, P.O. Box 469061, Denver, CO 80246-9061, USA;
telephone 303-331-7590. For information visit: http://www.va.gov/
hac/forbenefciaries/fmp/fmp.asp

Some Veterans traveling or living overseas can telephone the
Foreign Medical Program toll free from these countries: Germany
0800-1800-011; Australia 1800-354-965; Italy 800-782-655; United
Kingdom (England and Scotland) 0800-032-7425; Mexico 001-877-
345-8179; Japan 00531-13-0871; Costa Rica 0800-013-0759; and
Spain 900-981-776. (Note: Veterans in Mexico or Costa Rica must
frst dial the United States country code.)

On occasion Veterans will ask to have prescriptions mailed outside
the Unites States and its territories. VA Pharmacy Service will not
ship medications or medical/surgical supply items outside of the
Unites States or US Territories (Virgin Islands, Guam, American Samoa, and the Commonwealth of the Northern Mariana Islands). For
Veterans registered with the Foreign Medical Program, prescription
reimbursement is approved only for United States Food and Drug
Administration (FDA) approved medications.

Within the United States and prior to travel abroad, VA facilities
may opt to fll a Veteran patient's outpatient medications prior to the

normal dispensing date in the event that a Veteran will be traveling and unable to obtain medications while abroad. This may be done on a limited basis and requires prior consultation with the Veteran patient's VA provider prior to dispensing.

Online Health Services

VA offers Veterans, Servicemembers, their dependents and caregivers their own personal health record through My HealtheVet, found at www.myhealth.va.gov.

My HealtheVet's free, online Personal Health Record is available 24/7 with Internet access. Those with an upgraded account (obtained by completing the one-time in-person authentication* process) can:

- Participate in secure messaging with VA health care team members
- View key portions of DoD military service information
- Get VA wellness reminders
- View VA appointments
- View VA lab results
- View VA allergies, adverse reactions and other key portions of their VA electronic health record.
- View their VA Comprehensive Care Document (CCD)

With My HealtheVet, Veterans can access trusted health information to better manage personal health care and learn about other VA benefits and services.

My HealtheVet helps Veterans partner with VA health care teams by providing tools to make shared, informed decisions. Simply follow the directions on the Website to register. VA patients registered on My HealtheVet can begin to refll VA medications online. Veterans can also use the VA Blue Button to view, print, or download the health data currently in their My Health eVet account. Veterans can share this information with family, caregivers or others such as non-VA health care providers. It puts the Veteran in control of information stored in My Health eVet. Accessible through My HealtheVet, VA Blue Button also provides Veterans who were discharged from military service after 1979 access to DoD Military Service Information. This information may include Military Occupational Specialty (MOS) codes, pay details, service dates, deployment, and retirement periods.

*To access the advanced My HealtheVet features, Veterans will need to get an upgraded account by completing a one-time process at their VA facility called in-person authentication. Visit My HealtheVet at www.myhealth.va.gov, register and learn more about in-person authentication plus the many features and tools available with Internet access. Veterans with questions should contact the My HealtheVet Coordinator at their VA facility.

Caregiver Programs and Services

VA has long supported Family Caregivers as vital partners in providing care worthy of the sacrifces by America's Veterans and Servicemembers. Each VA medical center has a Caregiver Support Program coordinated by a Caregiver Support Coordinator (CSC). The CSC coordinates Caregiver activities and serve as a resource expert for Veterans, their families and VA providers. Several programs are available for all Veteran Caregivers including:

In-Home and Community Based Care: Skilled home health care, homemaker/home health aide services, community adult day health care and Home Based Primary Care.

Respite Care: Designed to relieve the family Caregiver from the constant burden of caring for a chronically ill or disabled Veteran at home. Services can include in-home care, a short stay in an institutional setting or adult day health care.

Caregiver Education and Training Programs: VA currently provides multiple training opportunities which include pre-discharge care instruction and specialized Caregiver programs in multiple severe traumas such as Traumatic Brain Injury (TBI), Spinal Cord Injury/Disorders, and Blind Rehabilitation. VA has a Caregiver web site, www.caregiver.va.gov, which provides tools, resources, and information to Family Caregivers.

Family Support Services: These support groups can be face-to-face or on the telephone. They include family counseling, spiritual and pastoral care, family leisure and recreational activities and temporary lodging in Fisher Houses.

Travel: VA's Comprehensive Assistance for Family Caregivers Program entitles the designated family caregiver to benefciary travel

benefts. These benefts include:
- Transport, lodging, and subsistence for period of Caregiver training
- Transport, lodging, and subsistence while traveling as Veteran's attendant to and from VA Healthcare as well as duration of care at VA or VA authorized facility.
- Mileage or common carrier transport.
- Lodging and/or subsistence at 50 percent of local federal employee rates

Other Benefts: VA provides durable medical equipment and prosthetic and sensory aides to improve function, fnancial assistance with home modifcation to improve access and mobility, and transportation assistance for some Veterans to and from medical appointments.

On May 5, 2010, the Caregivers and Veterans Omnibus Health Services Act of 2010 was signed into law. Title I of the Act will allow VA to provide unprecedented benefits to eligible Caregivers (a parent, spouse, child, step-family member, extended family member, or an individual who lives with the Veteran, but is not a family member) who support the Veterans who have given so much for this Nation. The law distinguishes between Veterans who incurred or aggravated a serious injury in the line of duty on or after Sept. 11, 2001 (post-9/11 Veterans), and those Veterans whose injuries were incurred prior to Sept. 11, 2001 (pre-9/11 Veterans).

The new services for this group include:
- Monthly stipend based on the personal care needs of the Veteran
- Travel expenses, including lodging and per diem while accompanying Veterans undergoing care
- Access to health care insurance through CHAMPVA if the Caregiver is not already entitled to care or services under a health plan
- Mental health services and counseling
- Comprehensive VA Caregiver training provided by Easter Seals
- Respite care
- Appropriate caregiving instruction and training

Chapter 2
Service-connected Disabilities

Disability Compensation
Disability compensation is a monetary beneft paid to Veterans who are disabled by an injury or illness that was incurred or aggravated during active military service. These disabilities are considered to be service connected.

For additional details on types of disability claims and how to apply, go to http://benefts.va.gov/benefts/

Monthly disability compensation varies with the degree of disability and the number of eligible dependents. Veterans with certain severe disabilities may be eligible for additional special monthly compensation (SMC). Disability compensation benefts are not subject to federal or state income tax.

The payment of military retirement pay, disability severance pay and separation incentive payments, known as Special Separation Beneft (SSB) and Voluntary Separation Incentive (VSI), may affect the amount of VA compensation paid to disabled Veterans.

To be eligible for compensation, the Veteran must have been separated or discharged under conditions other than dishonorable.

Receiving Disability Beneft Payments
The Department of Treasury has mandated that all recurring federal benefts be administered through either Electronic Funds Transfer (EFT) or Direct Express® Debit MasterCard®. Compensation and pension benefciaries can establish direct deposit through the Treasury's Go Direct helpline. Call toll-free 1-800-333-1795, or enroll online at www.GoDirect.org.

Veterans also have the option of receiving their benefts via a prepaid debit card, even if they do not have a bank account. There is no credit check, no minimum balance required, and basic services are free. To establish payments of federal benefts through Direct Express® Debit MasterCard® issued by Comerica Bank, call 1-888-213-1625 to enroll in the program.

2013 VA Disability Compensation Rates for Veterans

Disability Rating	Monthly Rate
10 percent	$129
20 percent	$255
30 percent*	$395
40 percent*	$569
50 percent*	$810
60 percent*	$1,026
70 percent*	$1,293
80 percent*	$1,503
90 percent*	$1,689
100 percent*	$2,816

*Veterans with disability ratings of at least 30 percent are eligible for additional allowances for dependents, including spouses, minor children, children between the ages of 18 and 23 who are attending school, children who are permanently incapable of self-support because of a disability arising before age 18, and dependent parents. The additional amount depends on the disability rating and the number of dependents.

Additional Monetary Benefits for Eligible Military Retirees
Concurrent Retirement and Disability Pay (CRDP) is a Department of Defense (DoD) program that allows some individuals to receive both military retired pay and VA disability compensation. This dual receipt was prohibited until the CRDP program began on Jan. 1, 2004. CRDP is a "phase in" of benefits that gradually restores a retiree's VA disability offset. This means that an eligible person's retired pay will gradually increase each year until the phase in is complete in Jan. 2014.

Effective Jan. 1, 2005, Veterans rated 100 percent disabled by VA, including those receiving benefits at the 100 percent rate due to individual unemployability (IU), are entitled to full CRDP without being phased in.

Eligibility: To qualify for CRDP, Veterans must:
• Have a VA service-connected rating of 50 percent or greater,

and:
* Be retired from military service based on longevity, including temporary Early Retirement Authority (TERA) retirees; or
* Be retired under Chapter 61 with 20 or more qualifying years of service; or
* Be retired from National Guard or Reserve service with 20 or more qualifying years; and
* Be eligible to receive retired pay (must be offset by VA payments).

Retirees do not need to apply for this benefit. Payment is coordinated between VA and the military pay center.

Combat-Related Special Compensation (CRSC) is a DoD program that provides tax-free monthly payments to eligible retired Veterans with combat-related disabilities. With CRSC, Veterans can receive both their military retirement pay and VA disability compensation for disabilities determined by the service department to be combat related.

Eligibility: To qualify for CRSC, Veterans must:
1. Be a military retiree.
2. Be entitled to and/or receiving military retired pay.
3. Have a compensable service-connected disability.

In addition, Veterans must be able to provide documentary evidence that their disabilities were the result of one of the following:
* Training that simulates war (e.g., exercises, feld training)
* Hazardous duty (e.g., fight, diving, parachute duty)
* An instrumentality of war (e.g., combat vehicles, weapons)
* Armed confict (e.g., gunshot wounds, Purple Heart)

Disabilities related to in-service exposure to hazards (e.g., Agent Orange, Gulf War illnesses, radiation exposure) for which VA awards compensation are considered combat-related for CRSC purposes.

For more information, visit www.defense.gov, or call the toll-free phone number for the Veteran's branch of service:

Army 1-866-281-3254, ,https://www.hrc.army.mil/site/crsc/index.html or e-mail at crsc.info@us.army.mil

Air Force 1-800-616-3775, http://www.retirees.af.mil/ or email at
AFPC.DPPDC.AFCRSC@us.af.mil

Navy/Marine Corps 1-877-366-2772, www.donhq.navy.mil/corb/
CRSCB/combatrelated.htm or email at DoN_CRSC@navy.mil

Coast Guard 1-202-493-1735, http://www.uscg.mil/adm1/crsc.asp or
email at Cassie.H.Sylvester@uscg.mil.

Disability Compensation for Presumptive Conditions
Certain chronic and tropical diseases (for example, multiple sclerosis, diabetes mellitus, and arthritis) may be service connected if the
disease becomes at least 10 percent disabling within the applicable
time limit following service. For a comprehensive list of these chronic
diseases, see 38 CFR 3.309; for applicable time limits, see 38 CFR
3.307.

All Veterans who develop Amyotrophic Lateral Sclerosis (ALS), also
known as Lou Gehrig's Disease, at any time after separation from
service may be eligible for compensation for that disability. To be
eligible, the Veteran must have served a minimum of 90 consecutive
days of active service.

Prisoners of War: For former POWs who were imprisoned for any
length of time, the following disabilities are presumed to be service
connected if they become at least 10 percent disabling anytime
after military service: psychosis, any of the anxiety states, dysthymic
disorder, organic residuals of frostbite, post-traumatic osteoarthri-
tis, atherosclerotic heart disease or hypertensive vascular disease
and their complications, stroke and its complications, and, effective
Oct.10, 2008, osteoporosis if the Veteran has post-traumatic stress
disorder (PTSD).

For former POWs who were imprisoned for at least 30 days, the
following conditions are also presumed to be service connected:
avitaminosis, beriberi, chronic dysentery, helminthiasis, malnutrition
(including optic atrophy associated with malnutrition), pellagra and/or
other nutritional defciencies, irritable bowel syndrome, peptic ulcer
disease, peripheral neuropathy except where related to infectious
causes, cirrhosis of the liver, and, effective Sept. 28, 2009, osteoporosis.

Veterans Exposed to Agent Orange and Other Herbicides: A Veteran who served in the Republic of Vietnam between Jan. 9, 1962, and May 7, 1975, is presumed to have been exposed to Agent Orange and other herbicides used in support of military operations. VA presumes the following diseases to be service-connected for such exposed Veterans: AL amyloidosis, chloracne or other acneform disease similar to chloracne, porphyria cutanea tarda, soft-tissue sarcoma (other than osteosarcoma, chondrosarcoma, Kaposi's sarcoma or mesothelioma), Hodgkin's disease, multiple myeloma, respiratory cancers (lung, bronchus, larynx, trachea), non-Hodgkin's lymphoma, prostate cancer, acute and subacute peripheral neuropathy, diabetes mellitus (Type 2), all chronic B-cell leukemias (including, but not limited to, hairy-cell leukemia and chronic lymphocytic leukemia), Parkinson's disease, and ischemic heart disease.

Veterans Exposed to Radiation: For Veterans who participated in radiation risk activities as defned in VA regulations while on active duty, active duty for training, or inactive duty training, the following conditions are presumed to be service connected: all forms of leukemia (except for chronic lymphocytic leukemia); cancer of the thyroid, breast, pharynx, esophagus, stomach, small intestine, pancreas, bile ducts, gall bladder, salivary gland, urinary tract (renal pelvis, ureter, urinary bladder and urethra), brain, bone, lung, colon, and ovary; bronchiolo-alveolar carcinoma; multiple myeloma; lymphomas (other than Hodgkin's disease), and primary liver cancer (except if cirrhosis or hepatitis B is indicated).

To determine service connection for other conditions or exposures not eligible for presumptive service connection, VA considers factors such as the amount of radiation exposure, duration of exposure, elapsed time between exposure and onset of the disease, gender and family history, age at time of exposure, the extent to which a non-service exposure could contribute to disease, and the relative sensitivity of exposed tissue.

Gulf War Veterans with Chronic Disabilities may receive disability compensation for chronic disabilities resulting from undiagnosed illnesses and/or medically unexplained chronic multi-symptom illnesses defned by a cluster of signs or symptoms. A disability is considered chronic if it has existed for at least six months.

The undiagnosed illness must have appeared either during active service in the Southwest Asia theater of operations during the Gulf War period of Aug. 2, 1990, to July 31, 1991, or to a degree of at least 10 percent at any time since then through Dec.31, 2016. This theater of operations includes Iraq, Kuwait, Saudi Arabia, the neutral zone between Iraq and Saudi Arabia, Bahrain, Qatar, the United Arab Emirates, Oman, the Gulf of Aden, the Gulf of Oman, the Persian Gulf, the Arabian Sea, the Red Sea, and the airspace above these locations.

Examples of symptoms of an undiagnosed illness and medically unexplained chronic multi-symptom illness defned by a cluster of signs and symptoms include: chronic fatigue syndrome, fbromyalgia, functional gastrointestinal disorders , fatigue, signs or symptoms involving the skin, headache, muscle pain, joint pain, neurological signs or symptoms, neuropsychological signs or symptoms, signs or symptoms involving the respiratory system (upper or lower), sleep disturbances, gastrointestinal signs or symptoms, cardiovascular signs or symptoms, abnormal weight loss, and menstrual disorders.

Presumptive service connection may be granted for the following in-fectious diseases if found compensable within a specifc time period: Brucellosis, Campylobacter jejuni, Coxiella burnetti (Q fever), Ma-laria, Mycobacterium tuberculosis, Nontyphoid Salmonella, Shigella, Visceral leishmaniasis, and West Nile virus. Qualifying periods of service for these infectious diseases include active military, naval, or air service in the above stated Southwest Asia theater of operations during the Gulf War period of Aug. 2, 1990, until such time as the Gulf War is ended by Congressional action or Presidential proclama-tion; and active military, naval, or air service on or after Sept. 19, 2001, in Afghanistan.

Housing Grants for Disabled Veterans Certain Servicemembers and Veterans with service-connected disabilities may be entitled to a housing grant from VA to help build a new specially adapted house, to adapt a home they already own, or buy a house and modify it to meet their disability-related requirements. Eligible Veterans or Servicemembers may now receive up to three grants, with the total dollar amount of the grants not to exceed the maximum allowable. Previous grant recipients who had received assistance of less than the current maximum allowable may be eligible for an additional grant.

Specially Adapted Housing (SAH) Grant Eligibility for up to
$64,960: VA may approve a grant of not more than 50 percent of
the cost of building, buying, or adapting existing homes or paying
to reduce indebtedness on a currently owned home that is being
adapted, up to a maximum of $64,960. In certain instances, the full
grant amount may be applied toward remodeling costs. Veterans and
Servicemembers must be determined eligible to receive compensation for permanent and total service-connected disability due to one
of the following:
1. Loss or loss of use of both lower extremities, which so affects the
    functions of balance or propulsion to preclude ambulating without
    the aid of braces, crutches, canes or a wheelchair.
    2. Loss or loss of use of both upper extremities at or above the
        elbow.
    3. Blindness in both eyes, having only light perception, plus loss
        or loss of use of one lower extremity.
    4. Loss or loss of use of one lower extremity together with (a)
        residuals of organic disease or injury, or (b) the loss or loss of
        use of one upper extremity which so affects the functions of
        balance or propulsion as to preclude locomotion without the
        use of braces, canes, crutches or a wheelchair.
    5. Severe burn injuries, which are defned as full thickness or
        subdermal burns that have resulted in contractures with
        limitation of motion of two or more extremities or of at least
        one extremity and the trunk.
    6. The loss, or loss of use of one or more lower extremities due
        to service
        on or after Sept. 11, 2001, which so affects the functions
        of balance or propulsion as to preclude ambulating without the
        aid of braces, crutches, canes, or a wheelchair.

Special Home Adaption (SHA) Grant: Eligibility for up to $12,992:
VA may approve a beneft amount up to a maximum of $12,992, for
the cost of necessary adaptations to a Servicemember's or Veteran's
residence or to help him/her acquire a residence already adapted
with special features for his/her disability, to purchase and adapt a
home, or for adaptations to a family member's home in which they
will reside.

To be eligible for this grant, Servicemembers and Veterans must be
entitled to compensation for permanent and total service-connected
disability due to one of the following:

1. Blindness in both eyes with 20/200 visual acuity or less.
2. Anatomical loss or loss of use of both hands.
3. Severe burn injuries (see above).

Temporary Residence Adaptation (TRA): Eligible Veterans and Servicemembers who are temporarily residing in a home owned by a family member may also receive a TRA grant to help the Veteran or Servicemember adapt the family member's home to meet his or her special needs. Those eligible for a $64,960 grant would be permitted to use up to $28,515 and those eligible for a $12,992 grant would be permitted to use up to $5,092. Grant amounts are adjusted Oct.1 every year based on a cost-of-construction index. These adjustments will increase the grant amounts or leave them unchanged; grant amounts will not decrease. Under the Honoring America's Veterans and Caring for Camp Lejeune Families Act of 2012, TRA grant amounts will not count against SAH grant maximum amounts starting Aug. 6, 2013.

The property may be located outside the United States, in a country or political subdivision which allows individuals to have or acquire a benefcial property interest, and in which the Secretary of Veterans Affairs, in his or her discretion, has determined that it is reasonably practicable for the Secretary to provide assistance in acquiring specially adapted housing. For more information on SAH, visit http://www.benefts.va.gov/homeloans/sah.asp.

Supplemental Financing: Veterans and Servicemembers with available loan guaranty entitlement may also obtain a guaranteed loan or a direct loan from VA to supplement the grant to acquire a specially adapted home. Amounts with a guaranteed loan from a private lender will vary, but the maximum direct loan from VA is $33,000. Additional information about the Specially Adapted Housing Program is available at http://www.benefts.va.gov/homeloans/sah.asp.

Automobile Allowance: As of Oct. 1, 2012, Veterans and Servicemembers may be eligible for a one-time payment of not more than $19,505 toward the purchase of an automobile or other conveyance if they have service-connected loss or permanent loss of use of one or both hands or feet, or permanent impairment of vision of both eyes to a certain degree.

They may also be eligible for adaptive equipment, and for repair, replacement, or reinstallation required because of disability or for the safe operation of a vehicle purchased with VA assistance. To apply, contact a VA regional offce at 1-800-827-1000 or the nearest VA health care facility.

Clothing Allowance: Any Veteran who has service-connected disabilities that require a prosthetic or orthopedic appliances may receive clothing allowances. This allowance is also available to any Veteran whose service-connected skin condition requires prescribed medication that irreparably damages outer garments. To apply, contact the prosthetic representative at the nearest VA medical center.

Allowance for Aid and Attendance or Housebound Veterans
A Veteran who is determined by VA to be in need of the regular aid and attendance of another person, or a Veteran who is permanently housebound, may be entitled to additional disability compensation or pension payments. A Veteran evaluated at 30 percent or more disabled is entitled to receive an additional payment for a spouse who is in need of the aid and attendance of another person.

Chapter 3
VR&E

Vocational Rehabilitation and Employment (VR&E): sometimes referred to as the Chapter 31 program. VR&E provides services to eligible Servicemembers and Veterans with service-connected disabilities to help them prepare for, obtain, and maintain suitable employment or achieve independence in daily living. Additional information is available at www.vetsuccess.gov.

Eligibility for Veterans: A Veteran must have a VA service-connected disability rated at least 20 percent with an employment handicap, or rated 10 percent with a serious employment handicap, and be discharged or released from military service under other than dishonorable conditions.

Eligibility for Servicemembers: Servicemembers are eligible to apply if they expect to receive an honorable discharge upon separation from active duty, obtain a rating of 20 percent percent or more from VA, obtain a proposed Disability Evaluation System (DES) rating of 20 percent percent or more from VA, or obtain a referral to a Physical Evaluation Board (PEB) through the Integrated Disability Evaluation System (IDES).

Entitlement: A Vocational Rehabilitation Counselor (VRC) works with the Veteran to determine if an employment handicap exists. An employment handicap exists if a Veteran's service- connected disability impairs his/her ability to prepare for, obtain, and maintain suitable career employment. After an entitlement decision is made, the Veteran and VRC work together to develop a rehabilitation plan. The rehabilitation plan outlines the rehabilitation services to be provided.

Services: Based on their individualized needs, Veterans work with a VRC to select one of fve vocational tracks of services. If a program of training is selected, the VA pays the cost of the approved training and services (except those coordinated through other providers) that are included in an individual's rehabilitation plan, including subsistence allowance.

VR&E's fve tracks of services are:
Reemployment with Previous Employer: For individuals who are separating from active duty or in the National Guard or Reserves and are returning to work for their previous employer.

Rapid Access to Employment: For individuals who either wish to obtain employment soon after separation or who already have the necessary skills to be competitive in the job market in an appropriate occupation.

Self-Employment: For individuals who have limited access to traditional employment, need fexible work schedules, or who require more accommodation in the work environment due to their disabling conditions or other life circumstances.

Employment Through Long-Term Services: For individuals who need specialized training and/or education to obtain and maintain suitable employment.

Independent Living Services: For Veterans who are not currently able to work and need rehabilitation services to live more independently.

Length of a Rehabilitation Program: The basic period of eligibility in which VR&E benfts may be used is 12 years from the latter of the following: 1). A Veteran's date of separation from active military service, or 2). The date VA frst notifed a Veteran that he/she have a compensable service-connected disability. Depending on the length of program needed, Veterans may be provided up to 48 months of full-time services or the part-time equivalent. Rehabilitation plans that only provide services to improve independence in daily living are limited to 30 months. These limitations may be extended in certain circumstances.

Intergrated Disability Evaluation System (IDES): VR&E is providing earlier access to VR&E benefts to wounded, ill or injured Servicemembers pending a medical separation from military service. Vocational Rehabilitation Counselors are assigned to military installations hosting an IDES site and provide VR&E services to assist Servicemembers in the transition from active-duty to entering the labor market in viable careers.

Current locations include: Joint Base Elmendorf-Richardson, Ft. Wainwright, Ft. Benning, Ft. Gordon, Robins AFB, Ft. Meade, Ft. Drum, BeauFt. NH, Ft. Jackson, Ft. Carson, Tripler AMC, Pearl Harbor NH, San Antonio JB (Sam Houston), Ft. Irwin, Ft. Knox, White-River Junction, Pensacola NH, Ft. Rucker, Redstone Arsenal, Ft. Sill, Sheppard AFB, Ft. Campbell, Ft. Polk, Travis AFB, Ft. Huachuca, Nellis AFB, Ft. Eustis, Portsmouth NMC, Ft. Lee, Langley JB, San Diego Navy Medical Center (Balboa), Ft. Lewis, Kitsap Naval Base, Fairchild AFB, Ft. Lewis (JB Lewis McChord), Ft. Leonard Wood, Jacksonville NH, Ft. Bliss, Ft. Hood, Bethesda NNMC/Walter Reed AMC, Andrews AFB, Ft. Belvoir, MCB Quantico, Ft. Riley, Camp Lejuene, Ft. Bragg, Seymour-Johnson AFB, and Cherry Point NH.

VetSuccess.gov: See page 57.

Work-Study Program: Refer to Chapter 5, "Education and Training"

Educational and Vocational Counseling Services: Refer to Chapter 10, "Transition Assistance"

Dependents and Survivors Educational Assistance: Refer to Chapter 12, "Dependents and Survivors Benefts"

Fiduciary Program: The fduciary program provides oversight of VA's most vulnerable benefciaries who are unable to manage their VA benefts because of injury, disease, the infrmities of advanced age, or being under 18 years of age. VA appoints fduciaries who manage VA benefts for these benefciaries and conducts oversight of VA-appointed fduciaries to ensure that they are meeting the needs of the benefciaries they serve.

VA closely monitors fduciaries for compliance with program responsibilities to ensure that VA benefts are being used for the purpose of meeting the needs, security, and comfort of benefciaries and their dependents. In deciding who should act as fduciary for a benefciary, VA will always select the most effective and least restrictive fduciary arrangement.

This means that VA will frst consider whether the benefciary can manage his/her VA benefts with limited supervision. VA will consider the choice of the benefciary as well as any family, friends and caregivers who are qualifed and willing to provide fduciary services for the benefciary without a fee.

As a last resort, VA will consider appointment of a paid fduciary. For more information about VA's fduciary program, please visit our website at http://benefts.va.gov/fduciary/index.asp.

Vocational Rehabilitation and Employment Subsistence Allowance: In some cases, a Veteran may require additional education or training to become employable. A subsistence allowance is paid each month during training and is based on the rate of attendance (full-time or part-time), the number of dependents, and the type of training.

Veterans who are eligible for both VR&E services and Post-9/11 GI Bill benefts may elect a special subsistence allowance that is based on the monthly basic allowance for housing paid to active duty military. The monthly amount varies depending on the ZIP code of the training facility and is usually greater than the following regular subsistence allowance rates that are available to Veterans with no Post-9/11 GI Bill eligibility who are using VR&E benefts.

Active-duty Servicemembers are not eligible for subsistence allowance until after Release from Active Duty date (RAD). 2012.

VR&E Subsistence Allowance Rates as of Oct. 1, 2012

Training	Time	No dependents	One dependent	Two dependents	Each Additional dependent
Institutional*	Full-Time	$585.11	$725.78	$855.28	$62.34
	3/4-Time	$439.64	$545.13	$639.45	$47.94
	1/2-Time	$294.17	$364.47	$428.42	$31.99
Farm Co-op Apprentice OJT**	Full-Time	$511.58	$618.65	$713.00	$46.38
Extended Evaluation Services in Rehab Facility	Full-Time	$585.11	$725.78	$855.28	$62.34
	3/4-Time	$439.64	$545.13	$639.45	$47.94
	1/2-Time	$294.17	$364.47	$428.42	$31.99
	1/4-Time	$147.06	$182.25	$214.21	$15.95
Independ. Living	Full-Time	$585.11	$725.78	$855.28	$62.34
	3/4-Time	$439.64	$545.13	$639.45	$47.94
	1/2-Time	$294.17	$364.47	$428.42	$31.99

For VR&E Training Programs Subsistence Allowance Rates, please go to http://www.vba.va.gov/bln/vre/sa.htm.

Chapter 4
VA Pensions

Eligibility for Veterans Pension
Low-income wartime Veterans may qualify for pension if they meet
certain service, income and net worth limits set by law; are age 65 or
older, permanently and totally disabled, a patient in a nursing home
receiving skilled nursing care, receiving Social Security Disability
Insurance, or receiving Supplemental Security Income. Generally,
a Veteran must have at least 90 days of active duty service, with at
least one day during a VA recognized wartime period. The 90-day active service requirement does not apply to Veterans discharged from
the military due to a service-connected disability. (Veterans may have
to meet longer minimum periods of active duty if they entered active
duty on or after Sept. 8, 1980, or, if they were offcers who entered
active duty on or after Oct. 16, 1981.) The Veteran's discharge must
have been under conditions other than dishonorable and the disability must be for reasons other than the Veteran's own willful misconduct.

Payments are made to bring the Veteran's total income, including other retirement or Social Security income, to a level set by
Congress. Unreimbursed medical expenses may reduce countable
income for VA purposes.

Protected Pension: Pension benefciaries, who were receiving a VA
pension on December 31, 1978, and do not wish to elect the Improved Pension, will continue to receive the pension rate received on
that date. This rate generally continues as long as the benefciary's
income remains within established limits, or net worth does not bar
payment, and the benefciary does not lose any dependents.

Benefciaries must continue to meet basic eligibility factors, such as
permanent and total disability for Veterans. VA must adjust rates for
other reasons, such as a Veteran's hospitalization in a VA facility.

Medal of Honor Pension: VA administers a pension beneft to recipients of the Medal of Honor. This entitlement is not based on income
level or need. Congress set the monthly pension at $1,259 for 2013.

Veterans Pension: Congress establishes the maximum annual Veterans Pension rates. Payments are reduced by the amount of countable income of the Veteran, spouse, and dependent children. When a Veteran without a spouse or a child is furnished nursing home or domiciliary care by VA, the pension is reduced to an amount not to exceed $90 per month after three calendar months of care. The reduction may be delayed if nursing-home care is being continued to provide the Veteran with rehabilitation services.

Aid and Attendance and Housebound Benefts (Special Monthly Pension): Veterans and surviving spouses who are eligible for VA pensions are eligible for higher maximum pension rates if they qualify for aid and attendance or housebound benefts. An eligible individual may qualify if he or she requires the regular aid of another person in order to perform personal functions required in everyday living, or is bedridden, a patient in a nursing home due to mental or physical incapacity, blind, or permanently and substantially confned to his/her immediate premises because of a disability.

Veterans and surviving spouses who are ineligible for basic pension based on annual income may still be eligible for VA Pension if they are eligible for aid and attendance or housebound benefts because a higher income limit applies. In addition, unreimbursed medical expenses for nursing home or home-health care may be used to reduce countable annual income, which may result in a higher pension beneft.

Claimants may apply for aid and attendance or housebound benefts by completing VA Form 21-2680 (available through www.va.gov). Claimants may also write to the nearest VA regional offce and include copies of any evidence, preferably a report from an attending physician or a nursing home, validating the need for aid and attendance or housebound care. The report should be in suffcient detail to determine whether there is disease or injury producing physical or mental impairment, loss of coordination, or conditions affecting the ability to dress and undress, to feed oneself, to attend to sanitary needs, and to keep oneself ordinarily clean and presentable. In addition, VA may need to determine whether the claimant is confned to the home or immediate premises.

VA also pays a special $90 monthly rate to pension-eligible Veterans or surviving spouses with no dependents who receive Medicaid-covered nursing home care. These funds are available for the beneficiary's personal use and may not be used to offset the cost of his or her care.

2012 VA Improved Pension - Veterans Rates

Status of Veteran's Family Situation and Caretaking Needs	Maximum Annual Rate
Veteran without dependents	$12,465
Veteran with one dependent	$16,324
Veteran permanently housebound, no dependents	$15,233
Veteran permanently housebound, one dependent	$19,093
Veteran needing regular aid and attendance, no dependents	$20,795
Veteran needing regular aid and attendance, one dependent	$24,652
Two Veterans married to one another	$16,324
Increase for each additional dependent child	$2,129

* Additional information can be found in the Pension Benefts section at www.benefts.va.gov/pension/

Chapter 5
Education and Training

This chapter provides a summary of VA educational and training benefts. Additional information can be found at www.gibill.va.gov/ or by calling 1-888-GI-BILL-1 (1-888-442-4551).

Post – 9/11 GI Bill

Eligibility: The Post- 9/11 GI Bill is an education beneft program for Servicemembers and Veterans who served on active duty after Sept. 10, 2001. Benefts are payable for training pursued on or after Aug. 1, 2009. No payments can be made under this program for training pursued before that date.

To be eligible, the Servicemember or Veteran must serve at least 90 aggregate days on active duty after Sept. 10, 2001, and remain on active duty or be honorably discharged. Active duty includes active service performed by National Guard members under title 32 U.S.C. for the purposes of organizing, administering, recruiting, instructing, or training the National Guard; or under section 502(f) for the purpose of responding to a national emergency. Veterans may also be eligible if they were honorably discharged from active duty for a service-connected disability after serving 30 continuous days after Sept. 10, 2001. Generally, Servicemembers or Veterans may receive up to 36 months of entitlement under the Post-9/11 GI Bill.

Eligibility for benefts expires 15 years from the last period of active duty of at least 90 consecutive days. If released for a service-connected disability after at least 30 days of continuous service, eligibility ends 15 years from when the member is released for the service-connected disability. If, on Aug.1, 2009, the Servicemember or Veteran is eligible for the Montgomery GI Bill; the Montgomery GI Bill – Selected Reserve; or the Reserve Educational Assistance Program, and qualifes for the Post-9/11 GI Bill, an irrevocable election must be made to receive benefts under the Post-9/11 GI Bill.

In most instances, once the election to receive benefts under the Post-9/11 GI Bill is made, the individual will no longer be eligible to receive benefts under the relinquished program.

Based on the length of active duty service, eligible participants are entitled to receive a percentage of the following:

1. Cost of in-state tuition and fees at public institutions and for the 2011-2012 academic year, up to $17,500 towards tuition and fee costs at private and foreign institutions (paid directly to the school);
2. Monthly housing allowance equal to the basic allowance for housing payable to a military E-5 with dependents, in the same Zip code as the primary school (paid directly to the Servicemember, Veteran, or eligible dependents);
3. Yearly books and supplies stipend of up to $1,000 per year (paid directly to the Servicemember, Veteran, or eligible dependents); and
4. A one-time payment of $500 paid to certain individuals relocating from highly rural areas.

* The housing allowance is not payable to individuals pursuing training at half time or less.

Approved training under the Post-9/11 GI Bill includes graduate and undergraduate degrees, vocational/technical training, on-the-job training, fight training, correspondence training, licensing and national testing programs, and tutorial assistance.

Individuals serving an aggregate period of active duty after Sept. 10, 2001 can receive the following percentages based on length of service:

Active Duty Service	Maximum Benefit
At least 36 months	100 percent
At least 30 continuous days and discharged due to service-connected disability	100 percent
At least 30 months < 36 months (1)	90 percent
At least 24 months < 30 months (1)	80 percent (3)
At least 18 months < 24 months (2)	70 percent
At least 12 months < 18 months (2)	60 percent
At least 6 months < 12 months (2)	50 percent
At least 90 days < 6 months (2)	40 percent

(1) Includes service on active duty in entry level and skill training. (2) Excludes service on active duty in entry level and skill training. (3) If the

individual would only qualify at the 70 percent level when service on active duty in entry level and skill training is excluded, then VA can only pay at the 70 percent level.

The Yellow Ribbon G.I. Education Enhancement Program was enacted to potentially assist eligible individuals with payment of their tuition and fees in instances where costs exceed the in-state tuition charges at a public institution or the national maximum payable at private and foreign institutions. To be eligible, the student must be: a Veteran receiving benefits at the 100 percent benefit rate payable, a transfer-of-entitlement-eligible dependent child, or a transfer-of-entitlement eligible spouse of a Veteran.

The school of attendance must have accepted VA's invitation to participate in the program, state how much student tuition will be waived (up to 50 percent) and how many participants will be accepted into the program during the current academic year. VA will match the school's percentage (up to 50 percent) to reduce or eliminate out-of-pocket costs for eligible participants.

Transfer of Entitlement (TOE): DoD may offer members of the Armed Forces on or after Aug.1, 2009, the opportunity to transfer benefits to a spouse or dependent children. DoD and the military services must approve all requests for this benefit. Members of the Armed Forces approved for the TOE may only transfer any unused portion of their Post-9/11 GI Bill benefits while a member of the Armed Forces, subject to their period of eligibility.

Marine Gunnery Sergeant John David Fry Scholarship: This scholarship entitles children of those who die in the line of duty on or after Sept. 11, 2001, to use Post-9/11 GI Bill benefits.

Eligible children:
- are entitled to 36 months of benefits at the 100 percent level
- have 15 years to use the benefit beginning on their 18th birthday
- may use the benefit until their 33rd birthday
- are not eligible for the Yellow Ribbon Program

Restoring GI Bill Fairness Act of 2011
The Restoring GI Bill Fairness Act of 2011 amended the Post-9/11 GI Bill. The provisions of the bill are applicable to training pursued under

the Post-9/11 GI Bill that began on or after Aug. 1, 2011.

The legislation authorizes VA to pay more than the national maximum set for private schools (currently $17,500 or the appropriately reduced amount based on eligibility percentage) in tuition and fees under the Post-9/11 GI Bill for certain students attending private colleges and universities in seven states - Arizona, Michigan, New Hampshire, New York, Pennsylvania, South Carolina and Texas.

To qualify for the increased payment (also referred to as the "grandfathered" tuition and fee amount), students must have been enrolled in the same college or university since Jan. 4, 2011, and have been enrolled in a program for which the combined amount of tuition and fees for full-time attendance during the 2010-2011 academic year exceeded $17,500.

VOW to Hire Heroes Act of 2011

Included in this new law is the Veterans Retraining Assistance Program (VRAP) for unemployed Veterans. VA and the Department of Labor (DoL) rolled out this new program on July 1, 2012. The program provides retraining for Veterans hardest hit by current economic conditions.

VRAP offers 12 months of training assistance to unemployed Veterans. To qualify, a Veteran must:
• Be at least 35, but no more than 60 years old
• Be unemployed (as determined by DoL)
• Have an other than dishonorable discharge
• Not be eligible for any other VA education benefit program (e.g., the Post-9/11 GI Bill, Montgomery GI Bill, Vocational Rehabilitation and Employment assistance)
• Not be in receipt of VA compensation due to unemployability
• Not be enrolled in a federal or state job-training program

The program is limited to 54,000 participants from Oct. 1, 2012, through March 31, 2014. Participants may receive up to 12 months of assistance at the full-time payment rate under the Montgomery GI Bill–Active Duty program (currently $1,564 per month). Applications will be submitted through DoL and benefits paid by VA. DoL provides employment assistance to every Veteran who participates upon completion of their program.

Participants must be enrolled in a VA-approved program of education offered by a community college or technical school. The program must lead to an associate degree, non-college degree, or a certifcation, and train the Veteran for a high-demand occupation.

More details will be available at www.gibill.va.gov and on VA's Facebook, which are updated regularly.

VetSuccess on Campus: is designed to provide on-campus benefts assistance and readjustment counseling to assist Veterans in completing their college educations and entering the labor market in viable careers. Under this program, a full-time, experienced Vocational Rehabilitation Counselor and a part-time Vet Center Outreach

Coordinator are assigned at each campus to provide VA benefits outreach, support, and assistance to ensure their health, educational, and beneft needs are met.

Current locations include Cleveland State University, Community College of Rhode Island, Rhode Island College, University of Maryland University College, Western Michigan University, Kalamazoo Valley Community College, Kellogg Community College, Eastern Michigan University, University of Michigan - Ann Arbor, Washtenaw Community College, University of South Florida, Middle Tennessee State University, Eastern Kentucky University, Norfolk State University, Tidewater Community College, Tidewater Community College – Chesapeake, Tidewater Community College – Portsmouth, Tidewater Community College - Virginia Beach, Tarrant County College District - South Campus, Tarrant County College District - Northeast Campus, Texas A&M University - Central Texas, Sam Houston State University, University of Texas-San Antonio, Arizona State University, Boise State University, Salt Lake Community College, University of Utah, Portland State University, San Diego State University, University of Alaska –Anchorage, Central New Mexico Community College, and University of New Mexico.

Educational and Vocational Counseling Services: Refer to Chapter 10, "Transition Assistance," for detailed information on available services.

Montgomery GI Bill

Eligibility: VA educational benefts may be used while the Servicemember is on active duty or after the Servicemember's separation from active duty with a fully honorable military discharge. Discharges "under honorable conditions" and "general" discharges do not establish eligibility.

Eligibility generally expires 10 years after the Servicemember's discharge. However, there are exceptions for disability, re-entering active duty, and upgraded discharges.
All participants must have a high school diploma, equivalency certifcate, or have completed 12 hours toward a college degree before applying for benefts.

Previously, Servicemembers had to meet the high school requirement before they completed their initial active duty obligation. Those who did not may now meet the requirement and reapply for benefts. If eligible, they must use their benefts within 10 years from the date of last discharge from active duty.

Additionally, every Veteran must establish eligibility under one of four categories.

Category 1: Service after June 30, 1985
For Veterans who entered active duty for the frst time after June 30, 1985, did not decline MGIB in writing, and had their military pay reduced by $100 a month for 12 months. Servicemembers can apply after completing two continuous years of service. Veterans must have completed three continuous years of active duty, or two continuous years of active duty if they frst signed up for less than three years or have an obligation to serve four years in the Selected Reserve (the 2x4 program) and enter the Selected Reserve within one year of discharge.

Servicemembers or Veterans who received a commission as a result of graduation from a service academy or completion of an ROTC scholarship are not eligible under Category 1 unless they received their commission:
    1. After becoming eligible for MGIB benefts (including completing the minimum service requirements for the initial period of active duty); or
    2. After Sept. 30, 1996, and received less than $3,400 during any one year under ROTC scholarship.

Servicemembers or Veterans who declined MGIB because they received repayment from the military for education loans are also ineligible under Category 1. If they did not decline MGIB and received loan repayments, the months served to repay the loans will be deducted from their entitlement.

Early Separation from Military Service: Servicemembers who did not complete the required period of military service may be eligible under:

Category 1: If discharged for one of the following:
1. Convenience of the government—with 30 continuous months of service for an obligation of three or more years, or 20 continuous months of service for an obligation of less than three years
2. Service-connected disability
3. Hardship
4. A medical condition diagnosed prior to joining the military
5. A condition that interfered with performance of duty and did not result from misconduct
6. A reduction in force (in most cases)
7. Sole Survivorship (if discharged after 9/11/01)

Category 2: Vietnam Era GI Bill Conversion
For Veterans who had remaining entitlement under the Vietnam Era GI Bill on Dec. 31, 1989, and served on active duty for any number of days during the period Oct. 19, 1984, to June 30, 1985, for at least three continuous years beginning on July 1, 1985; or at least two continuous years of active duty beginning on July 1, 1985, followed by four years in the Selected Reserve beginning within one year of release from active duty.

Veterans not on active duty on Oct. 19, 1984, may be eligible under Category 2 if they served three continuous years on active duty beginning on or after July 1, 1985, or two continuous years of active duty at any time followed by four continuous years in the Selected Reserve beginning within one year of release from active duty.

Veterans are barred from eligibility under Category 2 if they received a commission after Dec. 31, 1976, as a result of graduation from a service academy or completion of an ROTC scholarship.

However, such a commission is not disqualifying if they received the commission after becoming eligible for MGIB benefts, or received the commission after Sept. 30, 1996, and received less than $3,400 during any one year under ROTC scholarship.

Category 3: Involuntary Separation/Special Separation
For Veterans who meet one of the following requirements:
1. Elected MGIB before being involuntarily separated; or
2. were voluntarily separated under the Voluntary Separation Incentive or the Special Separation Beneft program, elected MGIB benefts before being separated, and had military pay reduced by $1,200 before discharge.

Category 4: Veterans Educational Assistance Program
For Veterans who participated in the Veterans Educational Assistance Program (VEAP) and:
1. Served on active duty on Oct. 9, 1996.
2. Participated in VEAP and contributed money to an account.
3. Elected MGIB by Oct. 9, 1997, and paid $1,200.

Veterans who participated in VEAP on or before Oct. 9, 1996, may also be eligible even if they did not deposit money in a VEAP account if they served on active duty from Oct. 9, 1996, through April 1, 2000, elected MGIB by Oct. 31, 2001, and contributed $2,700 to MGIB.

Certain National Guard Servicemembers may also qualify under Category 4 if they:
1. Served for the frst time on full-time active duty in the National Guard between June 30, 1985, and Nov. 29, 1989, and had no previous active duty service.
2. Elected MGIB during the nine-month window ending on July 9, 1997; and
3. Paid $1,200.

Payments: Effective Oct. 1, 2012, the rate for full-time training in college, technical or vocational school is $1,564 a month for those who served three years or more or two years plus four years in the Selected Reserve. For those who served less than three years, the monthly rate is $1,270

Benefts are reduced for part-time training. Payments for other types of training follow different rules. VA will pay an additional amount, called a "kicker" or "college fund," if directed by DoD. Visit www.gibill.

va.gov for more information. The maximum number of months Veterans can receive payments is 36 months at the full-time rate or the part-time equivalent.

The following groups qualify for the maximum: Veterans who served the required length of active duty, Veterans with an obligation of three years or more who were separated early for the convenience of the government and served 30 continuous months, and Veterans with an obligation of less than three years who were separated early for the convenience of the government and served 20 continuous months.

Types of Training Available:
1. Courses at colleges and universities leading to associate, bachelor or graduate degrees, including accredited independent study offered through distance education.
2. Courses leading to a certifcate or diploma from business, technical or vocational schools.
3. Apprenticeship or on-the-job training for those not on active duty, including self-employment training begun on or after June 16, 2004, for ownership or operation of a franchise
4. Correspondence courses, under certain conditions.
5. Flight training, if the Veteran holds a private pilot's license upon beginning the training and meets the medical requirements.
6. State-approved teacher certifcation programs.
7. Preparatory courses necessary for admission to a college or graduate school.
8. License and certifcation tests approved for Veterans.
9. Entrepreneurship training courses to create or expand small businesses.
10. Tuition assistance using MGIB as "Top-Up" (active duty Servicemembers).

Accelerated payments for certain high-cost programs are authorized.

Work-Study Program: Participants who train at the three-quarter or full-time rate may be eligible for a work-study program in which they work for VA and receive hourly wages. Students under the work-study program must be supervised by a VA employee, and all duties performed must relate to VA. The types of work allowed include:
Working in Veterans-related position at schools or other training

facilities.

Providing hospital or domiciliary care at a state home.

Working at national or state Veterans' cemeteries.

Various jobs within any VA facility.

Providing assistance in obtaining a beneft under title 38 U.S.C. at a state Veterans agency.

Assisting in the administration of chapters 1606 or 1607 of title 10 U.S.C. at a Department of Defense, Coast Guard, or National Guard facility.

Working in a Center for Excellence for Veterans Student Success.

Educational and Vocational Counseling Services: Refer to Chapter 10, "Transition Assistance", for detailed information on available services.

Veterans' Educational Assistance Program

Eligibility: Active duty personnel could participate in the Veterans' Educational Assistance Program (VEAP) if they entered active duty for the frst time after Dec. 31, 1976, and before July 1, 1985, and made a contribution prior to April 1, 1987.

The maximum contribution is $2,700. Active duty participants may make a lump-sum contribution to their VEAP account. For more information, visit www.gibill.va.gov.

Servicemembers who participated in VEAP are eligible to receive benefts while on active duty if:

1. At least three months of contributions are available, except for high school or elementary, in which only one month is needed.
2. And they enlisted for the frst time after Sept. 7, 1980, and completed 24 months of their frst period of active duty.

Servicemembers must receive a discharge under conditions other than dishonorable for the qualifying period of service. Servicemembers who enlisted for the frst time after Sept. 7, 1980, or entered active duty as an offcer or enlistee after Oct. 16, 1981, must have completed 24 continuous months of active duty, unless they meet a qualifying exception.

Eligibility generally expires 10 years from release from active duty, but can be extended under special circumstances.

Payments: DoD will match contributions at the rate of $2 for every $1 put into the fund and may make additional contributions, or "kickers," as necessary. For training in college, vocational or technical schools, the payment amount depends on the type and hours of training pursued. The maximum amount is $300 a month for full-time training.

Training, Work-Study, Counseling: VEAP participants may receive the same training, work-study benefts and counseling as provided under the MGIB with the exception of preparatory courses.

Employment Services

VetSuccess.gov
The Department of Veterans Affairs provides Veterans with employment and transition assistance through the VetSuccess.gov Website. VetSuccess.gov is a Veteran-centric tool, providing a number of employment and transition resources. Veterans can access VetSuccess.gov to:
    Browse job listings
    Post resumes
    Apply for positions

Employers can use VetSuccess.gov to hire Veterans by posting job openings or by searching a database of over 25,000 Veteran resumes. VetSuccess.gov provides links to millions of jobs on the VetCentral site and the Veterans Job Bank search engine, and links Veterans to Indeed, Google, Simply Hired, and other job search engines. Veterans may also apply for VA benefts, including Vocational Rehabilitation and Employment, through the site.

Veterans, Servicemembers, and their families can also access a variety of interactive tools and information available throughout the Veteran lifecycle from transition to college, career, retirement, and family life.

Servicemembers and Veterans with Disabilities
Eligible Veterans or Servicemembers with disabilities who require assistance with obtaining and maintaining employment may receive services through the Vocational Rehabilitation & Employment (VR&E) program (see chapter 2 for eligibility information).   VR&E staff assists Veterans and Servicemembers with achieving their employment goals by providing job development and placement ser-

vices, which include: on-the-job training, job-seeking skills, resume development, interviewing skills and direct placement. VR&E has partnerships with federal, state and private agencies to provide direct placement of Veterans or Servicemembers. VR&E can assist with placement using the following resources:

On the Job Training Program: Employers hire Veterans at an apprentice wage, and VR&E supplements the salary up the journey-man wage (up to maximum allowable under OJT). As the Veterans progress through training, the employers begin to pay more of the salary until the Veterans reach journeyman level and the employers are paying the entire salary. VR&E will also pay for any necessary tools. Employers are also eligible for a federal tax credit for hiring an individual who participated in a vocational rehabilitation program.

Non-Paid Work Experience: The Non-Paid Work Experience (NPWE) program provides eligible Veterans the opportunity to obtain training and practical job experience concurrently. This program is ideal for Veterans or Servicemembers who have a clearly estab-lished career goal, and who learn easily in a hands-on environment. This program is also well suited for Veterans who are having diffcul-ties obtaining employment due to lack of work experience. NPWE program may be established in a federal, state, or local (i.e. city, town, school district) government agencies only. The employer may hire the Veteran at any point during the NPWE.

Special Employer Incentive: The Special Employer Incentive (SEI) program is for eligible Veterans who face challenges in obtaining employment. Veterans approved to participate in the SEI program are hired by participating employers and employment is expected to continue following successful completion of the program. Employ-ers may be provided this incentive to hire Veterans. If approved, the employer will receive reimbursement for up to 50 percent of the Veteran's salary during the SEI program, which can last up to six months.

Chapter 6
Home Loan Guaranty

VA home loan guaranties are issued to help eligible Servicemembers, Veterans, Reservists, National Guard and certain unmarried surviving spouses obtain homes, condominiums, and manufactured homes, and to refnance loans. For additional information or to obtain VA loan guaranty forms, visit http://www.benefts.va.gov/homeloans/.

Loan Uses: A VA guaranty helps protect lenders from loss if the borrower fails to repay the loan. It can be used to obtain a loan to:
1. Buy or build a home.
2. Buy a residential condominium unit.
3. Repair, alter, or improve a residence owned by the Veteran and occupied as a home.
4. Refnance an existing home loan.
5. Buy a manufactured home and/or lot.
6. Install a solar heating or cooling system or other energy-effcient improvements.

Eligibility: In addition to the periods of eligibility and conditions of service requirements, applicants must have a good credit rating, suffcient income, a valid Certifcate of Eligibility (COE), and agree to live in the property in order to be approved by a lender for a VA home loan.

Lenders can apply for a COE online through the Veterans Information Portal (https://vip.vba.va.gov/portal/VBAH/Home). Active duty Servicemembers and Veterans can also apply online at http://www.ebenefts.va.gov. Although it's preferable to apply electronically, it is possible to apply for a COE using VA Form 26-1880, Request for Certifcate of Eligibility.

In applying for a hard-copy COE from the VA Eligibility Center using VA Form 26-1880, it is typically necessary that the eligible Veteran present a copy of his/her report of discharge or DD Form 214, Certifcate of Release or Discharge from Active Duty, or other adequate substitute evidence to VA. An eligible active duty Servicemember should obtain and submit to the VA Eligibility Center a statement of service signed by an appropriate military offcial. A completed VA Form 26-1880 and any associated documentation should be mailed to Atlanta Regional Loan Center, Attn: COE (262), P.O. Box 100034, Decatur, GA 30031.

Please note that while VA's electronic applications can establish eligibility and issue an online COE in a matter of seconds, not all cases can be processed online. The system can only process those cases for which VA has suffcient data in its records. If a COE cannot be issued immediately, users have the option of submitting an electronic application.

Periods of Eligibility: World War II: (1) active duty service after Sept.15, 1940, and prior to July 26, 1947; (2) discharge under other than dishonorable conditions; and (3) at least 90 days total service unless discharged early for a service-connected disability.

Post-World War II period: (1) active duty service after July 25, 1947, and prior to June 27, 1950; (2) discharge under other than dishonorable conditions; and (3) 181 days continuous active duty service unless discharged early for a service-connected disability.

Korean War: (1) active duty after June 26, 1950, and prior to Feb. 1, 1955; (2) discharge under other than dishonorable conditions; and (3) at least 90 days total service, unless discharged early for a service-connected disability.

Post-Korean War period: (1) active duty after Jan. 31, 1955, and prior to Aug. 5, 1964; (2) discharge under other than dishonorable conditions; (3) 181 days continuous service, unless discharged early for a service-connected disability.

Vietnam War: (1) active duty after Aug. 4, 1964, and prior to May 8, 1975; (2) discharge under other than dishonorable conditions; and (3) 90 days total service, unless discharged early for a service-connected disability. For Veterans who served in the Republic of Vietnam, the beginning date is Feb. 28, 1961.

Post-Vietnam period: (1) active duty after May 7, 1975, and prior to Aug. 2, 1990; (2) active duty for 181 continuous days, all of which occurred after May 7, 1975; and (3) discharge under conditions other than dishonorable or early discharge for service-connected disability.

24-Month Rule: If service was between Sept. 8, 1980, (Oct. 16, 1981, for offcers) and Aug. 1, 1990, Veterans must generally complete 24 months of continuous active duty service or the full period (at least 181 days) for which they were called or ordered to active duty, and be discharged under conditions other than dishonorable.

Exceptions are allowed if the Veteran completed at least 181 days of active duty service but was discharged earlier than 24 months for (1) hardship, (2) the convenience of the government, (3) reduction-in-force, (4) certain medical conditions, or (5) service-connected disability.

Gulf War: Veterans of the Gulf War era – Aug. 2, 1990, to a date to be determined – must generally complete 24 months of continuous active duty service or the full period (at least 90 days) for which they were called to active duty, and be discharged under other than dishonorable conditions.

Exceptions are allowed if the Veteran completed at least 90 days of active duty but was discharged earlier than 24 months for (1) hardship, (2) the convenience of the government, (3) reduction-in-force, (4) certain medical conditions, or (5) service-connected disability. Reservists and National Guard members are eligible if they were activated after Aug. 1, 1990, and completed the full period for which they were called to active duty, served at least 90 days, and were discharged under other than dishonorable conditions.

Active Duty Personnel: Until the Gulf War era is ended, persons on active duty are eligible after serving 90 continuous days.

Eligibility for Reserves and/or Guard (not activated): Members of the Reserves and National Guard who are not otherwise eligible for loan guaranty benefts are eligible upon completion of 6 years service in the Reserves or Guard (unless released earlier due to a service-connected disability). The applicant must have received an honorable (a general or under honorable conditions is not qualifying) discharge from such service unless he or she is either in an inactive status awaiting fnal discharge, or still serving in the Reserves or Guard.

Surviving Spouses: Some spouses of Veterans may have home loan eligibility. They are:

- the unmarried surviving spouse of a Veteran who died as a result of service or service-connected causes
- the surviving spouse of a Veteran who dies on active duty or from service-connected causes, who remarries on or after attaining age 57 and on or after Dec. 16, 2003
- the spouse of an active duty member who is listed as missing in action (MIA) or a prisoner of war (POW) for at least 90 days.

Eligibility under this MIA/POW provision is limited to one-time use only.

Surviving spouses of Veterans who died from non service-connected causes may also be eligible if any of the following conditions are met: The Veteran was rated totally disabled for 10 years or more immediately preceding death, or was rated totally disabled for not less than fve years from date of discharge or release from active duty to date of death, or was a former prisoner of war who died after Sept. 30, 1999, and was rated totally disabled for not less than one year immediately preceding death.

Under the Home Loan Guaranty Program, VA does not make loans to Veterans and Servicemembers; VA guarantees loans made by private-sector lenders. The guaranty amount is what VA could pay a lender should the loan go to foreclosure.

VA's guaranteed home loans have no maximum loan amount, only a maximum guaranty amount, which is set in law. However, due to secondary market requirements, lenders typically require that the VA guaranty, plus any downpayment provided by a Veteran, total 25 percent of the loan amount. As a result, an amount equal to four times VA's maximum guaranty amount is customarily referred to as a "loan limit." Loans for the loan limit or less are typically available to Veterans with no downpayment; loans for more than the loan limit generally require downpayments. VA's maximum guaranty amounts are established annually, and vary, depending on the size of the loan and the location of the property.

The following chart lists general information on VA's maximum guaranty. To see the county limits for 2013, select "Loan Limits" on the "Purchase & Cash-Out Refnance Loan" link on http://www.benefts.va.gov/homeloans.

Loan Amount	Maximum Guaranty	Special Provisions
Up to $45,000	50 percent of loan amount	25 percent on Interest Rate Reduction Refnancing Loans
$45,001 - $56,250	$22,500	Same as above
$56,251 - $144,000	40 percent of the loan amount, with a maximum of $36,000	Same as above
$144,000 or more	Up to an amount equal to 25 percent of the county loan limit	Same as above

An eligible borrower can use a VA-guaranteed Interest Rate Reduction Refnancing Loan to refnance an existing VA loan to lower the interest rate and payment. Typically, no credit underwriting is required for this type of loan. The loan may include the entire outstanding balance of the prior loan, the costs of energy-effcient improvements, as well as closing costs, including up to two discount points.

An eligible borrower who wishes to obtain a VA-guaranteed loan to purchase a manufactured home or lot can borrow up to 95 percent of the home's purchase price. The amount VA will guarantee on a manufactured home loan is 40 percent of the loan amount or the Veteran's available entitlement, up to a maximum amount of $20,000. These provisions apply only to a manufactured home that will not be placed on a permanent foundation.

VA Appraisals: No loan can be guaranteed by VA without frst being appraised by a VA-assigned fee appraiser. A lender can request a VA appraisal through VA systems. The Veteran borrower typically pays for the appraisal upon completion, according to a fee schedule approved by VA. This VA appraisal estimates the value of the property. It is not an inspection and does not guarantee the house is free of defects. VA guarantees the loan, not the condition of the property. A thorough inspection of the property by a reputable inspection frm may help minimize any problems that could arise after loan closing. In an existing home, particular attention should be given to plumbing, heating, electrical, and roofng components.

Closing Costs: For purchase home loans, payment in cash is required on all closing costs, including title search and recording fees, hazard insurance premiums and prepaid taxes. For refnancing loans, all such costs may be included in the loan, as long as the total loan does not exceed the reasonable value of the property. Interest rate reduction loans may include closing costs, including a maximum of two discount points.

2013 VA Funding Fees: A ffunding fee must be paid to VA unless the Veteran is exempt from such a fee. [See previous discussion in Closing Costs for specifc exemptions from the funding fee]. The fee may be paid in cash or included in the loan. Closing costs such as VA appraisal, credit report, loan processing fee, title search, title insurance, recording fees, transfer taxes, survey charges, or hazard insurance may not be included for purchase home loans.

All Veterans, except those who are specifed by law as exempt, are charged a VA funding fee (See chart on Page 66). Currently, exemptions from the funding fee are provided for those Veterans and Servicemembers receiving VA disability compensation, those who are rated by VA as eligible to receive compensation as a result of pre-discharge disability examination and rating, and those who would be in receipt of compensation, but who were recalled to active duty or reenlisted and are receiving active-duty pay in lieu of compensation. Additionally, unmarried surviving spouses in receipt of Dependency and Indemnity Compensation are exempt from the funding fee. For all types of loans, the loan amount may include this funding fee.

The VA funding fee and up to $6,000 of energy-effcient improvements can be included in VA loans. However, no other fees, charges, or discount points may be included in the loan amount for regular purchase or construction loans. For refnancing loans, most closing costs may be included in the loan amount.

Required Occupancy: To qualify for a VA home loan, a Veteran or the spouse of an active-duty Servicemember must certify that he or she intends to occupy the home. A dependent child of an active-duty Servicemember also satisfes the occupancy requirement when refnancing a VA-guaranteed loan solely to reduce the interest rate, a Veteran need only certify to prior occupancy.

Financing, Interest Rates and Terms: Veterans obtain VA-guaranteed loans through the usual lending institutions, including banks, credit unions, and mortgage brokers. VA-guaranteed loans can have either a fxed interest rate or an adjustable rate, where the interest rate may adjust up to one percent annually and up to fve percent over the life of the loan. VA does not set the interest rate. Interest rates are negotiable between the lender and borrower on all loan types.

Veterans may also choose a different type of adjustable rate mortgage called a hybrid ARM, where the initial interest rate remains fxed for three to 10 years. If the rate remains fxed for less than fve years, the rate adjustment cannot be more than one percent annually and fve percent over the life of the loan. For a hybrid ARM with an initial fxed period of fve years or more, the initial adjustment may be up to two percent. The Secretary has the authority to determine annual adjustments thereafter. Currently annual adjustments may be up to two percentage points and six percent over the life of the loan.

If the lender charges discount points on the loan, the Veteran may negotiate with the seller as to who will pay points or if they will be split between buyer and seller. Points paid by the Veteran may not be included in the loan (with the exception that up to two points may be included in interest rate reduction refnancing loans). The term of the loan may be for as long as 30 years and 32 days.

Loan Assumption Requirements and Liability: VA loans made on or after March 1, 1988, are not assumable without the prior approval of VA or its authorized agent (usually the lender collecting the monthly payments). To approve the assumption, the lender must ensure that the borrower is a satisfactory credit risk and will assume all of the Veteran's liabilities on the loan. If approved, the borrower will have to pay a funding fee that the lender sends to VA, and the Veteran will be released from liability to the federal government. A release of liability does not mean that a Veteran's guaranty entitlement is restored. That occurs only if the borrower is an eligible Veteran who agrees to substitute his or her entitlement for that of the seller. If a Veteran allows assumption of a loan without prior approval, then the lender may demand immediate and full payment of the loan, and the Veteran may be liable if the loan is foreclosed and VA has to pay a claim under the loan guaranty.

Loans made prior to March 1, 1988, are generally freely assumable, but Veterans should still request VA's approval in order to be released of liability. Veterans whose loans were closed after Dec. 31, 1989, usually have no liability to the government following a foreclosure, except in cases involving fraud, misrepresentation, or bad faith, such as allowing an unapproved assumption. However, for the entitlement to be restored, any loss suffered by VA must be paid in full.

2013 VA Funding Fee Rates

Loan Category	Active Duty and Veterans	Reservists and National Guard
Loans for purchase or construction with downpayments of less than 5 percent, refnancing, and home improvement	2.15 percent	2.40 percent
Loans for purchase or construction with downpayments of at least 5 percent but less than 10 percent	1.50 percent	1.75 percent
Loans for purchase or construction with downpayments of 10percent or more	1.25 percent	1.50 percent
Loans for manufactured homes	1 percent	1 percent
Interest rate reduction refnancing loans	.50 percent	.50 percent
Assumption of a VA-guaranteed loan	.50 percent	.50 percent
Second or subsequent use of entitlement with no downpayment	3.3 percent	3.3 percent

VA Assistance to Veterans in Default: VA urges all Veterans who are encountering problems making their mortgage payments to speak with their servicers as soon as possible to explore options to avoid foreclosure. Contrary to popular opinion, servicers do not want to foreclose because foreclosure costs a lot of money. Depending on a Veteran's specifc situation, servicers may offer any of the following options to avoid foreclosure:

- Repayment Plan – The borrower makes regular installment each month plus part of the missed installments.
- Special Forbearance – The servicer agrees not to initiate fore closure to allow time for borrowers to repay the missed installments. An example of when this would be likely is when a borrower is waiting for a tax refund.
- Loan Modifcation - Provides the borrower a fresh start by adding the delinquency to the loan balance and establishing a new payment schedule.
- Additional time to arrange a private sale – The servicer agrees to delay foreclosure to allow a sale to close if the loan will be paid off.
- Short Sale – When the servicer agrees to allow a borrower to sell his/her home for a lesser amount than what is currently required to payoff the loan.
- Deed-in-Lieu of Foreclosure - The borrower voluntarily agrees to deed the property to the servicer instead of going through a lengthy foreclosure process.

Servicemembers Civil Relief Act

Veteran borrowers may be able to request relief pursuant to the Servicemembers Civil Relief Act (SCRA). In order to qualify for certain protections available under the Act, their obligation must have originated prior to their current period of active military service. SCRA may provide a lower interest rate during military service and for up to one year after service ends, and provide forbearance, or prevent foreclosure or eviction up to nine months from period of military service.

Assistance to Veterans with VA-Guaranteed Home Loans

When a VA-guaranteed home loan becomes delinquent, VA may provide supplemental servicing assistance to help cure the default. The servicer has the primary responsibility of servicing the loan to resolve the default.

However, in cases where the servicer is unable to help the Veteran borrower, VA has loan technicians in eight Regional Loan Centers and two special servicing centers who take an active role in interceding with the mortgage servicer to explore all options to avoid foreclosure. Veterans with VA-guaranteed home loans can call 1-877 827-3702 to reach the nearest VA offce where loan specialists are prepared to discuss potential ways to help save the loan.

VA Acquired Property Foreclosures
VA acquires properties as a result of foreclosures VA-guaranteed and VA-owned loans. A private contractor is currently marketing the acquired properties through listing agents using local Multiple Listing Services. A listing of "VA Properties for Sale" may be found at http:// listings.vrmco.com/. Contact a real estate agent for information on purchasing a VA-acquired property.

Preventing Veteran Homelessness
Veterans who feel they may be facing homelessness as a result of losing their home can call 1-877-4AID VET (877-424-3838) or go to http://www.va.gov/HOMELESS/index.asp to receive assistance from VA.

Assistance to Veterans with Non-VA Guaranteed Home Loans
For Veterans or Servicemembers who have a conventional or sub-prime loan, VA has a network of eight Regional Loan Centers and two special servicing centers that can offer advice and guidance. Borrowers may visit www.benefts.va.gov/homeloans/, or call toll free -1-877-827-3702 to speak with a VA loan technician. However, unlike when a Veteran has a VA-guaranteed home loan, VA does not have the legal authority to intervene on the borrower's behalf. It is imperative that a borrower contact his/her servicer as quickly as possible.

VA Refnancing of a Non-VA Guaranteed Home Loan
Veterans with conventional home loans now have new options for refnancing to a VA-guaranteed home loan. These new options are available as a result of the Veterans' Benefts Improvement Act of 2008. Veterans who wish to refnance theii subprime or conventional mortgage may now do so for up t o 100 percent of the value of the property, which is up from the previous limit of 90 percent.

Additionally, Congress raised VA's maximum loan guaranty for these types of refnancing loans. Loan limits were effectively raised from $144,000 to $417,000. High-cost counties have even higher maximum loan limits. VA county loan limits can be found at http://www.benefts.va.gov/homeloans/. These changes will allow more qualifed Veterans to refnance through VA, allowing for savings on interest costs and avoiding foreclosure.

Other Assistance for Delinquent Veteran Borrowers
If VA is not able to help a Veteran borrower retain his/her home (whether a VA-guaranteed loan or not), the HOPE NOW Alliance may be of assistance. HOPE NOW is a joint alliance consisting of servicers, counselors, and investors whose main goal is to assist distressed borrowers retain their homes and avoid foreclosure. They have expertise in fnancial counseling, as well as programs that take advantage of relief measures that VA cannot. HOPE NOW provides outreach, counseling and assistance to homeowners who have the willingness and ability to keep their homes but are facing fnancial diffculty as a result of the crisis in the mortgage market. The HOPE NOW Alliance can be reached at (888) 995-HOPE (4673), or by visiting www.hopenow.com.

For more information go to http://www.benefts.va.gov/homeloans/, or call (877) 827-3702

Loans for Native American Veterans
Eligible Native American Veterans can obtain a loan from VA to purchase, construct, or improve a home on Federal Trust Land, or to reduce the interest rate on such a VA loan. Native American Direct Loans are only available if a memorandum of understanding exists between the tribal organization and VA.
Veterans who are not Native American, but who are married to Native American non-Veterans, may be eligible for a direct loan under this program. To be eligible for such a loan, the qualifed non-Native American Veteran and the Native American spouse must reside on Federal Trust Land, and both the Veteran and spouse must have a meaningful interest in the dwelling or lot.
The following safeguards have been established to protect Veterans:
    1. VA may suspend from the loan program those who take unfair advantage of Veterans or discriminate because of race, color, religion, sex, disability, family status, or national origin.
    2. The builder of a new home (or manufactured) is required to give the purchasing Veteran either a one-year warranty or a 10-year insurance-backed protection plan.
    3. The borrower obtaining a loan may only be charged closing

costs allowed by VA.
4. The borrower can prepay without penalty the entire loan or any part not less than one installment or $100.
5. VA encourages holders to extend forbearance if a borrower becomes temporarily
unable to meet the terms of the loan.

Chapter 7

VA Life Insurance

For complete details on government life insurance, visit the VA Internet site at www.insurance.va.gov/ or call VA's Insurance Center toll-free at 1-800-669-8477. Specialists are available between the hours of 8:30 a.m. and 6 p.m., Eastern Time, to discuss premium payments, insurance dividends, address changes, policy loans, naming benefciaries and reporting the death of the insured.

If the insurance policy number is not known, send whatever information is available, such as the Veteran's VA fle number, date of birth, Social Security number, military serial number or military service branch and dates of service to:

> Department of Veterans Affairs
> Insurance Center
> PO Box 42954
> Philadelphia, PA 19101

For information about Servicemembers' Group Life Insurance, Veterans Group Life Insurance, Servicemembers' Group Life Insurance Traumatic Injury Protection, or Servicemembers' Group Life Insurance Family Coverage, visit the Website above or call the Offce of Servicemembers' Group Life Insurance directly at 1-800-419-1473.

Servicemembers' Group Life Insurance: The following are automatically insured for $400,000 under Servicemembers' Group Life Insurance (SGLI)
  1. Active-duty members of the Army, Navy, Air Force, Marines and Coast Guard.
  2. Commissioned members of the National Oceanic and Atmospheric Administration (NOAA) and the Public Health Service (PHS).
  3. Cadets or midshipmen of the U.S. military academies.
  4. Members, cadets and midshipmen of the ROTC while engaged in authorized training and practice cruises.
  5. Members of the Ready Reserves/National Guard who are

scheduled to perform at least 12 periods of inactive training per year.

6. Members who volunteer for a mobilization category in the Individual Ready Reserve.

Individuals may elect in writing to be covered for a lesser amount or no coverage. SGLI coverage is available in $50,000 increments up to the maximum of $400,000.

Full-time Servicemembers on active duty are covered 365 days per year. Coverage is in effect during the period of active duty or inactive duty training and for 120 days following separation or release from duty. Reservists or National Guard members who have been assigned to a unit in which they are scheduled to perform at least 12 periods of inactive duty that is creditable for retirement purposes are also covered 365 days of the year and for 120 days following separation or release from duty.

Part-time coverage is provided for Reservists or National Guard members who do not qualify for the full-time coverage described above. Part-time coverage generally applies to Reservists/National Guard members who drill only a few days in a year. These individuals are covered only while on active duty or active duty for training, or traveling to and from such duty. Members covered part-time do not receive 120 days of free coverage after separation unless they incur or aggravate a disability during a period of duty

SGLI Traumatic Injury Protection: Members of the armed services serve our nation heroically during times of great need, but what happens when they experience great needs of their own because they have sustained a traumatic injury? Servicemembers' Group Life Insurance Traumatic Injury Protection (TSGLI) helps severely injured Servicemembers who have suffered physical losses through their time of need with a one-time payment. The amount varies depending on the loss, but it could make a difference in the lives of Servicemembers by allowing their families to be with them during their recovery. TSGLI helps them with unforeseen expenses or gives them a fnancial head start on life after recovery.

TSGLI is attached to Servicemembers' Group Life Insurance (SGLI). An additional $1.00 is added to the Servicemember's SGLI premium to cover TSGLI. After December 1, 2005, all Servicemembers who are covered by SGLI are automatically also covered by TSGLI. TSGLI cannot be declined unless the Servicemember also declines basic SGLI. TSGLI claims are adjudicated by the individual military branches of service.

In addition, there is retroactive TSGLI coverage for Servicemembers who sustained a qualifying loss between Oct. 7, 2001 and November 30, 2005, regardless of where it occurred . TSGLI coverage is payable to these Servicemembers regardless of whether they had SGLI coverage in force.

For more information, and branch of service contact information, visit www.insurance.va.gov/sgliSite/TSGLI/TSGLI.htm, or call 1-800-237-1336 (Army); 1-800-368-3202 (Navy); 1-877-216-0825 (Marine Corps); 1-800-433-0048 (Active Duty Air Force); 1-800-525-0102 (Air Force Reserves); 1-240-612-9072 (Air National Guard); 1-703-872-6647- (U.S. Coast Guard); 1-301-427-3280 (PHS); or 1-301-713-3444 (NOAA).

Servicemembers' Group Life Insurance Family Coverage: FSGLI Family Coverage consists of spousal coverage and dependent child coverage. FSGLI provides up to $100,000 of life insurance coverage for spouses of Servicemembers with full-time SGLI coverage, not to exceed the amount of SGLI the member has in force. FSGLI is a Servicemembers' beneft; the member pays the premium and is the only person allowed to be the benefciary of the coverage. FSGLI spousal coverage ends when: 1) the Servicemember elects in writing to terminate coverage on the spouse; 2) the Servicemember elects to terminate his or her own SGLI coverage; 3) the Servicemember dies; 4) the Servicemember separates from service; or 5) the Servicemember is divorced from the spouse. The insured spouse may convert his or her FSGLI coverage to a permanent policy offered by participating private insurers within 120 days of the date of any of the termination events noted above. FSGLI dependent coverage of $10,000 is also automatically provided for dependent children of Servicemembers insured under SGLI, with no premium required.

Veterans' Group Life Insurance: SGLI may be converted to Veterans' Group Life Insurance (VGLI), which provides renewable term coverage to:
    1. Veterans who had full-time SGLI coverage upon speration

from active duty or the reserves.

2. Members of the Ready Reserves/National Guard with part-time SGLI coverage who incur a disability or aggravate a pre-existing disability during a period of active duty or a period of inactive duty for less than 31 days that renders them uninsurable at standard premium rates.

3. Members of the Individual Ready Reserve and Inactive National Guard.

Servicemembers must apply for VGLI within one year and 120 days from separation . Servicemembers discharged on or after November 1, 2012 who apply for VGLI within 240 days of separation do not need to submit evidence of good health, while Servicemembers who apply after the 240-day period must submit evidence of insurability..

Effective April 11, 2011, VGLI insureds who are under age 60 and have less than $400,000 in coverage can purchase up to $25,000 of additional coverage on each fve-year anniversary of their coverage, up to the maximum $400,000. No medical underwriting is required for the additional coverage.

SGLI Disability Extension: Servicemembers who are totally dis-abled at the time of separation (unable to work), can apply for the SGLI Disability Extension, which provides free coverage for up to two years from the date of separation. To apply, Servicmembers must complete and return SGLV 8715, the SGLI Disability Extension Ap-plication.

Those covered under the SGLI Disability Extension are automati-cally converted to VGLI at the end of their extension period, subject to the payment of premiums. VGLI is convertible at any time to a permanent plan policy with any participating commercial insurance company.

Accelerated Death Benefts: Like many private life insurance companies, the SGLI, FSGLI and VGLI programs offer an acceler-ated benfts option to terminally ill insureds. An insured member is considered to be terminally ill if he or she has a written medical prognosis of 9 months or less to live. All terminally ill members are eligible to receive up to 50 percent of their SGLI or VGLI cover-age in a lump sum. Accelerated benfts paid prior to death are not, of course, available for payment to survivors. To apply, an insured

member must submit SGLV 8284, Servicemember/Veteran Accelerated Beneft Option Form.

Service-Disabled Veterans' Insurance: Veterans who separated
from Service on or after April 25, 1951 under other than dishonorable
conditions who have service-connected disabilities, even zero percent, disability but are otherwise in good health, may apply to VA for
up to $10,000 in life insurance coverage under the Service-Disabled
Veterans' Insurance (S-DVI) program. Applications must be submitted within two years from the date of being notifed of the approval of
a new service-connected disability by VA. .
Veterans who are totally disabled may apply for a waiver of premiums and additional supplemental insurance coverage of up to
$30,000. However, premiums cannot be waived on the additional
supplemental insurance. To be eligible for this type of supplemental
insurance, Veterans must meet all of the following three requirements:
1. Be under age 65.
2. Be eligible for a waiver of premiums due to total disability.
3. Apply for additional insurance within one year from the date of
   notifcation of waiver approval on the basic S-DVI policy.

Veterans' Mortgage Life Insurance: VMLI is mortgage protection
insurance available to severely disabled Veterans who have been
approved by VA for a Specially Adapted Housing Grant (SAH). Maximum coverage is the smaller of the existing mortgage balance or
$200,000, and is payable only to the mortgage company. Protection
is issued automatically following SAH approval, provided the Veteran
submits mortgage information required to establish a premium and
does not decline coverage. Coverage automatically terminates when
the mortgage is paid off. If a mortgage is disposed of through sale
of the property, VMLI may be obtained on the mortgage of another
home.

Other Insurance Information
The following information applies to policies issued to World War
II, Korean, and Vietnam-era Veterans and any Service-Disabled
Veterans Insurance policies. Policies in this group are prefxed by the
letters K, V, RS, W, J, JR, JS, or RH.

Insurance Dividends Issued Annually: World War II, and Korean-era Veterans with active policies beginning with the letters V, RS, W, J, JR, JS, or K earn tax-free dividends annually on the policy anniversary date. (Policies prefxed by RH do not earn dividends.) Policyholders do not need to apply for dividends, but may select from among the following dividend options:

1. Cash: The dividend is paid directly to the insured either by a mailed check or by direct deposit to a bank account.
2. Paid-Up Additional Insurance: The dividend is used to purchase additional insurance coverage.
3. Credit or Deposit: The dividend is held in an account for the policyholder with interest. Withdrawals from the account can be made at any time. The interest rate may be adjusted.
4. Net Premium Billing Options: These options use the dividend to pay the annual policy premium. If the dividend exceeds the premium, the policyholder has options to choose how the remainder is used. If the dividend is not enough to pay an annual premium, the policyholder is billed the balance.
5. Other Dividend Options: Dividends can also be used to repay a loan or pay premiums in advance.

Reinstating Lapsed Insurance: Lapsed term policies may be reinstated within fve years from the date of lapse. A fve-year term policy that is not lapsed at the end of the term is automatically renewed for an additional fve years. Lapsed permanent plans may be reinstated within certain time limits and with certain health requirements. Reinstated permanent plan policies require repayment of all back premiums, plus interest.

Converting Term Policies: Term policies are renewed automatically every fve years, with premiums increasing at each renewal. Premiums do not increase after age 70. Term policies may be converted to permanent plans, which have fxed premiums for life and earn cash and loan values.

Dividends on Capped Term Policies: Effective Sept. 2000, VA provides either a cash dividend or paid-up insurance on term policies whose premiums have been capped. Veterans with National Service Life Insurance (NSLI) term insurance that has renewed at age 71 or older and who stop paying premiums on their policies will be given a "termination dividend." This dividend can either be received as a cash payment or used to purchase a reduced amount of paid-up insurance, which insures the Veteran for life with no premium payments required. The amount of the reduced paid-up insurance remains level. This does not apply to S-DVI (RH) policies.

Borrowing on Policies: Policyholders with permanent plan policies may borrow up to 94 percent of the cash surrender value of their insurance after the insurance is in force for one year or more. Interest is compounded annually. The loan interest rate is variable and may be obtained by calling toll-free 1-800-669-8477.

Chapter 8

Burial and Memorial Benefts

Veterans discharged from active duty under conditions other than dishonorable; Servicemembers who die while on active duty, active duty for training, or inactive duty training; and spouses and dependent children of Veterans and active duty service members, may be eligible for VA burial and memorial benefts. (For the purposes of this chapter, the term "Veteran" includes eligible persons who die during active duty service.) The Veteran does not have to die before a spouse or dependent child can be eligible for burial or memorial benefts.

Burial in VA National Cemeteries

Burial in a VA national cemetery is available for eligible Veterans, spouses and dependents at no cost and includes the gravesite, grave-liner, opening and closing of the grave, a headstone or marker, and perpetual care as part of a national shrine. For Veterans, benefts may also include a burial fag (with case for active duty), and military funeral honors.

With certain exceptions, active duty service beginning after Sept. 7, 1980, as an enlisted person, and after Oct. 16, 1981, as an offcer, must be for a minimum of 24 consecutive months or the full period of active duty (as in the case of reservists or National Guard members called to active duty for a limited duration). Active duty for training, by itself, while serving in the reserves or National Guard, is not suffcient to confer eligibility. Reservists and National Guard members, as well as their spouses and dependent children, are eligible if they were entitled to retired pay at the time of death, or would have been upon reaching requisite age. See Chapter 8 for more information.

Certain otherwise eligible individuals found to have committed federal or state capital crimes are barred from burial or memorialization in a VA national cemetery, and from receipt of Government-furnished headstones, markers, medallions, burial fags, and Presidential Memorial Certifcates. Veterans and other claimants for VA burial benefts have the right to appeal decisions made by VA regarding eligibility for national cemetery burial or other memorial benefts. Chapter 13 discusses the procedures for appealing VA claims. This chapter contains information on the full range of VA burial and memorial benefts. Readers with questions may contact the nearest national cemetery, listed by state in the VA Facilities section of this book, call 1-800-827-1000, or visit the web site at www.cem.va.gov/.

Surviving spouses of Veterans who died on or after Jan. 1, 2000, do not lose eligibility for burial in a national cemetery if they remarry. Unmarried dependent children of Veterans who are under 21 years of age, or under 23 years of age if a full-time student at an approved educational institution, are eligible for burial. Unmarried adult children who become physically or mentally disabled and incapable of self-support before age 21, or age 23 if a full-time student, also are eligible.

Certain Parents of servicemembers who die as a result of hostile activity or from combat training-related injuries may be eligible for burial in a national cemetery with their child. The biological or adopted parents of a servicemember who died in combat or while performing training in preparation for a combat mission, who leaves no surviving spouse or dependent child, may be buried with the deceased servicemember if there is available space. Eligibility is limited to servicemembers who died on or after Oct. 7, 2001, and biological or adoptive parents who died on or after Oct. 13, 2010.

The next of kin or authorized representative (e.g., funeral director) makes interment arrangements at time of need by contacting the National Cemetery Scheduling Offce (see information available at http://www.cem.va.gov/bbene/need.asp) or, in some cases, the national cemetery in which burial is desired. VA normally does not conduct burials on weekends. Gravesites cannot be reserved; however, VA will honor reservations made before 1973 by the Department of the Army.

VA's National Cemetery Scheduling Offce or local national cemetery directors verify eligibility for burial. A copy of the Veteran's discharge document that specifes the period(s) of active duty and character of service is usually suffcient to determine eligibility. A copy of the deceased's death certifcate and proof of relationship to the Veteran (for eligible family members) may be required.

VA operates 131 national cemeteries, of which 72 are currently open for both new casket and cremation interments and 18 may accept new interment of cremated remains only. Burial options are limited to those available at a specifc cemetery and may include in-ground casket, or interment of cremated remains in a columbarium, in-ground, or in a scattering area. Contact the national cemetery directly, or visit our website at http://www.cem.va.gov to determine if a particular cemetery is open for new burials, and what other options are available.

Headstones, Markers and Medallions

Veterans, Veterans, active duty service members, and retired Reservists and National Guard service members, are eligible for an inscribed headstone or marker for their unmarked grave at any cemetery – national, state veterans, tribal, or private. VA will deliver a headstone or marker at no cost, anywhere in the world.

For eligible Veterans or service members buried in a private ceme-tery whose deaths occurred on or after Nov. 1, 1990, VA may furnish a government headstone or marker (even if the grave is already marked with a private one); or VA may furnish a medallion to affx to an already existing privately-purchased headstone or marker.

Spouses and dependent children are eligible for a government head-stone or marker only if they are buried in a national or State Veterans cemetery.

Flat markers are available in bronze, granite or marble. Upright headstones come in granite or marble. The style provided will be consistent with existing monuments at the place of burial. Niche markers are available to mark columbaria used for inurnment of cremated remains. Medallions are made of bronze and are available in three sizes: 5-inch, 3-inch, and 1 ½-inches. Headstones, mark-ers and medallions previously furnished by the government may be replaced at the government's expense if badly deteriorated, illegible, vandalized or stolen.

Headstones or markers for VA national cemeteries will be ordered by the cemetery director using information provided by the next of kin or authorized representative.

Headstones or Markers for private cemeteries: Before ordering, the next of kin or authorized representative should check with the cemetery to ensure that the Government-furnished headstone or marker will be accepted. All installation fees at private cemeteries are the responsibility of the applicant. To submit a claim for a headstone or marker for a gravesite in a private cemetery, use VA Form 40-1330, Application for Standard Government Headstone or Marker (available at http://www.va.gov/vaforms/). A copy of the Veteran's military discharge document is required. Mail forms to Memorial Programs Service, Department of Veterans Affairs, 5109 Russell Road, Quantico, VA 22134-3903. The form and supporting documents may also be faxed toll free to 1-800-455-7143.

"In Memory Of" Markers: VA provides memorial headstones and markers with "In Memory Of" as the frst line of inscription for those whose remains have not been recovered or identifed, were buried at sea, donated to science or cremated and scattered. Eligibility is the same as for regular headstones and markers. There is no fee when the "In Memory Of" marker is placed in a national cemetery. All installation fees at private cemeteries are the responsibility of the applicant. Memorial headstones/markers for spouses and dependents can be provided only for placement in a national or State veterans cemetery.

Inscriptions: Headstones and markers must be inscribed with the name of the deceased, branch of service, and year of birth and death. They also may be inscribed with other optional information, including an emblem of belief and, space permitting, additional text including military rank; war service such as "World War II;" complete dates of birth and death; military awards; military organizations; civilian or Veteran affliations; and personalized words of endearment.

Medallion in lieu of government headstone or marker for private cemeteries: For Veterans or service members whose death occurred on or after Nov. 1, 1990, VA is authorized to provide a medallion instead of a headstone or marker if the grave is in a private cemetery and already marked with a privately-purchased headstone or marker. To submit a claim for a medallion to be affxed to a private headstone/marker in a private cemetery, use VA Form 40-1330M, Claim for Government Medallion (available at http://www.va.gov/vaforms). A copy of the Veteran's military discharge document is required. Mail forms to Memorial Programs Service, Department of Veterans Affairs, 5109 Russell Road, Quantico, VA 22134-3903. The form and supporting documents may also be faxed toll free to 1-800-

455-7143.

To check the status of a claim for a headstone or marker for placement in a national, state, or tribal Veterans cemetery, please call
the cemetery. To check the status of one being placed in a private
cemetery, please contact the Applicant Assistance Unit at 1-800-697-
6947 or via email at mps.headstone@va.gov.

Other Memorialization
Presidential Memorial Certifcates are issued to recognize the
military service of honorably discharged deceased Veterans and persons who died in the active military, naval, or air service. Next of kin,
relatives and other loved ones may apply for a certifcate by mailing,
or faxing a completed and signed VA Form 40-0247, Presidential
Memorial Certifcate Request Form (available at http://www.va.gov/
vaforms/), along with a copy of the Veteran's military discharge
documents or proof of honorable military service. The processing of
requests sent without supporting documents will be delayed until eligibility can determined. Eligibility requirements can be found at www.
cem.va.gov.

Burial Flags: Generally, VA will furnish a U.S. burial fag to memorialize Veterans who received an other than dishonorable discharge.
This includes certain persons who served in the organized military
forces of the Commonwealth of the Philippines while in service of
the U.S armed forces and who died on or after April 25, 1951. Also
eligible for a burial fag are Veterans who were entitled to retired pay
for service in the Reserve or National Guard, or would have been
entitled if over age 60; and members or former members of the Selected Reserve who served their initial obligation, or were discharged
for a disability incurred or aggravated in the line of duty, or died while
a member of the Selected Reserve. The next of kin may apply for the
fag at any VA regional offce or U.S. Post Offce by completing VA
Form 21-2008, Application for United States Flag for Burial Purposes
(available at http://www.va.gov/vaforms/). In most cases, a funeral
director will help the family obtain the fag.

Reimbursement of Burial Expenses: VA will pay a burial allowance
up to $2,000 if the Veteran's death is service-connected. In such
cases, the person who bore the Veteran's burial expenses may claim
reimbursement from VA.

112

In some cases, VA will pay the cost of transporting the remains of a Veteran whose death was service-connected to the nearest national cemetery with available gravesites. There is no time limit for fling reimbursement claims in service-connected death cases.

Burial Allowance: VA will pay a burial and funeral allowance of up to $2,000 for Veterans who die from service-connected causes. VA will pay a burial and funeral allowance of up to $300 for Veterans who, at the time of death from nonservice-connected causes, were entitled to receive pension or compensation or would have been entitled if they were not receiving military retirement pay. VA will pay a burial and funeral allowance of up to $722 when the Veteran's death occurs in a VA facility, a VA-contracted nursing home or a state Veterans nursing home. In cases in which the Veteran's death was not service con-nected, claims must be fled within two years after burial or crema-tion.

Plot Allowance: VA will pay a plot allowance of up to $722 when a Veteran is buried in a cemetery not under U.S. government ju-risdiction if: the Veteran was discharged from active duty because of disability incurred or aggravated in the line of duty; the Veteran was receiving compensation or pension or would have been if the Veteran was not receiving military retired pay; or the Veteran died in a VA facility. The plot allowance may be paid to the state for the cost of a plot or interment in a state-owned cemetery reserved solely for Veteran burials if the Veteran is buried without charge. Burial expenses paid by the deceased's employer or a state agency will not be reimbursed.

Military Funeral Honors: Upon request, DoD will provide military funeral honors consisting of folding and the presenting of the United States fag and the playing of "Taps." A funeral honors detail consists of two or more uniformed members of the armed forces, with at least one member from the deceased's branch of service.

Family members should inform their funeral director if they want military funeral honors. DoD maintains a toll-free number (1-877-MIL-HONR) for use by funeral directors only to request honors. VA can help arrange honors for burials at VA national cemeteries. Veterans service organizations or volunteer groups may help provide honors. For more information, visit www.militaryfuneralhonors.osd.mil/.

Veterans Cemeteries Administered by Other Agencies

Department of the Army: Administers Arlington National Cemetery and other Army installation cemeteries. Eligibility is generally more restrictive than at VA national cemeteries. For information, call (703) 607-8000, write Superintendent, Arlington National Cemetery, Arlington, VA 22211, or visit www.arlingtoncemetery.mil/.

Department of the Interior: Administers two active national cemeteries – Andersonville National Cemetery in Georgia and Andrew Johnson National Cemetery in Tennessee. Eligibility is similar to VA national cemeteries. For information, call (202) 208-4747, write Department of Interior, National Park Service 1849 C. St. NW, Washington, D.C. 20240.

State and Tribal Veterans Cemeteries: Currently 87 state and four Tribal Veterans cemeteries offer burial options for Veterans and their families. These cemeteries have similar eligibility requirements and some require state residency. Some services, particularly for family members, may require a fee. Contact the state or tribal veterans cemetery or the state veterans affairs offce for information. To locate a State or Tribal Veterans cemetery, visit www.cem.va.gov/cem/scg/lsvc.asp.

Chapter 9
Reserve and National Guard

Eligibility for VA Benefts

Reservists who serve on active duty establish Veteran status and may be eligible for the full range of VA benefts, depending on the length of active military service and a discharge or release from active duty under conditions other than dishonorable. In addition, Reservists not activated may qualify for some VA benefts.

National Guard members can establish eligibility for VA benefts if activated for federal service during a period of war or domestic emergency. Activation for other than federal service does not qualify National Guard members for all VA benefts. Claims for VA benefts based on federal service fled by members of the National Guard should include a copy of the military orders, presidential proclamation, or executive order that clearly demonstrates the federal nature of the service.

Qualifying for VA Health Care

Under the "Combat Veteran" authority, Combat Veterans who were discharged or released from active service on or after Jan. 28, 2003, are eligible for enrollment in Priority Group 6, unless eligible for enrollment in a higher priority group. This authority provides a 5-year enrollment period, which begins on the discharge or separation date. These Combat Veterans are eligible for health care services and community living care for conditions possibly related to their military service, and are not required to disclose their income information unless they would like to be considered for a higher priority status, benefciary travel benefits, or exemption of co-pays for care unrelated to their military service.

Activated Reservists and members of the National Guard are eligible if they served on active duty in a theater of combat operations after Nov. 11, 1998, and were discharged under other than dishonorable conditions.

Veterans who enroll with VA under this authority will continue to be enrolled even after their enhanced eligibility period ends. At the end of their enhanced eligibility period, Veterans enrolled in Priority Group 6 may be shifted to a lower priority group depending on their income level. For additional information, call 1-877-222-VETS (8387).

OEF/OIF/OND Veterans may be eligible for a one-time dental evaluation and treatment following separation from service, if they did not have a dental exam prior to separation. Veterans must request a dental appointment within the frst 180 days post separation from active duty.

Disability Benefts
VA pays monthly compensation benefts for disabilities incurred or aggravated during active duty, or active duty for training as a result of injury or disease, or inactive duty training for disabilities due to injury, heart attack, or stroke. Additionally, the discharge must be under other than dishonorable conditions. For additional information see Chapter 2, "Service-connected Disabilities."

Montgomery GI Bill – Selected Reserve
Members of reserve elements of the Army, Navy, Air Force, Marine Corps and Coast Guard, and members of the Army National Guard and the Air National Guard, may be entitled to up to 36 months of educational benefts under the Montgomery GI Bill (MGIB) – Selected Reserve. To be eligible, the participant must:
1. Have a six-year obligation in the Selected Reserve or National Guard signed after June 30, 1985, or, if an offcer, agree to serve six years in addition to the original obligation.
2. Complete initial active duty for training (IADT).
3. Meet the requirement to receive a high school diploma or equivalency certifcate before Completing IADT..
4. Remain in good standing in a Selected Reserve or National Guard unit.

Reserve components determine eligibility for benefts. VA does not make decisions about eligibility and cannot make payments until the Reserve component has determined eligibility and notifed VA.

Period of Eligibility: Benefts generally end the day a reservist or National Guard member separates from the military. Additionally, if in the Selected Reserve and called to active duty, VA can generally extend the eligibility period by the length of time on active duty plus four

116

months for each period of active duty. Once this extension is granted, it will not be taken awayafter leaving the Selected Reserve.

Eligible members separated because of unit deactivation, a disability that was not caused by misconduct, or otherwise involuntarily separated during Oct. 1, 1991, through December 31, 2001, have 14 years after their eligibility date to use benefits. Similarly, members involuntarily separated from the Selected Reserve due to a deactivation of their unit between Oct. 1, 2007, and Sept. 30, 2014, may receive a 14-year period of eligibility.

Payments: The rate for full-time training effective Oct. 1, 2012, is $356 a month for 36 months. Part-time benefts are reduced proportionately. For complete current rates, visit www.gibill.va.gov. DoD may make additional contributions.

Training: Participants may pursue training at a college or university, or take technical training at any approved facility. Training includes undergraduate, graduate, or post-graduate courses; state licensure and certifcation; courses for a certifcate or diploma from business, technical or vocational schools; cooperative training; apprenticeship or on-the-job training; correspondence courses; independent study programs; fight training; entrepreneurship training; remedial, defciency or refresher courses needed to complete a program of study; or preparatory courses for tests required or used for admission to an institution of higher learning or graduate school.
Accelerated payments for certain high-cost programs are authorized effective Jan. 28, 2008

Work-Study: See page 55

Educational and Vocational Counseling: Refer to Chapter 10, "Transition Assistance", for detailed information on available services.

Reserve Educational Assistance Program (REAP)
This program provides educational assistance to members of National Guard and Reserve components who are called or ordered to active duty service in response to a war or national emergency as declared by the President or Congress. Visit www.gibill.va.gov for more information.

Eligibility: Eligibility is determined by DoD or the Department of Homeland Security. Generally, a Servicemember who serves on active duty on or after Sept. 11, 2001, for at least 90 consecutive days, or accumulates a total of three or more of years of service is eligible.

Payments: Reserve or National Guard members whose eligibility is based upon continuous service receive a payment rate based upon their number of continuous days on active duty. Members who qualify after the accumulation of three or more years of aggregate active duty service receive the full payment allowable.

Reserve Educational Assistance Rates

Active Duty Service	Monthly Payment Rate for Full-Time Students
90 days but less than one year	$625.60
One year but less than two years	$938.40
Two or more continuous years	$1,251.20

Training: Participants may pursue training at a college or university, or take technical training at any approved facility. Training includes undergraduate, graduate, or post-graduate courses; state licensure and certifcation courses; courses for a certifcate or diploma from business, technical or vocational schools; cooperative training; apprenticeship or on-the-job training; correspondence courses; independent study programs; fight training; entrepreneurship training; remedial, defciency, or refresher courses needed to complete a program of study; or preparatory courses for tests required or used for admission to an institution of higher learning or graduate school. Accelerated payments for certain high-cost programs are authorized.

Period of Eligibility: Prior to Jan. 28, 2008, members of the Selected Reserve called to active duty were eligible as long as they continued to serve in the Selected Reserve. They lost eligibility if they went into the Inactive Ready Reserve (IRR). Members of the IRR called to active duty were eligible as long as they stayed in the IRR or Selected Reserve.

Effective Jan. 28, 2008, members who are called up from the Selected Reserve, complete their REAP-qualifying period of active duty service, and then return to the Selected Reserve for the remainder of their service contract, have 10 years to use their benefts after separation.

In addition, members who are called up from the IRR or Inactive National Guard (ING), complete their REAP-qualifying period of active duty service, and then enter the Selected Reserve to complete their service contract, have 10 years to use their benefts after separation.

Work-Study Program: See page 55.

Educational and Vocational Counseling: Refer to Chapter 10, "Transition Assistance", for detailed information on available services.

Home Loan Guaranty

National Guard members and reservists are eligible for a VA home loan if they have completed at least six years of honorable service, are mobilized for active duty service for a period of at least 90 days, or are discharged because of a service-connected disability.

Reservists who do not qualify for VA housing loan benefts may be eligible for loans on favorable terms insured by the Federal Housing Administration (FHA), part of HUD. Additional information can be found in Chapter 5 – "Home Loan Guaranty."

Life Insurance

National Guard members and reservists are eligible to receive Servicemembers' Group Life Insurance (SGLI), Veterans' Group Life Insurance (VGLI), and Family Servicemembers' Group Life Insurance (FSGLI). They may also be eligible for SGLI Traumatic Injury Protection if severely injured and suffering a qualifying loss, Service-Disabled Veterans Insurance if they receive a service-connected disability rating from VA, and Veterans' Mortgage Life Insurance if approved for a Specially Adapted Housing Grant. Complete details can be found in Chapter 6 – "VA Life Insurance."

Burial and Memorial Benefts

VA provides a burial fag to memorialize members or former members of the Selected Reserve who served their initial obligation, or were discharged for a disability incurred or aggravated in the line of duty, or died while a member of the Selected Reserve.

Reservists and National Guard members may be eligible for additional burial benefts if their death was due to an injury or disease that developed during, or was aggravated during, active duty, active duty for training, or inactive duty for training. Burial benefts may include burial in a national cemetery; an inscribed headstone, marker, or medallion; a Presidential Memorial Certifcate; and an allowance to partially reimburse burial and funeral costs. Additional information about burial benefts that may be available can be found in Chapter 7 – "Burial and Memorial Benefts".

Re-employment Rights

A person who left a civilian job to enter active duty in the armed forces is entitled to return to the job after discharge or release from active duty if they:

1. Gave advance notice of military service to the employer.
2. Did not exceed fve years cumulative absence from the civilian job (with some exceptions).
3. Submitted a timely application for re-employment.
4. Did not receive a dishonorable or other punitive discharge.

The law calls for a returning Veteran to be placed in the job as if he/she had never left, including benefts based on seniority such as pensions, pay increases and promotions. The law also prohibits discrimination in hiring, promotion or other advantages of employment on the basis of military service. Veterans seeking re-employment should apply, verbally or in writing, to the company's hiring offcial and keep a record of their application. If problems arise, contact the Department of Labor's Veterans' Employment and Training Service (VETS) in the state of the employer.

Federal employees not properly re-employed may appeal directly to the Merit Systems Protection Board. Non-federal employees may fle complaints in U.S. District Court. For information, visit www.dol.gov/vets/programs/userra/main.htm.

Transition Assistance Advisor Program

The Transition Assistance Advisor (TAA) program is a partnership between the National Guard and VA to assist Veterans. The TAA Program, housed within the National Guard (NG) Offce of Warrior Support, places a NG/VA trained expert at the NG Headquarters in each of the 50 states as well as PR, GU, VI, and the District of Columbia. The advisor serves as an advocate for Guard members and their families, as well as other geographically dispersed military members and families. In collaboration with state and local coalition partners, the TAA Program provides VA beneft enrollment assistance, referrals, and assists in facilitating access for Veterans through the overwhelming maze of programs, with the compassion of someone who knows what it is like to transition from the Guard to active duty and then back to civilian status.

Advisors receive annual training from VA experts in VA health care and benefts to assist Guard members and their families with access to VA health care facilities and TRICARE facilities within their network. To fnd a local Transition Assistance Advisor call 1-877-577-6691 or go to http://www.taapmo.com.

Outreach for OEF/OIF/New Dawn Veterans
VA's OEF/OIF/New Dawn Outreach Teams focus on improving outreach to members of the National Guard and Reserve by engaging them throughout the deployment cycle with targeted messages and face-to-face encounters with VA staff. These outreach teams are located at VA Medical Centers to help ease the transition from military to civilian life. To learn more, visit www.oefoif.va.gov. Veterans can also call the toll-free OEF/OIF/New Dawn Help Line at 1-866-606-8216 for answers to questions about VA benefts, health care, and enrollment procedures.

Air Reserve Personnel Center
The Air Reserve Personnel Center (ARPC) is available to assist with various personnel issues, including requests for personnel records, copies of DD Form 214, or other military documents. Many Veterans fle an Air Force Board Correction of Military Records (AFBCMR) or write their Congressman to get these basic issues resolved, which requires that the request be routed through appropriate authorities, sometimes taking up to 180 days. Alternately, the ARPC routinely handles these actions on a much quicker basis. Members should call the ARPC for assistance at 1-800-525-0102 or logon to https://gum-crm.csd.disa.mil.

Chapter 10
Special Groups of Veterans

Homeless Veterans

VA's homeless programs constitute the largest integrated network of homeless assistance programs in the country, offering a wide array of services to help Veterans recover from homelessness and live as self-suffciently and independently as possible.

The *VA Health Care for Homeless Veterans (HCHV) Program* provides a gateway to VA and community supportive services for eligible Veterans. Through the HCHV Program, Veterans are provided with case management and residential treatment in the community. The program also conducts outreach to homeless Veterans who are not likely to come to VA facilities on their own.

Homeless Veterans Supported Employment Program (HVSEP) provides vocational assistance, job development and placement, and ongoing employment supports designed to improve employment outcomes among homeless Veterans. HVSEP is coordinated between CWT and the continuum of Homeless Veterans Programs for the purpose of providing community-based vocational and employment services. All of the HVSEP vocational rehabilitation specialists (VRS) hired to provide employment services for the program consists of homeless, formerly homeless, or at risk of homelessness Veterans.

The **National Call Center for Homeless Veterans** (NCCHV) assists homeless Veterans, at-risk Veterans, their families and other interested parties with linkages to appropriate VA and community-based resources. The call center provides trained VA staff members 24 hours a day, seven days a week to assess a caller's needs and connect them to appropriate resources. The call center can be accessed by dialing 1-877-4AID VET (1-877-424-3838).

The **VA's Homeless Providers Grant and Per Diem Program** provides funds to non-proft community agencies providing transitional housing (up to 24 months) and/or offering services to homeless Veterans, such as case management, education, crisis intervention, counseling, and services targeted towards specialized populations including homeless women Veterans. The goal of the program is to help homeless Veterans achieve residential stability, increase their skill levels and/or income, and obtain greater self-determination.

The **Housing and Urban Development-Veterans Affairs Support-ive Housing** (HUD-VASH) Program provides permanent housing and ongoing case management for eligible homeless Veterans who would not be able to live independently otherwise. This program allows eligible Veterans to live in Veteran-selected housing units with a "Housing Choice" voucher. These vouchers are portable to support the Veteran's choice of housing in communities served by their VA medical facility where case management services can be provided. HUD-VASH services include outreach and case management to ensure integration of services and continuity of care. This program enhances the ability of VA to serve homeless women Veterans, and homeless Veterans with families.

Through the **Supportive Services for Veteran Families Program**, VA aims to improve very low-income Veteran families' housing stability by providing supportive services in, or transitioning to, permanent housing. VA funds community-based organizations to provide eligible Veteran families with outreach, case management and assistance in obtaining VA and other benefts. Grantees may also provide time-limited payments to third parties (e.g., landlords, utility companies, moving companies and licensed child care providers) if these payments help Veterans' families stay in or acquire permanent housing on a sustainable basis.

In **VA's Compensated Work Therapy/Transitional Residence** (CWT/TR) Program, disadvantaged, at-risk, and homeless Veterans live in CWT/TR community-based supervised group homes while working for pay in VA's CWT Program, to learn new job skills, relearn successful work habits, and regain a sense of self-esteem and self-worth.

The **Health Care for Re-Entry Veterans (HCRV) Program** offers outreach, referrals and short-term case management assistance for incarcerated Veterans who may be at risk for homelessness upon their release.

For more information on VA homeless programs and services, Veterans currently enrolled in VA health care can speak with their VA mental health or health care provider. Other Veterans and interested parties can fnd a complete list of VA health care facilities at www. va.gov, or they can call VA's general information hotline at 1-800-827-1000. If assistance is needed when contacting a VA facility, ask to speak to the Health Care for Homeless Veterans Program or the Mental Health service manager. Information is also available on the VA Homeless program website at www.va.gov/homeless.

Filipino Veterans

World War II era Filipino Veterans are eligible for certain VA benefts. Generally, Old Philippine Scouts are eligible for VA benefits in the same manner as U.S. Veterans. Commonwealth Army Veterans, including certain organized Filipino guerrilla forces and New Philippine Scouts residing in the United States who are citizens or lawfully admitted for permanent residence, are also eligible for VA health care in the United States on the same basis as U.S. Veterans.

Certain Commonwealth Army Veterans and new Philippine Scouts may be eligible for disability compensation and burial benefits. Other Veterans of recognized guerrilla groups also may be eligible for certain VA benefits. Survivors of World War II era Filipino Veterans may be eligible for dependency and indemnity compensation. Eligibility and the rates of benefts vary based on the recipient's citizenship and place of residence. Call 1-800-827-1000 for additional information.

VA Benefts for Veterans Living Overseas

VA monetary benefts, including disability compensation, pension, educational benefts, and burial allowances are generally payable overseas. Some programs are restricted. Home loan guaranties are available only in the United States and selected U.S. territories and possessions. Educational benefts are limited to approved, degree-granting programs in institutions of higher learning. Benefciaries living in foreign countries should contact the nearest American embassy or consulate for help. In Canada, contact an offce of Veterans Affairs Canada. For information, visit http://www.vba.va.gov/bln/21/Foreign/index.htm.

World War II Era Merchant Marine Seamen

Certain Merchant Marine seamen who served in World War II may qualify for Veterans benefits. When applying for medical care, seamen must present their discharge certifcate from the Department of Defense. Call 1-800-827-1000 for help obtaining a certifcate.

Allied Veterans Who Served During WWI or WWII

VA may provide medical care to certain Veterans of nations allied or associated with the United States during World War I or World War II if authorized and reimbursed by the foreign government. VA also may provide hospitalization, outpatient care and domiciliary care to former members of the armed forces of Czechoslovakia or Poland who fought in World War I or World War II in armed confict against an enemy of the United States if they have been U.S. citizens for at least 10 years.

World War Service by Particular Groups

A number of groups who provided military-related service to the United States can receive VA benefts. A discharge by the Secretary of Defense is needed to qualify. Service in the following groups has been certifed as active military service for benefts purposes:

1. Women Air Force Service Pilots (WASPs).
2. World War I Signal Corps Female Telephone Operators Unit.
3. World War I Engineer Field Clerks.
4. Women's Army Auxiliary Corps (WAAC).
5. Quartermaster Corps female clerical employees serving with the American Expeditionary Forces in World War I.
6. Civilian employees of Pacifc naval air bases who actively participated in defense of Wake Island during World War II.
7. Reconstruction aides and dietitians in World War I.
8. Male civilian ferry pilots.
9. Wake Island defenders from Guam.
10. Civilian personnel assigned to OSS secret intelligence.
11. Guam Combat Patrol.
12. Quartermaster Corps members of the Keswick crew on Corregidor during World War II.
13. U.S. civilians who participated in the defense of Bataan.
14. U.S. merchant seamen on block ships in support of Operation Mulberry in the World War II invasion of Normandy.
15. American merchant marines in oceangoing service during World War II.
16. Civilian Navy IFF radar technicians who served in combat areas of the Pacifc during World War II.
17. U.S. civilians of the American Field Service who served overseas in World War I.
18. U.S. civilians of the American Field Service who served overseas under U.S. armies and U.S. army groups in World War II.

19. U.S. civilian employees of American Airlines who served overseas in a contract with the Air Transport Command between Dec. 14, 1941, and Aug. 14, 1945.
20. Civilian crewmen of U.S. Coast and Geodetic Survey vessels who served in areas of immediate military hazard while conducting cooperative operations with and for the U.S. armed forces between Dec. 7, 1941, and Aug. 15, 1945 Qualifying vessels are: the Derickson, Explorer, Gilber, Hilgard, E. Lester Jones, Lydonia Patton, Surveyor, Wainwright, Westdahl, Oceanographer, Hydrographer and Pathfnder.
21. Members of the American Volunteer Group (Flying Tigers) who served between Dec. 7, 1941, and July 18, 1942.
22. U.S. civilian fight crew and aviation ground support employees of United Air Lines who served overseas in a contract with Air Transport Command between Dec. 14, 1941, and Aug.14, 1945.
23. U.S. civilian fight crew, including pursers, and aviation ground support employees of Transcontinental and Western Air, Inc. who served overseas in a contract with the Air Transport Command between Dec. 14, 1941, and Aug. 14, 1945.
24. U.S. civilian fight crew and aviation ground support employees of Consolidated Vultee Aircraft Corp. who served overseas in a contract with Air Transport Command between Dec. 14, 1941, and Aug. 14, 1945.
25. U.S. civilian fight crew and aviation ground support employees of Pan American World Airways and its subsidiaries and affliates, who served overseas in a contract with the Air Transport Command and Naval Air Transport Service between Dec. 14, 1941, and Aug. 14, 1945.
26. Honorably discharged members of the American Volunteer Guard, Eritrea Service Command, between June 21, 1942, and March 31, 1943.
27. U.S. civilian fight crew and aviation ground support employees of Northwest Airlines who served overseas under the airline's contract with Air Transport Command from Dec. 14, 1941, through Aug. 14, 1945.
28. U.S. civilian female employees of the U.S. Army Nurse Corps who served in the defense of Bataan and Corregidor between Jan. 2, 1942, and Feb. 3, 1945.
29. U.S. fight crew and aviation ground support employees of

Northeast Airlines Atlantic Division, who served overseas as a result of Northeast Airlines' contract with the Air Transport Command from Dec. 7, 1941, through Aug. 14, 1945.
30. U.S. civilian fight crew and aviation ground support employees of Braniff Airways, who served overseas in the North Atlantic or under the jurisdiction of the North Atlantic Wing, Air Transport Command, as a result of a contract with the Air Transport Command between Feb. 26, 1945, and Aug. 14, 1945.
31. Chamorro and Carolina former native police who received military training in the Donnal area of central Saipan and were placed under command of Lt. Casino of the 6th Provisional Military Police Battalion to accompany U.S. Marines on active, combat patrol from Aug. 19, 1945, to Sept. 2, 1945.
32. Three scouts/guides, Miguel Tenorio, Penedicto Taisacan, and Cristino Dela Cruz, who assisted the United States Marines in the offensive operations against the Japanese on the Northern Mariana Islands from June 19, 1944, through Sept. 2, 1945.
33. The operational Analysis Group of the Offce of Scientifc Research and Development, Offce of Emergency Management, which served overseas with the U.S. Army Air Corps from Dec. 7, 1941, through Aug. 15, 1945.
34. Service as a member of the Alaska Territorial Guard during World War II or any individual who was honorably discharged under section 8147 of the Department of Defense Appropriations Act of 2001.

Incarcerated Veterans

VA benefts are affected if a benefciary is convicted of a felony and imprisoned for more than 60 days. Disability or death pension paid to an incarcerated benefciary must be discontinued. Disability compensation paid to an incarcerated Veteran rated 20 percent or more disabled is limited to the 10 percent rate. For a Veteran whose disability rating is 10 percent, the payment is reduced to half of the rate payable to a Veteran evaluated as 10 percent disabled.

Any amounts not paid to the Veteran while incarcerated may be apportioned to eligible dependents. Payments are not reduced for participants in work-release programs, residing in halfway houses or under community control.

Failure to notify VA of a Veteran's incarceration can result in overpay-ment of benefts and the subsequent loss of all VA fnancial benefts until the overpayment is recovered. VA benefts will not be provided to any Veteran or dependent wanted for an outstanding felony war-rant.

The Health Care for Reentry Veterans Program (HCRV) offers outreach to Veterans incarcerated in state and federal prisons, and referrals and short-term case management assistance upon release from prison.

The Veterans Justice Outreach Program (VJO) offers outreach and case management to Veterans involved in law enforcement encounters, overseen by treatment courts, and incarcerated in local jails. Visit www.va.gov/homeless/ to locate an outreach worker.

Chapter 11
Transition Assistance

Joint Transition Assistance

The Departments of Veterans Affairs, Defense, and Labor re-launched a new and improved website for wounded warriors – the National Resource Directory (NRD). This directory (www.nrd.gov) provides access to thousands of services and resources at the national, state and local levels to support recovery, rehabilitation and community reintegration. The NRD is a comprehensive online tool available nationwide for wounded, ill and injured Servicemembers, Veterans and their families.

The NRD includes extensive information for Veterans seeking resources on VA benefits such as disability benefits, pensions for Veterans and their families, VA health care insurance and the GI Bill. The NRD's design and interface is simple, easy-to-navigate and intended to answer the needs of a broad audience of users within the military, Veteran and caregiver communities.

Transition From Military to VA

VA has personnel stationed at major military hospitals to help seriously injured Servicemembers returning from Operations Enduring Freedom, Iraqi Freedom, and New Dawn (OEF/OIF/OND) as they transition from military to civilian life. OEF/OIF Servicemembers who have questions about VA benefits or need assistance in fling a VA claim or accessing services can contact the nearest VA offce or call 1-800-827-1000.

eBenefts

The eBenefts portal (www.ebenefts.va.gov) provides Servicemembers, Veterans, their families, and Caregivers with self-service access to beneft applications, benefts information, and access to personal information such as offcial military personnel fle documents. The portal provides two main services; it catalogs links to information on other websites about military and Veteran benefts, and it provides a personalized workspace called My Dashboard, which gives quick access to all the online tools currently integrated into eBenefts.

Transition Assistance Program:consists of comprehensive work-shops at military installations designed to assist Servicemembers as they transition from military to civilian life. The program includes job search, employment and training information, as well as VA benefts information for Servicemembers who are within 18 months of sepa-ration or retirement. The VA Benefit Briefngs are comprised of two briefngs focusing on education, benefts. and VA health care and dis-ability compensation. Servicemembers can sign up for one-on-one appointments with a VA representative. Interested Servicemembers should contact their local TAP Manager to sign up for this program.

VOW to Hire Heroes Act
Improving the Transition Assistance Program (TAP): The VOW to Hire Heroes Act of 2011 ("the Act") made TAP, including attendance at the VA Beneft Briefngs, mandatory for most Servicemembers transitioning to civilian status, upgraded career counseling options, and tailored TAP for the 21st Century job market.

Facilitating Seamless Transition: The Act allows Servicemembers to begin the federal employment process prior to separation in order to facilitate a truly seamless transition from the military to jobs at VA, Department of Homeland Security, and the many other federal agen-cies seeking to hire Veterans.

Expanding Education and Training: The Act provides nearly 100,000 unemployed Veterans of past eras and wars with up to one year of assistance (equal to the full-time payment rate under the Montgomery GI Bill-Active Duty program) to qualify for jobs in high-demand sectors. It also provides disabled Veterans up to one year of additional Vocational Rehabilitation and Employment benefts.

Translating Military Skills and Training: The Act requires the Department of Labor take a hard look at military skills and training equivalencies that are transferrable to the civilian sector and make it easier to obtain licenses and certifcations.

Veterans Tax Credits: The Act provides tax credits for hiring Veter-ans and disabled Veterans who are out of work.

The inTransition
Servicemembers and Veterans may receive assistance from the in-Transition Program when they are receiving mental health treatment

and are making transitions from military service, location or a health care system. This program provides access to transitional support, motivation, and healthy lifestyle assistance and advice from qualifed coaches through the toll-free telephone number 1-800-424-7877. For more information about The inTransition Program, please log onto www.health.mil/inTransition.

Pre-Discharge Program
The Pre-Discharge Program is a joint VA and DoD program that affords Servicemembers the opportunity to fle claims for disability compensation and other benefts up to 180 days prior to separation or retirement.

The two primary components of the Pre-Discharge Program, Benefts Delivery at Discharge (BDD) and Quick Start, may be utilized by separating and retiring Servicemembers on active duty, including members of the Coast Guard, and members of the National Guard and Reserves (activated under Titles 10 or 32) in CONUS and some overseas locations. BDD is offered to accelerate receipt of VA disability benefits after release or discharge from active duty.

To participate in the BDD program, Servicemembers must:
1. have at least 60 days, but not more than 180 days, remaining on active duty.
2. have a known date of separation or retirement.
3. provide VA with service treatment records, originals or photocopies.
4. be available to complete all necessary examinations prior to leaving the point of separation.

Quick Start is offered to Servicemembers who have less than 60 days remaining on active duty or are unable to complete the necessary examinations prior to leaving the point of separation.

To participate in the Quick Start Program, Servicemembers must:
1. have at least one day remaining on active duty.
2. have a known date of separation or retirement.
3. provide VA with service treatment records, originals or photocopies.

Servicemembers should contact the local Transition Assistance Offce or Army Career Alumni Program Center to schedule appointments to attend VA benefts briefngs and learn how to initiate a pre-discharge claim. Servicemembers can obtain more information by calling VA toll-free at 1-800-827-1000 or by visiting www.vba.va.gov/predischarge.

Integrated Disability Evaluation System (IDES)

A third component of the Pre-Discharge program is the Integrated Disability Evaluation System. The IDES program covers Service-members who are referred to a Medical Evaluation Board.
The IDES program has three goals:

1. a single seiers of disability exams conducted to VA standards that is used by both Departments;

2. a single disability rating completed by VA that is binding upon both Departments; and

3. expeditious payment of VA benefts after a Servicemember's separation from service.

VA Form 21-0819, VA/DoD Joint Disability Evaluation Board Claim, is initiated by the Military Service Coordinator jointly with Servicemem-ber (SM), when the SM is initially referred to IDES. The VA Form 21-0819, will not only refect the military referred/unftting medical conditions, but all claimed medical conditions affecting the uniformed member. This approach provides a comprehensive view of the SM's health at the time of the IDES evaluation process.

Federal Recovery Coordination Program

The Federal Recovery Coordination Program (FRCP), a joint pro-gram of DoD and VA, helps coordinate and access federal, state and local programs, benefits and services for seriously wounded, ill, and injured Servicemembers, and their families through recovery, reha-bilitation, and reintegration into the community.

Federal Recovery Coordinators (FRCs) have the delegated author-ity for oversight and coordination of the clinical and non-clinical care identifed in each client's Federal Individual Recovery Plan (FIRP). Working with a variety of case managers, FRCs assist their clients in reaching their FIRP goals. FRCs remain with their clients as long as they are needed regardless of the client's location, duty or health status. In doing so, they often serve as the central point of contact and provide transition support for their clients.

Military Services Provide Pre-Separation Counseling

Servicemembers may receive pre-separation counseling 24 months prior to retirement or 12 months prior to separation from active duty. These sessions present information on education, training, employment assistance, National Guard and Reserve programs, medical benefts, and fnancial assistance.

Verifcation of Military Experience and Training

The Verifcation of Military Experience and Training (VMET) Document, DD Form 2586, helps Servicemembers verify previous experience and training to potential employers, negotiate credits at schools, and obtain certifcates or licenses. VMET documents are available only through each military branch support offces and are intended for Servicemembers who have at least six months of active service. Servicemembers should obtain VMET documents from their Transition Support Offce within 12 months of separation or 24 months of retirement.

Transition Bulletin Board

To fnd business opportunities, a calendar of transition seminars, job fairs, information on Veterans associations, transition services, training and education opportunities, as well as other announcements at www.turbotap.org

DoD Transportal

To fnd locations and phone numbers of all Transition Assistance Offces as well as mini-courses on conducting successful job-search campaigns, writing resumes, using the internet to fnd a job, and links to job search and recruiting Websites, visit the DoD Transportal at www.Veteranprograms.com/index.html

Educational and Vocational Counseling

The Vocational Rehabilitation and Employment (VR&E) Program provides educational and vocational counseling to Servicemembers, Veterans, and certain dependents (U.S.C. Title 38, Section 3697) at no charge. These counseling services are designed to help an individual choose a vocational direction, determine the course needed to achieve the chosen goal, and evaluate the career possibilities open to them.

Assistance may include interest and aptitude testing, occupational exploration, setting occupational goals, locating the right type of training program, and exploring educational or training facilities which can be utilized to achieve an occupational goal.

133

Counseling services include, but are not limited to, educational and vocational counseling and guidance; testing; analysis of and recommendations to improve job-marketing skills; identifcation of employment, training, and fnancial aid resources; and referrals to other agencies providing these services.

Eligibility: Educational and vocational counseling services are available during the period the individual is on active duty with the armed forces and within 180 days of the estimated date of his or her discharge or release from active duty. The projected discharge must be under conditions other than dishonorable.

Servicemembers are eligible even if they are only considering whether or not they will continue as members of the armed forces. Veterans are eligible if not more than one year has elapsed since the date they were last discharged or released from active duty.

Veterans and dependents who are eligible for VA education benefts may receive educational and vocational counseling at any time during their eligibility period. This service is based on having eligibility for a VA program such as Chapter 30 (Montgomery GI Bill); Chapter 31 (Vocational Rehabilitation and Employment); Chapter 32 (Veterans Education Assistance Program – VEAP); Chapter 33 (Post-9/11 GI Bill); Chapter 35 (Dependents' Educational Assistance Program) for certain spouses and dependent children; Chapter 18 (Spina Bifda Program) for certain dependent children; and Chapter 1606 and 1607 of Title 10.

Veterans and Servicemembers may apply for counseling services using VA Form 28-8832, Application for Counseling. Veterans and Servicemembers may also write a letter expressing a desire for counseling services.

Upon receipt of either type of request for counseling from an eligible individual, an appointment for counseling will be scheduled. Counseling services are provided to eligible persons at no charge.

Veterans' Workforce Investment Program
Recently separated Veterans and those with service-connected disabilities, signifcant barriers to employment or who served on active duty during a period in which a campaign or expedition badge was authorized can contact the nearest state employment offce for em-

134

ployment help through the Veterans Workforce Investment Program. The program may be conducted through state or local public agencies, community organizations or private, nonproft organizations.

State Employment Services

Veterans can fnd employment information, education and training opportunities, job counseling, job search workshops, and resume preparation assistance at state Workforce Career or One-Stop Centers. These offces also have specialists to help disabled Veterans fnd employment.

Unemployment Compensation

Veterans who do not begin civilian employment immediately after leaving military service may receive weekly unemployment compensation for a limited time. The amount and duration of payments are determined by individual states. Apply by contacting the nearest state employment offce listed in the local telephone directory.

Veterans Preference for Federal Jobs

Since the time of the Civil War, Veterans of the U.S. armed forces have been given some degree of preference in appointments to federal jobs. Veterans' preference in its present form comes from the Veterans' Preference Act of 1944, as amended, and now codifed in Title 5, United States Code. By law, Veterans who are disabled or who served on active duty in the U.S. armed forces during certain specifed time periods or in military campaigns are entitled to preference over others when hiring from competitive lists of eligible candidates, and also in retention during a reduction in force (RIF).

To receive preference, a Veteran must have been discharged or released from active duty in the U.S. armed forces under honorable conditions (honorable or general discharge). Preference is also provided for certain widows and widowers of deceased Veterans who died in service; spouses of service-connected disabled Veterans; and mothers of Veterans who died under honorable conditions on active duty or have permanent and total service-connected disabilities. For each of these preferences, there are specifc criteria that must be met in order to be eligible to receive the Veterans' preference.

Recent changes in Title 5 clarify Veterans preference eligibility criteria for National Guard and Reserve members. Veterans eligible for preference include Reservists and National Guard members who served on active duty as defned by Title 38 at any time in the armed forces for a period of more than 180 consecutive days, any part of which occurred during the period beginning on Sept. 11, 2001, and ending on the date prescribed by Presidential proclamation or by law as the last date of OEF/OIF. Reservists and National Guardsmen must have been discharged or released from active duty in the armed forces under honorable conditions.

Another recent change involves Veterans who earned the Global War on Terrorism Expeditionary Medal for service in OEF/OIF/OND. Under Title 5, service on active duty in the armed forces during a war or in a campaign or expedition for which a campaign badge has been authorized also qualifes for Veterans preference. Any Armed Forces Expeditionary medal or campaign badge qualifes for preference. Medal holders must have served continuously for 24 months or the full period called or ordered to active duty. For additional information, visit the Offce of Personnel Management (OPM) website at www. fedshirevets.gov.

In 2011, President Obama signed the VOW (Veterans Opportunity to Work) To Hire Heroes Act. VOW amends Chapter 21 of Title 5, United States Code (U.S.C.) by adding section 2108a, "Treatment of certain individuals as Veterans, disabled Veterans, and preference eligibles." Section 2108a requires Federal agencies to treat active duty Servicemembers as Veterans, disabled Veterans, or preference eligibles for purposes of appointment in the competitive service when these Servicemembers submit a certifcation of expected discharge or release from active duty under honorable conditions along with their applications for Federal employment. A certifcation is any written document from the armed forces that certifes the Servicemember is expected to be discharged or released from active duty service in the armed forces under honorable conditions not later than 120 days from the date the certifcation is signed.

Veterans' preference does not require an agency to use any particular appointment process. Agencies can pick candidates from a number of different special hiring authorities or through a variety of different sources. For example, the agency can reinstate a former federal employee, transfer someone from another agency, reassign someone from within the agency, make a selection under merit promotion procedures or through open, competitive exams, or appoint someone noncompetitively under special authority such as a Veterans Readjustment Appointment or special authority for 30 percent or more disabled Veterans. The decision on which hiring authority the agency desires to use rests solely with the agency. When applying for federal jobs, eligible Veterans should claim preference on their application or resume. Veterans should apply for a federal job by contacting the personnel offce at the agency in which they wish to work. For more information, visit www.usajobs.gov for job openings or help creating a federal resume.

Veterans' Employment Opportunities Act: When an agency accepts applications from outside its own workforce, the Veterans' Employment Opportunities Act of 1998 allows preference eligible candidates or Veterans to compete for these vacancies under merit promotion procedures.Veterans who are selected are given career or career-conditional appointments. Veterans are those who have been separated under honorable conditions from the U.S. armed forces with three or more years of continuous active service. For information, visit www.usajobs.gov or www.fedshirevets.gov.

Veterans' Recruitment Appointment: Allows federal agencies to appoint eligible Veterans to jobs without competition. These appointments can be converted to career or career-conditional positions after two years of satisfactory work. Veterans should apply directly to the agency where they wish to work. For information,www.fedshirevets.gov/.

Small Businesses
VA's Center for Veterans Enterprise helps Veterans interested in forming or expanding small businesses and helps VA contracting offces identify Veteran-owned small businesses. For information, write the U.S. Department of Veterans Affairs (OOVE), 810 Vermont Avenue, N.W., Washington, DC 20420-0001, call toll-free 1-866-584-2344 or visit www.vetbiz.gov. Small Business Contracts: Like other federal agencies, VA is required to place a portion of its contracts and purchases with small and disadvantaged businesses. VA has a special offce to help small and disadvantaged businesses get information on VA acquisition opportunities. For information, write the U.S. Department of Veterans Affairs (OOSB), 810 Vermont Avenue, N.W., Washington, DC 20420-0001, call toll-free 1-800-949-8387 or visit www.va.gov/osdbu/.

Chapter 12

Dependents and Survivors Health Care

Civilian Health and Medical Program of the Department of Veterans Affairs (CHAMPVA). Under CHAMPVA, certain dependents and survivors can receive reimbursement for most medical expenses – inpatient, outpatient, mental health, prescription medication, skilled nursing care and durable medical equipment.

Eligibility: To be eligible for CHAMPVA, an individual cannot be eligible for TRICARE (the medical program for civilian dependents provided by DoD) and must be one of the following:
1. The spouse or child of a Veteran whom VA has rated permanently and totally disabled due to a service-connected disability.
2. The surviving spouse or child of a Veteran who died from a VA-rated service-connected disability, or who, at the time of death, was rated permanently and totally disabled.
3. The surviving spouse or child of a Veteran who died on active duty service and in the line of duty, not due to misconduct. However, in most of these cases, these family members are eligible for TRI-CARE, not CHAMPVA.

A surviving spouse under age 55 who remarries loses CHAMPVA eligibility at midnight of the date on remarriage. He/she may re-establish eligibility if the remarriage ends by death, divorce or annulment effective the frst day of the month following the termination of the remarriage or Dec. 1, 1999, whichever is later. A surviving spouse who remarries after age 55 does not lose eligibility upon remarriage.

For those who have Medicare entitlement or other health insurance, CHAMPVA is a secondary payer. Benefciaries with Medicare must be enrolled in Parts A&B to maintain CHAMPVA eligibility. For additional information, contact Purchased Care at the VA Health Administration Center, CHAMPVA, P.O. Box 469028, Denver, CO 80246, call 1-800-733-8387 or visit www.va.gov/hac/forbenefciaries/champva/champva.asp.

Many VA health care facilities provide services to CHAMPVA benefciaries under the CHAMPVA In-house Treatment Initiative (CITI) program. Contact the nearest VA health care facility to determine if it participates. Those who use a CITI facility incur no cost for services; however, services are provided on a space-available basis, after the needs of Veterans are met. Not all services are available at all times. The coverage of services is dependent upon the CHAMPVA beneft coverage. CHAMPVA benefciaries who are covered by Medicare cannot use CITI.

VA's Comprehensive Assistance for Family Caregivers Program en- titles the designated Primary Family Caregiver, who is without health insurance coverage, CHAMPVA benefts. Some of the health plans that would make a Primary Family Caregiver ineligible for CHAMP- VA benefts include Medicare, Medicaid, commercial health plans through employment and individual plans.

Children Born with Spina Bifda to Certain Vietnam or Korea Veterans: The Spina Bifda Program (SB) is a comprehensive health care benefts program administered by the Department of Veterans Affairs for birth children of certain Vietnam and Korea Veterans who have been diagnosed with spina bifda (except spina bifda occulta). The SB program provides reimbursement for inpatient and outpa- tient medical services, pharmacy, durable medical equipment, and supplies. Purchased Care at the VA's Health Administration Center in Denver, Colorado manages the SB Program, including the autho- rization of benefts and the subsequent processing and payment of claims. For more information about spina bifda health care benefts, call 1-888-820-1756 or visit www.va.gov/hac/forbenefciaries/spina/ spina.asp

Eligibility: To be eligible for the SB Program, Veterans must be eligible for a monetary award under the Veterans Benefts Adminis- tration (VBA). The Denver VA Regional Offce makes the determina- tion regarding this entitlement. The VBA notifes Purchased Care at the VA Health Administration Center after an award is made and the eligible child is enrolled in SB.

Children of Women Vietnam Veterans (CWVV) Born with Certain Birth Defects: The CWVV Health Care Program is a federal health benefts program administered by the Department of Veterans Af- fairs for children of women Vietnam Veterans born with certain birth defects. The CWVV Program provides reimbursement for medical care related to covered birth defects and conditions associated with the covered birth defect except for spina bifda. For more information about benefts for children with birth defects, call 1-888-820-1756 or visit www.va.gov/hac/forbenefciaries and select Spina Bifda/Children of Women Vietnam Veterans (CWVV.)

Eligibility: To be eligible for the CWVV Program, Veterans must have received an award under VBA. The Denver VA Regional Offce makes determination regarding this entitlement. The VBA notifes Purchased Care at the VA Health Administration Center after an award is made and the eligible child is enrolled in CWVV.

Bereavement Counseling: VA Vet Centers provide bereavement counseling to all family members including spouses, children, parents, and siblings of Servicemembers who die while on active duty. This includes federally activated members of the National Guard and reserve components. Bereavement services may be accessed by calling (202) 461-6530.

Bereavement Counseling related to Veterans: Bereavement counseling is available through any VA medical center to immediate family members of Veterans who die unexpectedly or while participating in a VA hospice or similar program, as long as the immediate family members had been receiving family support services in connection with or in furtherance of the Veteran's treatment. (In other cases, bereavement counseling is available to the Veteran's legal guardian or the individual with whom the Veteran had certifed an intention to live, as long as the guardian or individual had been receiving covered family support services.) This bereavement counseling is of limited duration and may only be authorized up to 60 days. However, VA medical center directors have authority to approve a longer period of time when medically indicated. Contact the Social Work Service at the nearest VA medical center to access bereavement counseling.

Chapter 13
Dependents and Survivors Benefts

Death Gratuity Payment
Military services provide payment, called a death gratuity, in the amount of $100,000 to the next of kin of Servicemembers who die while on active duty (including those who die within 120 days of separation) as a result of service-connected injury or illness.

If there is no surviving spouse or child, then parents or siblings designated as next of kin by the Servicemember may be provided the payment. The payment is made by the last military command of the deceased. If the benefciary is not paid automatically, application may be made to the military service concerned.

Dependency and Indemnity Compensation
Eligibility: For a survivor to be eligible for Dependency and Indemnity Compensation (DIC), one of the following must have directly caused or contributed to the Veteran's death:
1. A disease or injury incurred or aggravated in the line of duty while on active duty or active duty for training.
2. An injury, heart attack, cardiac arrest, or stroke incurred or aggravated in the line of duty while on inactive duty for training.
3. A service-connected disability or a condition directly related to a service-connected disability.

DIC also may be paid to certain survivors of Veterans who were totally disabled from service-connected conditions at the time of death, even though their service-connected disabilities did not cause their deaths. The survivor qualifes if the Veteran was:
1. Continuously rated totally disabled for a period of 10 years immediately preceding death; or
2. Continuously rated totally disabled from the date of military discharge and for at least 5 years immediately preceding death; or
3. A former POW who was continuously rated totally disabled for a period of at least on a year immediately preceding death.

Payments will be offset by any amount received from judicial pro-

141

ceedings brought on by the Veteran's death. When the surviving spouse is eligible for payments under the military's Survivor Beneft Plan (SBP), only the amount of SBP greater than DIC is payable. If DIC is greater than SBP, only DIC is payable. The Veteran's discharge must have been under conditions other than dishonorable.

Payments for Deaths After Jan. 1, 1993: Surviving spouses of Veterans who died on or after Jan. 1, 1993, receive a basic rate, plus additional payments for dependent children, for the aid and attendance of another person if they are patients in a nursing home or require the regular assistance of another person, or if they are permanently housebound.

Aid and Attendance and Housebound Benefts

Surviving Surviving spouses who are eligible for DIC or survivors pension may also be eligible for Aid and Attendance or Housebound benefts. They may apply for these benefts by writing to their VA regional offce. They should include copies of any evidence, preferably a report from an attending physician or a nursing home, validating the need for aid and attendance or housebound care. The report should contain suffcient detail to determine whether there is disease or injury producing physical or mental impairment, loss of coordination, or conditions affecting the ability to dress and undress, to feed oneself, to attend to sanitary needs, and to keep oneself ordinarily clean and presentable. In addition, it is necessary to determine whether the surviving spouse is confned to the home or immediate premises.

2013 DIC Payment Rates for Surviving Spouses

DIC rates (Veteran died on or after Jan. 1, 1993.)

Allowances	Monthly Rate
Basic Payment Rate	$1,215
Additional Allowances:	
Each Dependent Child	$301
Aid and Attendance	$301
Housebound	$141

Special Allowances: Add $258 if the Veteran was totally disabled eight continuous years prior to death.

Add $263 to the additional allowance if there are dependent children under age 18 for the initial two years of entitlement for DIC awards commencing on or after Jan. 1, 2005.

Payments for Deaths Prior to Jan. 1, 1993: Surviving spouses of Veterans who died prior to Jan. 1, 1993, receive an amount based on the deceased's military pay grade.

DIC Rates (Veteran who died prior to Jan. 1, 1993)

Enlisted	Rate	Warrant Offcer	Rate	Offcer	Rate
E-1	$1,215	W-1	$1,283	O-1	$1,283
E-2	$1,215	W-2	$1,334	O-2	$1,327
E-3	$1,215	W-3	$1,373	O-3	$1,418
E-4	$1,215	W-4	$1,453	O-4	$1,503
E-5	$1,215			O-5	$1,654
E-6	$1,215			O-6	$1,865
E-7	$1,257			O-7	$2,013
E-8	$1,327			O-8	$2,211
E-9	$1,384			O-9	$2,365
				O-10	$2,594

Parents' DIC: VA provides an income-based monthly beneft to the surviving parent(s) of a Servicemember or Veteran whose death was service-related. When countable income exceeds the limit set by law, no benefts are payable. The spouse's income must also be included if living with a spouse.

A spouse may be the other parent of the deceased Veteran, or a spouse from remarriage. Unreimbursed medical expenses may be used to reduce countable income. Beneft rates and income limits change annually.

Restored Entitlement Program for Survivors: Survivors of Veterans who died of service-connected causes incurred or aggravated prior to Aug. 13, 1981, may be eligible for a special beneft payable in addition to any other benefts to which the family may be entitled. The amount of the beneft is based on information provided by the Social Security Administration.

Survivors Pension

VA provides pension benefts to qualifying surviving spouses and unmarried children of deceased Veterans with wartime service.

Eligibility: To be eligible, spouses must not have remarried and children must be under age 18, or under age 23 if attending a VA-approved school, or have become permanently incapable of self-support because of disability before age 18. Surviving spouses and children must have qualifying income.

The Veteran must have been discharged under conditions other than dishonorable and must have had 90 days or more of active military service, at least one day of which was during a period of war, or a service-connected disability justifying discharge. Longer periods of service may be required for Veterans who entered active duty on or after Sept. 8, 1980, or Oct. 16, 1981, if an offcer. If the Veteran died in service but not in the line of duty, survivors pension may be payable if the Veteran completed at least two years of honorable service.

Children who become incapable of self-support because of a disability before age 18 may be eligible for survivors pension as long as the condition exists, unless the child marries or the child's income exceeds the applicable limit.

Payment: Survivors pension provides a monthly payment to bring an eligible person's income to a level established by law. The payment is reduced by the annual income from other sources such as Social Security. The payment may be increased if the recipient has unreimbursed medical expenses that can be deducted from countable income.

Aid and Attendance and Housebound Benefts

Surviving spouses who are eligible for VA survivors pension are eligible for a higher maximum pension rate if they qualify for aid and attendance or housebound benefts. An eligible individual may qualify if he or she requires the regular aid of another person in order to perform personal functions required for everyday living, or is bedridden, a patient in a nursing home due to mental or physical incapacity, blind, or permanently and substantially confned to his/her immediate premises because of a disability.

Surviving spouses who are ineligible for basic survivors pension

115 *Dependents and Survivors Benefts*

based on annual income may still be eligible for survivors pension if they are eligible for aid and attendance or housebound benefts because a higher income limit applies. In addition, unreimbursed medical expenses for nursing-home or home-health care may be used to reduce countable annual income, which may result in a higher pension beneft.

To apply for aid and attendance or housebound benefts, write to a VA regional offce. Please include copies of any evidence, preferably a report from an attending physician or a nursing home, validating the need for aid and attendance or housebound type care. The report should contain suffcient detail to determine whether there is disease or injury producing physical or mental impairment, loss of coordination, or conditions affecting the ability to dress and undress, to feed oneself, to attend to sanitary needs, and to keep oneself ordinarily clean and presentable. In addition, it is necessary to determine whether the claimant is confned to the home or immediate premises.

2013 Survivors Pension Rates

Recipient of Pension	Maximum Annual Rate
Surviving spouse	$8,359
(With dependent child)	$10,942
Permanently housebound	$10,217
(With dependent child)	$12,796
Needs regular aid & attendance	$13,362
(With dependent child)	$15,940
Each additional dependent child	$2,129
Pension for each surviving child	$2,129

Survivors' & Dependents' Educational Assistance

Eligibility: VA provides educational assistance to qualifying dependents as follows:

1. The spouse or child of a Servicemember or Veteran who either died of a service-connected disability, or who has permanent and total service-connected disability, or who died while such a disability existed.
2. The spouse or child of a Servicemember listed for more than 90 days as currently Missing in Action (MIA), captured in the line of duty by a hostile force, or detained or interned by a

foreign government or power.
3. The spouse or child of a Servicemember who is hospitalized or receives outpatient care or treatment for a disability that is determined to be totally and permanently disabling, incurred or aggravated due to active duty, and for which the service member is likely to be discharged from military service.

Surviving spouses lose eligibility if they remarry before age 57 or are living with another person who has been recognized publicly as their spouse. They can regain eligibility if their remarriage ends by death or divorce or if they cease living with the person. Dependent children do not lose eligibility if the surviving spouse remarries. Visit www.gibill.va.gov/ for more information.

Period of Eligibility: The period of eligibility for Veterans' spouses expires 10 years from either the date they become eligible or the date of the Veteran's death. Children generally must be between the ages of 18 and 26 to receive educational benefits. VA may grant extensions to both spouses and children.

The period of eligibility for spouses of Servicemembers who died on active duty expires 20 years from the date of death. This is a change in law that became effective Dec. 10, 2004. Spouses of Servicemembers who died on active duty whose 10-year eligibility period expired before Dec. 10, 2004, now have 20 years from the date of death to use educational benefits. Effective Oct. 10, 2008, Public Law 110-389 provides a 20-year period of eligibility for spouses of Veterans with a permanent and total service-connected disability rating effective within 3 years of release from active duty.

Payments: The payment rate effective Oct. 1, 2012, is $987 a month for full-time school attendance, with lesser amounts for part-time. Benefts are paid for full-time training up to 45 months or the equivalent in part-time training.

Training Available: Benefits may be awarded for pursuit of associate, bachelor, or graduate degrees at colleges and universities; independent study; cooperative training study abroad certifcate or diploma from business, technical or vocational schools, apprenticeships, on-the-job training programs; farm cooperative courses; and preparatory courses for tests required or used for admission to an institution of higher learning or graduate school. Benefts for correspondence courses under certain conditions are available to spouses only. Benefciaries without high-school degrees can pursue secondary schooling, and those with a defciency in a subject may receive tutorial assistance if enrolled half-time or more.

Special Benefts: Dependents over age 14 with physical or mental disabilities that impair their ability to pursue an education may receive specialized vocational or restorative training, including speech and voice correction, language retraining, lip reading, auditory training, Braille reading and writing, and similar programs. Certain disabled or surviving spouses are also eligible.

Marine Gunnery Sergeant John David Fry Scholarship
Children of those who died in the line of duty on or after Sept. 11, 2001, are potentially eligible to use Post-9/11 GI Bill benefits. Refer to Chapter 4, "Education and Training", for more details.

Work-Study: See page 55

Counseling: VA may provide counseling to help participants pursue an educational or vocational objective.

Montgomery GI Bill (MGIB) Death Beneft: VA will pay a special MGIB death benefit to a designated survivor in the event of the service-connected death of a Servicemember while on active duty or within one year after discharge or release. The deceased must either have been entitled to educational assistance under the MGIB program or a participant in the program who would have been so entitled but for the high school diploma or length-of-service requirement. The amount paid will be equal to the participant's actual military pay reduction, less any education benefts paid.

Children of Veterans Born with Certain Birth Defects Children of Vietnam or Korean Veterans Born with Spina Bifda: Biological children of male and female Veterans who served in Vietnam at any time during the period beginning Jan. 9, 1962 and ending May 7, 1975, or who served in or near the Korean demilitarized zone (DMZ) during the period beginning Sept. 1, 1967 and ending Aug. 31, 1971, born with spina bifda may be eligible for a monthly monetary allowance, and vocational training if reasonably feasible.
The law defnes "child" as the natural child of a Vietnam Veteran, regardless of age or marital status. The child must have been con-

ceived after the date on which the Veteran frst entered the Republic of Vietnam. For more information about benefts for children with birth defects, visit www.va.gov/hac/forbenefciaries/spina/spina.asp.

A monetary allowance is paid at one of three disability levels based on the neurological manifestations that defne the severity of disability: impairment of the functioning of extremities, impairment of bowel or bladder function, and impairment of intellectual functioning.

2012 VA Benefits for Children of Vietnam or Korean Veterans Born with Spina Bifda

	Level I	Level II	Level III
Monthly Rate	$303	$1,038	$1,769

Children of Women Vietnam Veterans Born with Certain Birth Defects: Biological children of women Veterans who served in Vietnam at any time during the period beginning on Feb. 28, 1961 and ending on May 7, 1975, may be eligible for certain benefts because of birth defects associated with the mother's service in Vietnam that resulted in a permanent physical or mental disability.

The covered birth defects do not include conditions due to family disorders, birth-related injuries, or fetal or neonatal infrmities with well-established causes. A monetary allowance is paid at one of four disability levels based on the child's degree of permanent disability.

2013 VA Benefits for Children of Women Vietnam Veterans Born with Certain Birth Defects

	Level I	Level II	Level III	Level IV
Monthly Rate	$139	$303	$1,038	$1,769

Vocational Training: VA provides vocational training, rehabilitation services, and employment assistance to help these children prepare for and attain suitable employment. To qualify, an applicant must be a child receiving a VA monthly allowance for spina bifda or another covered birth defect and for whom VA has determined that achievement of a vocational goal is reasonably feasible. A child may not begin vocational training before his/her 18th birthday or the date he/she completes secondary schooling, whichever comes frst. Depending on need and eligibility, a child may be provided up to 24 months of full-time training with the possibility of an extension of up to 24 months if it is needed to achieve the identifed employment goal.

Other Benefts for Survivors

VA Home Loan Guaranty
A VA loan guaranty to acquire a home may be available to an unmarried spouse of a Veteran or Servicemember who died as a result of service-connected disabilities, a surviving spouse who remarries after age 57, or to a spouse of a Servicemember offcially listed as MIA or who is currently a POW for more than 90 days. Spouses of those listed MIA/POW are limited to one loan. Surviving spouses of certain totally disabled Veterans whose disability may not have been the cause of death, may also be eligible for the VA loan guaranty.

"No-Fee" Passports
"No-fee" passports are available to immediate family members (spouse, children, parents, brothers and sisters) for the expressed purpose of visiting their loved one's grave or memorialization site at an American military cemetery on foreign soil. For additional information, write to the American Battle Monuments Commission, Courthouse Plaza II, Suite 500, 2300 Clarendon Blvd., Arlington, VA 22201, or telephone 703-696-6897, or visit www.abmc.gov

Burial and Memorial Benefts for Survivors
The Department of Veterans Affairs offers several burial and memorial benefts for eligible survivors and dependents. These benefts may include internment at a state or national Veterans cemetery, plot, marker and more. To learn more about these and other benefts please refer to Chapter 7 of this guide.

Chapter 14
Appeals of VA Claims Decisions

Veterans and other claimants for VA benefts have the right to appeal decisions made by a VA regional offce, medical center or National Cemetery Administration (NCA) offce. Typical issues appealed are disability compensation, pension, education benefts, recovery of overpayments, reimbursement for unauthorized medical services, and denial of burial and memorial benefts.

A claimant has one year from the date of the notifcation of a VA decision to fle an appeal. The frst step in the appeal process is for a claimant to fle a written notice of disagreement with the VA regional offce, medical center or national cemetery offce that made the decision.

Following receipt of the written notice, VA will furnish the claimant a "Statement of the Case" describing what facts, laws, and regulations were used in deciding the case. To complete the request for appeal, the claimant must fle a "Substantive Appeal" within 60 days of the mailing of the Statement of the Case, or within one year from the date VA mailed its decision, whichever period ends later.

Board of Veterans' Appeals
The Board of Veterans' Appeals ("the Board") makes decisions on appeals on behalf of the Secretary of Veterans Affairs. Although it is not required, a veterans service organization, an agent, or an attorney may represent a claimant. Appellants may present their cases in person to a member of the Board at a hearing in Washington, D.C., at a VA regional offce or by videoconference.

Decisions made by the Board can be found at www.index.va.gov/search/va/bva.html. The pamphlet, "Understanding the Appeal Process," is available on the website or may be requested by writing: Mail Process Section (014), Board of Veterans' Appeals, 810 Vermont Avenue, NW, Washington, DC 20420.

121   Appeals of VA Claims Decisions

U.S. Court of Appeals for Veterans Claims

A fnal Board of Veterans' Appeals decision that does not grant a claimant the benefts desired may be appealed to the U.S. Court of Appeals for Veterans Claims. The court is an independentbody, not part of the Department of Veterans Affairs.

Notice of an appeal must be received by the court with a postmark that is within 120 days after the Board of Veterans' Appeals mailed its decision. The court reviews the record considered by the Board of Veterans' Appeals. It does not hold trials or receive new evidence.

Appellants may represent themselves before the court or have lawyers or approved agents as representatives. Oral argument is held only at the direction of the court. Either party may appeal a decision of the court to the U.S. Court of Appeals for the Federal Circuit and may seek review in the Supreme Court of the United States.

Published decisions, case status information, rules and procedures, and other special announcements can be found at http:// www.uscourts.cavc.gov/. The court's decisions can also be found in West's Veterans Appeals Reporter, and on the Westlaw and LEXIS online services. For questions, write the Clerk of the Court, 625 Indiana Ave. NW, Suite 900, Washington, DC 20004, or call (202) 501-5970.

Chapter 15
Military Medals and Records

Replacing Military Medals

Medals awarded while in active service are issued by the individual military services if requested by Veterans or their next of kin. Requests for replacement medals, decorations, and awards should be directed to the branch of the military in which the Veteran served. However, for Air Force (including Army Air Corps) and Army Veterans, the National Personnel Records Center (NPRC) verifes awards and forwards requests and verifcation to appropriate services.

Requests for replacement medals should be submitted on Standard Form 180, "Request Pertaining To Military Records," which may be obtained at VA offces or the Internet at www.va.gov/vaforms/. Forms, addresses, and other information on requesting medals can be found on the Military Personnel Records section of NPRC's Website at www.archives.gov/st-louis/military-personnel/index.html. For questions, call Military Personnel Records at (314) 801-0800 or e-mail questions to: MPR.center@nara.gov.

When requesting medals, type or clearly print the Veteran's full name, include the Veteran's branch of service, service number or Social Security number and provide the Veteran's exact or approximate dates of military service. The request must contain the signature of the Veteran or next of kin if the Veteran is deceased. If available, include a copy of the discharge or separation document, WDAGO Form 53-55 or DD Form 214.

If discharge or separation documents are lost, Veterans or the next of kin of deceased Veterans may obtain duplicate copies through the eBenefts portal (www.ebenefts.va.gov) or by completing forms found on the Internet at www.archives.gov/research/index.html and mailing or faxing them to the NPRC.

Alternatively, write the National Personnel Records Center, Military

Personnel Records, One Archives Drive, St. Louis, MO 63138-1002. Specify that a duplicate separation document is needed. The Veteran's full name should be printed or typed so that it can be read clearly, but the request must also contain the signature of the Veteran or the signature of the next of kin, if the Veteran is deceased. Include the Veteran's branch of service, service number or Social Security number and exact or approximate dates and years of service. Use Standard Form 180, "Request Pertaining To Military Records."

It is not necessary to request a duplicate copy of a Veteran's discharge or separation papers solely for the purpose of fling a claim for VA benefts. If complete information about the Veteran's service is furnished on the application, VA will obtain verifcation of service.

Correcting Military Records

The Secretary of a military department, acting through a Board for Correction of Military Records, has authority to change any military record when necessary to correct an error or remove an injustice. A correction board may consider applications for correction of a military record, including a review of a discharge issued by court-martial.

The Veteran, survivor, or legal representative must fle a request for correction within three years of discovering an alleged error or injustice. The board may excuse failure to fle within this time, however, if it fnds it would be in the interest of justice. It is an applicant's responsibility to show why the fling of the application was delayed and why it would be in the interest of justice for the board to consider it despite the delay.

To justify a correction, it is necessary to show to the satisfaction of the board that the alleged entry or omission in the records was in error or unjust. Applications should include all available evidence, such as signed statements of witnesses or a brief of arguments supporting the correction. Application is made with DD Form 149, available at VA offces, Veterans organizations or visit www.dtic.mil/whs/directives/infomgt/forms/formsprogram.htm.

Review of Discharge from Military Service

Each of the military services maintains a discharge review board with authority to change, correct or modify discharges or dismissals not issued by a sentence of a general court-martial. The board has no authority to address medical discharges.

The Veteran or, if the Veteran is deceased or incompetent, the surviving spouse, next of kin or legal representative, may apply for a review of discharge by writing to the military department concerned, using DD Form 293 – "Application for the Review of Discharge from the Armed Forces of the United States." This form may be obtained at a VA regional offce, from Veterans organizations or online at www. dtic.mil/whs/directives/infomgt/forms/formsprogram.htm.

However, if the discharge was more than 15 years ago, a Veteran must petition the appropriate Service's Board for Correction of Military Records using DD Form 149 – "Application for Correction of Military Records Under the Provisions of Title 10, U.S. Code, Section 1552." A discharge review is conducted by a review of an applicant's record and, if requested, by a hearing before the board.

Discharges awarded as a result of a continuous period of unauthorized absence in excess of 180 days make persons ineligible for VA benefts regardless of action taken by discharge review boards, unless VA determines there were compelling circumstances for the absence. Boards for the Correction of Military Records also may consider such cases.

Veterans with disabilities incurred or aggravated during active duty may qualify for medical or related benefts regardless of separation and characterization of service. Veterans separated administratively under other than honorable conditions may request that their discharge be reviewed for possible recharacterization, provided they fle their appeal within 15 years of the date of separation.

Questions regarding the review of a discharge should be addressed to the appropriate discharge review board at the address listed on DD Form 293.

Physical Disability Board of Review

Veterans separated due to disability from Sept. 11, 2001, through Dec. 31, 2009, with a combined rating of 20 percent or less, as determined by the respective branch of service Physical Evaluation Board (PEB), and not found eligible for retirement, may be eligible for a review by the Physical Disability Board of Review (PDBR).

154

The PDBR was established to reassess the accuracy and fairness of certain PEB decisions, and where appropriate, recommend the correction of discrepancies and errors. A PDBR review will not lower the disability rating previously assigned by the PEB, and any correction may be made retroactively to the day of the original disability separation. As a result of the request for review by the PDBR, no further relief from the Board of Corrections of Military Records may be sought, and the recommendations by the PDBR, once accepted by the respective branch of service, is fnal. A comparison of these two boards, along with other PDBR information, can be viewed at www.health.mil/pdbr.

The Veteran or, if the Veteran is deceased or incompetent, the spouse or surviving spouse, next of kin or legal representative, may apply for a review using DD Form 294, "Application for a Review by the Physical Disability Board of Review (PDBR) of the Rating Awarded Accompanying a Medical Separation from the Armed Forces of the United States." As part of the review process, the PDBR considers the rating(s) previously awarded by VA. The completion of VA Form 3288, "Request for and Consent to Release of Information from Individual's Records," along with DD Form 294, allows the PDBR to request VA records. Both forms can be downloaded from the PDBR website at www.health.mil/pdbr. These forms may also be obtained at a VA Regional Offce (VARO), from a veterans service organization (VSO) or online at www.dtic.mil/whs/directives/infomgt/forms/formsprogram.htm.

Chapter 16
Benefts Provided by Other Federal Agencies

Internal Revenue Service

This year many workers will qualify for the Earned Income Credit (EIC) because their income declined or they became unemployed. Tax refunds through the EIC and Child Tax Credit can help low- and moderate-income families cover day-to-day expenses such as utilities, rent, and child care. To learn more,   visit www.irs.gov or consult a tax preparer.

Special Tax Considerations for Veterans

Disabled veterans may be eligible to claim a federal tax refund based on: an increase in the veteran's percentage of disability from VA or the combat-disabled veteran applying for, and being granted, Combat-Related Special Compensation, after an award for Concurrent Retirement and Disability. To do so, the disabled veteran will need to fle the amended return, Form 1040X, Amended U.S. Individual Income Tax Return, to correct a previously fled Form 1040, 1040A or 1040EZ. An amended return cannot be e-fled. It must be fled as a paper return. Disabled veterans should include all documents from VA and any information received from Defense Finance and Accounting Services explaining proper tax treatment for the current year.

If needed, veterans should seek assistance from a competent tax professional before fling amended returns based on a disability determination. Refund claims based on an incorrect interpretation of the tax law could subject the veteran to interest and/or penalty charges. Complete information and requirements can be found at http://www. irs.gov/Individuals/Military/Special-Tax-Considerations-for-Veterans.

USDA Provides Loans for Farms and Homes

The U.S. Department of Agriculture (USDA) provides loans and guarantees to buy, improve or operate farms. Loans and guarantees are generally available for housing in towns with a population up to 20,000. Applications from Veterans have preference. For further information, contact Farm Service Agency or Rural Development, USDA, 1400 Independence Ave., S.W., Washington, DC 20250, or apply at local Department of Agriculture offces, usually located in county seats.

HUD Veteran Resource Center (HUDVET)

Housing and Urban Development (HUD) sponsors the Veteran Resource Center (HUDVET), which works with national Veterans service organizations to serve as a general information center on all HUD-sponsored housing and community development programs and services. To contact HUDVET, call 1-800-998-9999, TDD 800-483-2209, or visit www.hud.gov/hudvet.

Veterans Receive Naturalization Preference

Honorable active-duty service in the U.S. armed forces during a designated period of hostility allows an individual to naturalize without being required to establish any periods of residence or physical presence in the United States. A Servicemember who was in the United States, certain territories, or aboard an American public vessel at the time of enlistment, re-enlistment, extension of enlistment or induction, may naturalize even if he or she is not a lawful permanent resident.

On July 3, 2002, the president issued Executive Order 13269 establishing a new period of hostility for naturalization purposes beginning Sept. 11, 2001, and continuing until a date designated by a future Executive Order. Qualifying members of the armed forces who have served at any time during a specifed period of hostility may immediately apply for naturalization using the current application, Form N-400, "Application for Naturalization". Additional information about fling and requirement fees and designated periods of hostility are available on the U.S. Citizenship and Immigration Services Website at www.uscis.gov.

Individuals who served honorably in the U.S. armed forces, but were no longer serving on active duty status as of Sept. 11, 2001, may still be naturalized without having to comply with the residence and physical presence requirements for naturalization if they fled Form N-400 while still serving in the U.S. armed forces or within six months of termination of their active duty service.

An individual who fles the application for naturalization after the six-month period following termination of active-duty service is not exempt from the residence and physical presence requirements, but can count any period of active-duty service towards the residence and physical presence requirements. Individuals seeking naturalization under this provision must establish that they are lawful permanent residents (such status not having been lost, rescinded or abandoned) and that they served honorably in the U.S. armed forces for at least one year.

If a Servicemember dies as a result of injury or disease incurred or aggravated by service during a time of combat, the Servicemember's survivor(s) can apply for the deceased Servicemember to receive posthumous citizenship at any time within two years of the Servicemember's death. The issuance of a posthumous certifcate of citizenship does not confer U.S. citizenship on surviving relatives. However, a non-U.S. citizen spouse or qualifying family member may fle for certain immigration benefts and services based upon their relationship to a Servicemember who died during hostilities or a non-citizen Servicemember who died during hostilities and was later granted posthumous citizenship.

For additional information, USCIS has developed a web page,www.uscis.gov/military, that contains information and links to services specifcally for the military and their families. Members of the U.S. military and their families stationed around the world can also call USCIS for help with immigration services and benefts using a dedicated, toll-free help line at 1-877-CIS-4MIL (1-877-247-4645).

Small Business Administration (SBA)

Historically, Veterans do very well as small business entrepreneurs. Veterans interested in entrepreneurship and small business ownership should look to the U.S. Small Business Administration's Offce of Veterans Business Development (OVBD) for assistance. OVBD conducts comprehensive outreach to Veterans, service-disabled Veterans, and Reservists of the U.S. military. OVBD also provides assistance to Veteran- and Reservist-owned small businesses. SBA is the primary federal agency responsible for assisting Veterans who own or are considering starting their own small businesses.

Among the services provided by SBA are business-planning assistance, counseling, and training through community based Veterans Business Outreach Centers. For more information, go to www.sba. gov/aboutsba/sbaprograms/ovbd/OVBD_VBOP.html. More than 1,000 university-based Small Business Development Centers; nearly 400 SCORE chapters (www.score.org/Veteran.html) with 11,000 volunteer counselors, many of whom are Veterans; and 100 Women's Business Centers.

SBA also manages a range of special small business lending programs at thousands of locations, ranging from Micro Loans to the Military-community-targeted Patriot Express Pilot Loan, to venture capital and Surety Bond Guarantees (www.sba.gov/services/fnancialassistance/index.html). Veterans also participate in all SBA federal procurement programs, including a special 3 percent federal procurement goal specifcally for service-connected disabled Veterans, and SBA supports Veterans and others participating in international trade.

A special Military Reservist Economic Injury Disaster Loan (www.sba. gov/reservists) is available for self-employed Reservists whose small businesses may be damaged through the absence of the owner or an essential employee as a result of Title 10 activation to Active Duty.

A Veterans Business Development Offcer is stationed at every SBA District Offce to act as a guide to Veterans, and SBA offers a full range of self-paced small business planning assistance at www.sba. gov/survey/checklist/index.cgi for Veterans, Reservists, discharging Servicemembers, and their families. Information about the full range of services can be found at http://www.sba.gov/about-offces-content/1/2985, or by calling 202-205-6773 or 1-800-U-ASK-SBA (1-800-827-5722).

Social Security Administration

Monthly retirement, disability and survivor benefts under Social Security are payable to Veterans and dependents if the Veteran has earned enough work credits under the program. Upon the Veteran's death, a one-time payment of $255 also may be made to the Veteran's spouse or child. In addition, a Veteran may qualify at age 65 for Medicare's hospital insurance and medical insurance. Medicare protection is available to people who have received Social Security

disability benefts for 24 months, and to insured people and their
dependents who need dialysis or kidney transplants, or who have
amyotrophic lateral sclerosis (more commonly known as Lou Gehrig's disease).

Since 1957, military service earnings for active duty (including active
duty for training) have counted toward Social Security and those
earnings are already on Social Security records. Since 1988, inactive
duty service in the Reserve Component (such as weekend drills) has
also been covered by Social Security. Servicemembers and Veterans
are credited with $300 credit in additional earnings for each calendar
quarter in which they received active duty basic pay after 1956 and
before 1978.

Veterans who served in the military from 1978 through 2001 are
credited with an additional $100 in earnings for each $300 in active
duty basic pay, up to a maximum of $1,200 a year. No additional
Social Security taxes are withheld from pay for these extra credits.
Veterans who enlisted after Sept. 7, 1980, and did not complete at
least 24 months of active duty or their full tour of duty, may not be
able to receive the additional earnings. Check with Social Security
for details. Additional earnings will no longer be credited for military
service periods after 2001.

Also, non-contributory Social Security earnings of $160 a month may
be credited to Veterans who served after Sept. 15, 1940, and before
1957, including attendance at service academies. For information,
call 1-800-772-1213 or visit www.socialsecurity.gov/. (Note: Social
Security cannot add these extra earnings to the record until an application is fled for Social Security benefts).

Armed Forces Retirement Homes

Veterans are eligible to live in the Armed Forces Retirement Homes
located in Gulfport, Miss., or Washington, D.C., if their active duty
military service is at least 50 percent enlisted, warrant offcer or limited duty offcer if they qualify under one of the following categories:

1. Are 60 years of age or older; and were discharged or released
   under honorable conditions after 20 or more years of active
   service.
2. Are determined to be incapable of earning a livelihood

160

because of a service-connected disability incurred in the line of duty.

3. Served in a war theater during a time of war declared by Congress or were eligible for hostile-fre special pay and were discharged or released under honorable conditions; and are determined to be incapable of earning a livelihood because of injuries, disease or disability.

4. Served in a women's component of the armed forces before June 12, 1948; and are determined to be eligible for admission due to compelling personal circumstances.

Eligibility determinations are based on rules prescribed by the Home's Chief Operating Offcer. Veterans are not eligible if they have been convicted of a felony or are not free from alcohol, drug or psychiatric problems. Married couples are welcome, but both must be eligible in their own right. At the time of admission, applicants must be capable of living independently.

The Armed Forces Retirement Home is an independent federal agency. For information, call 1-800-332-3527 or 1-800-422-9988, or visit www.afrh.gov/.

Commissary and Exchange Privileges

Unlimited commissary and exchange store privileges in the United States are available to honorably discharged Veterans with a service-connected disability rated at 100 percent or totally disabling, and to the unremarried surviving spouses and dependents of Servicemembers who die on active duty, military retirees, recipients of the Medal of Honor, and Veterans whose service-connected disability was rated 100 percent or totally disabling at the time of death. Certifcation of total disability is done by VA. National Guard Reservists and their dependents may also be eligible. Privileges overseas are governed by international law and are available only if agreed upon by the foreign government concerned

Though these benefts are provided by DOD, VA does provide assistance in completing DD Form 1172, "Application for Uniformed Services Identifcation and Privilege Card." For detailed information, contact the nearest military installation.

U.S. Department of Health and Human Services

The U.S. Department of Health and Human Services provides funding to states to help low-income households with their heating and home energy costs under the Low Income Home Energy Assistance Program (LIHEAP). LIHEAP can also assist with insulating homes to make them more energy effcient and reduce energy costs. The LIHEAP program in your community determines if your household's income qualifes for the program. To fnd out where to apply call 1-866-674-6327 or e-mail energy@ncat.org 7 a.m.- 5 p.m. (Mountain Time). More information can be found at www.acf.hhs.gov/programs/ocs/liheap/#index.html

VA Facilities

Patients should call the telephone numbers listed to obtain clinic hours of operation and services.

For more information or to search for a facility by zip code, visit www1.va.gov/directory/guide/home.asp?isFlash=1

ALABAMA

Regional Offce:
Montgomery 36109 (345 Perry Hill Rd., statewide 1-800-827-1000)

VA Medical centers:
BBirmingham 35233 (700 S. 19th St., 205-933-8101 or 800-872-0328)
Montgomery 36109-3798 (215 Perry Hill Rd., 334-260-4100 or 800-214-8387)
Tuscaloosa 35404 (3701 Loop Rd., East, 205-554-2000 or 888-269-3045)
Tuskegee 36083-5001 (2400 Hospital Rd., 334-725-3085 or 800-214-8387

Clinics:
Bessemer 32055 (975 9th Ave., SW-Suite 400 at UAB West Medical Center West Bessemer, 205-428-3495)
Childersburg 35044 (151 9Th Ave NW, 256-378-9026)
Dothan 36301 (2020 Alexander Dr., 334-673-4166)
Dothan Mental Health Center 36303 (3753 Ross Clark Cir Ste 4, 334-678-1933)
Ft. Rucker 36362 (301 Andrews Ave., 334-503-7831)
Gadsden 35906 (206 Rescia Ave., 256-413-7154)
Guntersville 35976 (100 Judy Smith Drive, 205-933-8101)
Huntsville 35801 (301 Governor's Dr., 256-535-3100)
Jasper 35501 (1454 Jone Dairy Rd., 205-221-7384)
Madison 35758 (8075 Madison Blvd., Suite 101, 256-772-6220)
Mobile 36604 (1504 Springhill Ave, 251-219-3900/888-201-0110)
Tuscaloosa MOC 35404 (3701 Loop Road East, 205-554-3581)
Oxford 36203 (96 Ali Way Creekside South, 256-832-4141)
Sheffeld 35660 (Florence Shoals Area: 422 DD Cox Blvd., 256-381-9055)

Vet Centers:
Birmingham 35233 (1500 5th Ave. S., 205-731-0550)
Mobile 36607 (3221 Springhill Avenue, Building 2, Suite C, 251-478-5906)
Montgomery 36109 (4405 Atlanta HWY, 334-273-7796)

National Cemeteries:
Alabama 35115 (3133 Hwy. 119, Montevallo, 205-665-9039)

Fort Mitchell 36856 (553 Hwy. 165, Fort Mitchell, 334-855-4731)
Mobile 36604 (1202 Virginia St., 850-453-4846)

ALASKA
VA Medical Center:
Anchorage 99504 (1201 N. Muldoon Rd., 888-353-7574/907-257-4700)

Clinics:
Fort Wainwright 99703 (Bldg 4076, Neeley Rd., Room 1J-101, Mailing Address: P.O. Box 74570, Fairbanks, AK 99707, 907-361-6370 or 888-353-5242)
Kenai 99611 (11312 Kenai Spur Highway, #39, 907-395-4100 or 1-877-797-8924)
Wasilla 99654 (Mat-Su) (865 N. Seward Meridian Parkway, Suite 105, 907-631-3100 or 1-866-323-8648)

Juneau VA Outreach Clinic (Located in the Juneau Federal Building 709 West 9th Street Mailing Address: P.O. Box 20069, Juneau, AK 99802, 907-796-4300 or 1-888-308-7890 (Note: This site is a VA Outreach Clinic, and VAST currently does not track Outreach Clinics).

Regional Offce:
Anchorage 99508-2989 (1201 N. Muldoon Rd., statewide 1-800-827-1000)

Vet Centers:
Anchorage 99508 (4201 Tudor Centre Dr., Suite 115, 907-563-6966)
Fairbanks 99701 (540 4th Ave., Suite 100, 907-456-4238)
Kenai 99669 (Red Diamond Ctr., Bldg. F, Suite 4, 43335 Kalifornsky Beach Rd., 907-260-7640)
Wasilla 99654 (851 E. West Point Dr., Suite 111, 907-376-4318)

National Cemeteries:
Fort Richardson 99505-5498 (Building 997, Davis Hwy., 907-384-7075)
Sitka 99835 (803 Sawmill Creek Rd., 907-384-7075)

AMERICAN SAMOA
Clinics:
Pago Pago 96799 (Fiatele Teo Army Reserve Bldg, Mailing Address: PO Box 1005, Pago Pago, AS 96799, 684-699-3730)

Benefts Offce:
Pago Pago 96799 (PO Box 1005, 684-633-5073)

Vet Centers:
Pago Pago 96799 (Ottoville Rd., PO Box 982942, 648-699-3730)

164

ARIZONA

VA Medical centers:
Prescott 86313 (500 N. Hwy 89, 928-445-4860 or 800-949-1005)

Tucson 85723 (3601 South 6th Avenue, 520-792-1450 or 800-470-8262)

Phoenix 85012 (650 E. Indian School Rd., 602-277-5551 or 800-554-7174)

Clinics:
Anthem 85086 (Anthem Medical Plaza, 3618 W. Anthem Way, Building D, #120, 623-551-6092)

Buckeye 85326 (213 E. Monroe Ave., 623-386-6093)

Casa Grande 85222 (1876 E. Sabin Drive, 520-629-4900 or 800-470-8262)

Chinle 86403 (Hwy 191 and Hospital Drive, (928-674-7675)

Cottonwood 86326 (501 S Willard Street, 928-649-1523 or 1532)

Flagstaff 86001 (1300 West University Avenue #200, Local Phone: 928-226-1056)

Fort Defance 86504 (Community PTSD Outreach Service, Fort Defance Indian Hospital/Board, Inc. 928-729-8048) The 2 PTSD Outreach Services listed in red are not tracked in VAST.

Globe-Miami 85502 (5860 S. Hospital Dr., Suite 111, 602-277-5551)

Green Valley 85614 (380 West Vista Hermosa Drive Suite #140, 520-399-2291 or 800-470-8262)

Holbrook (Primary Care Outpatient Telehealth Clinic) 86025 (33 West Vista Drive, (928-524-1050)

Kingman 86401 (1726 Beverly Ave., 928-692-0080 or 928-445-4860x6830)

Lake Havasu City 86403 (2035 Mesquite, Suite E, 928-680-0090 or 928-445-4860 ext. 7300)

Northwest 85374 (13985 W. Grand Ave., Suite 101, 623-251-2884)

Page 86040 (801 N. Navajo Dr., Ste-B, (928-645-4966)

Payson 85541 (1106 N. Beeline Highway, 928-472-3148)

Safford 85546 (711 South 14th Ave., 928-428-8010)

Second Mesa 86043 (Community PTSD Outreach Service, Hopi Guidance Center, 928-737-2685) (currently VAST does not track Outreach Clinics).

Show Low 85901 (2450 Show Low Lake Rd, Suite 1 & 3, 928-532-1069 ext. 2001 or 2002)

Sierra Vista 85635 (101 North Coronado Dr., Suite A, 520-459-1529 or 800-470-8262)

(Mesa CBOC in VAST) Southeast 85212 (6950 E. Williams Field Rd., Bldg. 23, 602-222-6568)

Thunderbird 85021 (9424 N. 25th Ave, 602-633-6900)

Tucson 85741 (2945 W. Ina Rd., 520-219-2418)

Tucson 85747 (7395 S. Houghton Rd. Ste. 129, 520-664-1836 or 800-470-8262)

Yuma 85365 (3111 S. 4th Avenue, 928-317-9973)

Regional Offce:
Phoenix 85012 (3333 N. Central Ave., statewide 1-800-827-1000)
Benefts Offces:
Tucson 85746 Voc Rehab (1360 W. Irvington Rd., Ste. 150, 602-627-0020)
Flagstaff 86001 Voc Rehab (123 N. San Francisco, Suite 103, 928-226-1845)

Vet Centers:
Chinle 86503 (Navajo [Indn] Rt. 7, Old CBI Bldg., (928) 647-3682)
Hopi 86030 (1 Main St. Hotevilla, 928-734-5166)
Phoenix 85012 (77 E. Weldon Ave., Suite 100, 602-640-2981)
Phoenix-East Valley 85202 (1303 S. Longmore, Suite 5, Mesa, 480-610-6727)
Prescott 86303 (3180 Stillwater Dr., Suite A, 928-778-3469)
Tucson 85719 (3055 N. 1st Ave., 520-882-0333

National Cemeteries:
Nat. Mem. Cem. of Arizona 85024 (23029 N. Cave Creek Rd., Phoenix, 480-513-3600)
Prescott 86301 (500 Hwy. 89 N., 480-513-3600)

ARKANSAS
VA Medical centers:
Fayetteville 72703 (1100 N. College Ave., 479-443-4301 or 800-691-8387)
Little Rock 72205-5484 (4300 West 7th St., 501-257-1000)
North Little Rock 72114-1706 (2200 Fort Roots Dr., 501-257-1000)

Clinics:
Conway 72032 (1520 East Dave Ward Drive, 501-548-0500)
El Dorado 71730 (460 W Oak St, 870-881-4488)
Ft Smith 72917 (1500 Dodson Ave Sparks Medical Plaza, 479-441-2600 or 1-877-604-0798)
Harrison 72601 (707 N Main St., 870-741-3592)
Helena 72342 (812B Newman Drive, 870-338-6200)
Hot Springs 71913 (177 Sawtooth Oak St., 501-520-6250 or 1-855-291-9762)
Jonesboro 72401 (1901 Woodsprings Road, 870- 268-6962)
Little Rock Veterans Day Treatment Center (1000 S. Main St., 501-244-1900)
Mena 71953 (1706 Hwy. 71 N, 479-394-4800)
Mountain Home CBOC 72653 (# 10 Medical Plaza, 870-424-4109) The Veterans are seen at this location.
Mountain Home 72653 (405 Buttercup Dr., 870-425-3030) this is a private clinic where Veterans used to be seen per business offce at the facility.
Ozark 72949 (2713 West Commercial, 479-508-1000 or 877-760-8387)
Paragould 72450 (2420 Linwood Drive Suite #3, 870-236-9756)
Pine Bluff 71603 (4747 Dusty Lake Drive, 870-541-9300)
Russellville 72801(3106 West 2nd Court, 479-880-5100)

Searcy 72143 (1120 South Main, 501-207-4700)
Texarkana 71854 (910 Realtor Rd.,870-216-2242)

Regional Offce:
North Little Rock 72114 (2200 Fort Roots Dr., Bldg. 65, statewide 1-800-827-1000

Vet Center:
Fayetteville 72703 (1416 College Avenue, 479-582-7152)
North Little Rock 72114 (201 W. Broadway, Suite A, 501-324-6395)

National Cemeteries:
Fayetteville 72701 (700 Government Ave., 479-444-5051)
Fort Smith 72901 (522 Garland Ave., 479-783-5345)
Little Rock 72206 (2523 Confederate Blvd., 501-324-6401)

CALIFORNIA

Benefts Offce:
Sacramento 95827 (10365 Old Placerville Rd., 916-364-6500)

VA Medical centers:
Fresno 93703 (2615 E. Clinton Ave., 559-225-6100 or 888-826-2838)
Livermore 94550 (4951 Arroyo Rd., 925-373-4700)
Loma Linda 92357 (11201 Benton St., 909-825-7084 or 800-741-8387)
Long Beach 90822 (5901 E. 7th St., 562-826-8000 or 888-769-8387)
Los Angeles 90073 (11301 Wilshire Blvd., 310-478-3711 or 800-952-4852)
Sacramento 95655 (10535 Hospital Way, Mather, 800-382-8387 or 916-366-5366)
Menlo Park 94025 (795 Willow Rd., 650-614-9997)
Palo Alto 94304-1290 (3801 Miranda Avenue, 650-493-5000 or 800-455-0057)
San Diego 92161 (3350 La Jolla Village Drive, 858-552-8585 or 800-331-8387)
San Francisco 94121-1598 (4150 Clement Street, 415-221-4810 or 800-733-0502)

Clinics:
Anaheim 92801 (Professional Center, 3rd Floor, Suite 303, 1801 W. Romneya Dr., 714-780-5400)
Atwater 95301-5140 (3605 Hospital Road, Suite D, 209-381-0105)
Auburn 95603 (11985 Heritage Oaks Place, 530-889-0872 or 888-227-5404)
Bakersfeld 93301 (1801 Westwind Dr., 661-632-1800)
Blythe 92225 (1273 W. Hobson Way 760-921-1224)

Imperial Valley 92243 (El Centro, 1600 South Imperial Ave., 760-352-1506)
Capitola 95010-3906 (1350 N. 41st St., Suite 102, 831-464-5519)
Chico 95926 (280 Cohasset Rd., 800-382-8387 or 530-879-5000)
Chula Vista 91910 (835 3rd Ave., 877-618-6534)
City of Commerce 90040 (East Los Angeles, 5426 E. Olympic Blvd., 323-725-7557)
Clearlake 95422 (15145 Lakeshore Drive, 707-995-7200)
Corona 92879 (800 Magnolia Ave., #101, 951-817-8820)
Escondido 92025 (815 E. Pennsylvania Ave., 760-466-7020)
Eureka 95501 (714 F St., 707-442-5335)
Fairfeld 94535 (103 Bodin Circle, Travis Air Force Base, 800-382-8387 or 707-437-1800)
Fremont 94538 (39199 Liberty Street, Fremont, 510-791-4000)
French Camp 95231 (Stockton Clinic, 7777 South Freedom Dr., 209-946-3400)
Gardena 90247 (1251 Redondo Beach Blvd, 3rd Floor, 310-851-4705)
Imperial Valley Clinic 92243 (El Centro, 1600 South Imperial Ave., 760-352-1506
Laguna Hills 92653 (25292 McIntyre St., 949-269-0700)
Lancaster 93536 (Antelope Valley, 547 West Lancaster Blvd., 661-729-8655 or 800-515-0031)
Long Beach 90806 (Villages at Cabrillo: 2001 River Ave, Bldg 28, 562-388-8000)
Los Angeles 90012 (351 East Temple St., 213-253-2677)
Los Angeles 90073 (West Los Angeles Ambulatory Care Center, 11301 Wilshire Blvd., 310-268-3526)
Martinez 94553 (Community Living Center - Clinic and Center for Rehabilitation & Extended Care, 150 Muir Rd., 800-382-8387 or 925-372-2000)
Mission Valley 92108 (8810 Rio San Diego Dr., 619-400-5000)
Modesto 95350 (1524 McHenry Ave., 209-557-6200)
Monterey 93955 (3401 Engineer Lane, Seaside, 831-883-3800)
Murrieta 92563 (28078 Baxter Road, Suite 540, 951-290-6500)
North Hills 91343: (Sepulveda Clinic and Nursing Home, 16111 Plummer St., 818-891-7711 or 800-516-4567)
Oakland 94612 (Behavioral Health Clinic, 525 21st St., 800-382-8387 or 510-587-3400)
Oakland 94612 (Clinic, 2221 Martin Luther King Jr. Way, 800-382-8387 or 510-267-7800)
Oceanside 92056 (1300 Rancho del Oro Dr., 760-643-2000)
Oxnard 93036 (2000 Outlet Center Drive., Ste 225, 805-604-6969, 800-310-5001)
Palm Desert 92211 (41-990 Cook St., Bldg. F, Suite 1004, 760-341-5570)
Rancho Cucamonga 91730 (8599 Haven Ave., Suite 102, 909-946-5348)
Redding 96002 (351 Hartnell Ave., 800-382-8387 or 530-226-7555)
Sacramento 95655 (Mental Health Clinic at Mather, 10535 Hospital Way., 800-382-8387 or 916-366-5420)

Sacramento 95652 (McClellan Dental Clinic, 5401 Arnold Ave., 800-382-8387 or 916-561-7800)

Sacramento 95652 (McClellan Outpatient Clinic, 5342 Dudley Blvd., 800-382-8387 or 916-561-7400)

San Bruno 94066 (1001 Sneath Lane, Suite 300, Third Floor, 650-615-6000)

San Francisco 94107 (Downtown Clinic, 401 3rd St., 415-221-5100)

San Gabriel 91776 (Pasadera, 420 W. Las Tunas Drive, 626-289-5973)

San Jose 95119 (80 Great Oaks Boulevard, 408-363-3011)

San Luis Obispo 93401 (Pacifc Medical Plaza, 1288 Morro St., Ste.200, 805-543-1233)

Santa Ana 92704 (1506 Brookhollow Drive, 714-434-4600)Santa Barbara 93110 (4440 Calle Real, 805-683-1491)

Santa Fe Springs 90670 (10210 Orr & Day Rd., 562-864-5565)

Santa Maria 93454 (1550 East Main St., 805-354-6000)

Santa Rosa 95403 (3841 Brickway Blvd., 707-569-2300)

Seaside 93955 (Monterey Clinic, 3401 Engineering Lane, 831-883-3800)

Sonora 95370 (13663 Mono Way 209-588-2600)

Stockton 95231 (500 West Hospital Rd., 209-946-3400)

Susanville 96130 (Diamond View Outpatient Clinic: 110 Bella Way, 775-328-1453)

Tulare 93274 (VA South Valley Clinic, 1050 N. Cherry St., 559-684-8703)

Ukiah 95482 (630 Kings Court 707-468-7700)

Vallejo 94592 (Mare Island Clinic, 201 Walnut Ave., 800-382-8387 or 707-562-8200)

Ventura 93001 (790 E. Santa Clara St. Suite 100, 805-585-1860)

Victorville 92395 (12138 Industrial Boulevard, Suite 120, 760-951-2599)

Yreka 96067 (Rural Outreach Clinic, 101 E. Oberlin Road, 530-226-7500

North Hills 91343 (16111 Plummer Street, 818-891-7711) – formerly known as Sepulveda

San Luis Obispo 93401 (1070 Southwood Drive, 805-210-6634) – moved)

Regional Offce:

Los Angeles 90024 (Fed. Bldg., 11000 Wilshire Blvd., serving counties of Inyo, Kern, Los Angeles, San Bernardino, San Luis Obispo, Santa Barbara and Ventura, statewide 1-800-827-1000)

Oakland 94612 (1301 Clay St., Rm. 1300 North, serving all CA counties not served by the Los Angeles, San Diego, or Reno VA Regional Offces, 1-800-827-1000)

San Diego 92108 (8810 Rio San Diego Dr., serving Imperial, Orange, Riverside and San Diego, statewide 1-800-827-1000). The counties of Alpine, Lassen, Modoc, and Mono are served by the Reno, NV, Regional Offce.

Benefts Offce:

Sacramento 95827 (10365 Old Placerville Rd., 1-800-827-1000)

Camp Pendleton 92055 (Family Services, Bldg 13150, Rm 226, 760-385-

0416, VR&E 619-980-6113)

Camp Pendleton 92055 (Wounded Warrior Transition Ctr, Santa Margarita Rd, 760-870-4428, VR&E 760-909-7291)

Hemet 92543 (VR&E, Work Force Development Center, 1075 N. State Street, 951-791-3503)

Laguna Hills 92653 (Outbased Clinic, 25292 McIntyre St, 949-269-0700, VR&E 562-826-8582)

Riverside 92507 (VR&E Riverside County Government Offces, 1153 Spruce Street, Suite A, 951-955-3032)

San Diego 92134 (Balboa Career Transition Ctr, Naval Medical Ctr, Bldg 26, 619-532-5122, VR&E 619-532-8194)

San Diego 92136 (Naval Station San Diego, Dolphin Alley, Bldg 270, 619-230-0393, VR&E 619-230-0390)

San Diego 92140 (Marine Corps Recruit Depot, 4025 Tripoli Ave, Bldg 14, 619-524-8233)

San Diego 92145 (MCAS Miramar, Bldg 5305, 858-689-2141)

San Diego 92182 (VR&E San Diego State University, Student Services West, 5500 Campanile Dr, 619-594-2444)

Vet Centers:

Anaheim 92805 (859 S. Harbor Blvd., 714-776-0161)

Colton 92324 (1325 E. Cooley Dr., Suite 101, 909-801-5762)

Chico 95926 (280 Cohasset Rd., Suite 100, 530-899-8549)

Chula Vista 91902 (180 Otay Lakes Road, Ste. 108, 858-404-8380)

Citrus Heights 95610 (5650 Sunrise Blvd., Suite 150, 916-535-0420)

Concord 94520 (1333 Willow Pass Rd., Suite 106, 925-680-4526)

Corona 92879 (800 Magnolia Ave., 110, 951-734-0525)

East Los Angeles 90022 (5400 E. Olympic Blvd., 140, 323-728-9966)

Eureka 95503 (930 West Harris St., 707-444-8271)

Fresno 93726 (3636 N. 1st St., Suite 112, 559-487-5660)

Gardena 90247 (1045 W. Redondo Beach Blvd., 150, Gardena, 310-767-1221)

West Los Angeles 90230 (5730 Uplander Way, Suite 100, Culver City, 310-641-0326)

Modesto 95351 (1225 Oakdale Rd., 209-557-6200)

North Orange County 92840 (12453 Lewis Street, 562-596-3101)

Oakland 94612 (1504 Franklin St., Suite 200, 510-763-3904)

Redwood City 94062 (2946 Broadway St., 650-299-0672)

Rohnert Park 94928 (6225 State Farm Dr., Suite 101, 707-586-3295)

Sacramento 95825 (1111 Howe Ave., Suite 390, 916-566-7430)

San Diego 92103 (2790 Tructon Rd. Suite 130, 858-642-1500)

San Francisco 94102 (505 Polk St., 415-441-5051)

San Jose 95112 (278 N. 2nd St., 408-993-0729)

San Luis Obispo 93401 (801 Grande Ave., 805-210-6634)

San Marcos 92069 (1 Civic Center Dr., Suite 140, 760-744-6914)

Santa Cruz 95010 (1350 41st Ave., Suite 102, 831-464-5477)

Sepulveda 91343 (9737 Haskell Ave., 818-892-9227)

South Orange County 92691 (26431 Crown Valley Parkway, 949-348-6700)

Temecula 92591 (40935 County Center Dr. Suite A, 951-302-4849)

Ventura 93001 (790 E. Santa Clara, Suite 100, 805-585-1860)

Victorville 92394 (15095 Amargosa Rd. Suite 107, 760-261-5925)

National Cemeteries:

Bakersfeld 93203 (30338 E. Bear Mountain Blvd., Arvin, 661-867-8850)

Fort Rosecrans 92106 (P.O. Box 6237, Point Loma, San Diego, 619-553-2084)

Golden Gate 94066 (1300 Sneath Ln., San Bruno, 650-589-7737)

Los Angeles 90049 (950 South Sepulveda Blvd., 310-268-4675)

Miramar 92122 (5795 Nobel Dr.., San Diego, 619-553-2084)

Riverside 92518 (22495 Van Buren Blvd., 951-653-8417)

Sacramento Valley VA 95620 (5810 Midway Rd., Dixon, 707-693-2460)

San Francisco 94129 (1 Lincoln Blvd., Presidio of San Francisco, 650-589-7737)

San Joaquin Valley 95322 (32053 West McCabe Rd., Santa Nella, 209-854-1040)

COLORADO

Medical centers:

Denver 80220 (1055 Clermont Street, 303-399-8020 or toll free: 888-336-8262)

Grand Junction 81501 (2121 North Avenue, 970-263-2800 or toll free 866-206-6415)

Health Administration Center:

Denver 80209 (3773 Cherry Creek North Dr., 303-331-7500)

Clinics:

Alamosa 81101 (San Luis Valley Clinic/Sierra Blanca Med. Ctr.: 622 Del Sol Drive, 719-587-6800 or toll free 1-866-659-0930)

Aurora 80045 (13701 East Mississippi Ave , Gateway Medical Bld. 200, 2nd Floor, West Wing, 303-398-6340

Burlington 80807 (1177 Rose Avenue, 719-346-5239)

Colorado Springs 80905 (25 North Spruce St., 719-327-5660 or toll free 800-278-3883)

Craig 81625 (585 Russell St, Suite 400, 970-824-6721 or 970-242-0731)

Durango 81301 (1970 E Third Ave, 970-247-2214)

Fort Collins 80526 (2509 Research Blvd. 970-224-1550 Or 888-481-8828)

Greeley 80631 (2001 70th Ave Suite# 200 970-313-0027 Or 888-481-4065

La Junta 81050 (1100 Carson Ave., Suite 104, 719-383-5195)

Lakewood 80225 (155 Van Gordon St., Suite 395, 303-914-2680)

Lamar 81052 (High Plains Community Health Center 201 Kendall Dr., 719-336-5972)

Montrose 81401 (4 Hillcrest Plaza Way, 970-249-7791 or 970-242-0731)

Pueblo 81008 (4112 Outlook Boulevard, 719-553-1000 or 800-369-6748)
Salida 81201 (920 Rush Drive, 719-539-8666)

Regional Offce:
Denver 80225 (Mailing Address: PO Box 25126. Physical Address: 155 Va n
Gordon St., Lakewood, 80228, statewide 1-800-827-1000)

Vet Centers:
Boulder 80302 (2336 Canyon Blvd., Suite 103, 303-440-7306)
Colorado Springs 80903 (602 S. Nevada Ave., 719-471-9992)
Denver 80230 (7465 E First Ave., Ste. B, 303-326-0645)
Fort Collins 80526 (702 W Drake, Bldg. C, 970-221-5176)
Grand Junction 81505 (2472 F. Rd. Unit 16, 970-245-4156)
Pueblo 81008 (1515 Fortino Blvd., Suite 130, 719-583-4058)

VHA Chief Business Offce:
Health Administration Center: Denver 80209 (3773 Cherry Creek North Dr., 303-331-7500)
Project HERO: Denver 80209 (3773 Cherry Creek North Dr., 303-370-7755)

National Cemeteries:
Fort Logan 80236 (4400 W. Kenyon Ave., Denver, 303-761-0117)
Fort Lyon 81504 (15700 County Road HH, Las Animas, 303-761-0117)

CONNECTICUT
VA Medical centers:
Newington 06111 (555 Willard Ave., 860-666-6951)
West Haven 06516 (950 Campbell Avenue, 203-932-5711)

Clinics:
Danbury 06810 (7 Germantown Rd., Suite 2B, 203-798-8422)
New London 06320 (4 Shaw's Cove , 860-437-3611)
Stamford 06905 (1275 Summer St, Suite 102, 203-325-0649)
Waterbury 06706 (95 Scovill St., 203-465-5292)
Willimantic 06226 (1320 Main Street Tyler Square, 860-450-7583)
Winsted 06908 (Winsted Health Center, 115 Spencer St., 860-738-6985)

Regional Offce:
Hartford (PO Box 310909, Newington, CT 06131),1-800-827-1000)

For UPS shipments :
VA Regional Offce – 308, Building 2E - Room 5137, 555 Willard Ave., Newington, CT 06111

Vet Centers:
Danbury 06831 (457 N Main St., 203-790-4000)
Rocky Hill 06067 (25 Elm St. 860-563-8800)
Norwich 06360 (2 Cliff St., 860-887-1755)
West Haven 06516 (141 Captain Thomas Blvd., 203-932-9899)

DELAWARE

VA Medical Center:
Wilmington 19805 (1601 Kirkwood Highway, 302-994-2511 or
800-461-8262)

Clinics:
Dover 19901 (1198 S. Governors Ave., 302-994-2511 x2400)
Georgetown 19947 (15 Georgetown Plaza, 302-994-2511 x5251

Regional Offce:
Wilmington 19805 (1601 Kirkwood Hwy., local, 1-800-827-1000)

Vet Center:
Wilmington 19805 (2710 Centerville Rd. Suite 103, 302-994-1660)

DISTRICT OF COLUMBIA

VA Medical Center:
Washington 20422 (50 Irving Street, NW, 202-745-8000 or 888-553-0242)

VHA Chief Business Offce:
Disability and Medical Assessment DMA (810 Vermont Ave., NW,
Washington, 202-461-6699)

Clinic:
Washington 20032 (820 Chesapeake Street, S.E., 202-745-8685)

Appeals Management Center:
Washington, D.C., 20421 (1722 I St., N.W., local, 1-800-827-1000)

Regional Offce:
Washington, D.C., 20421 (1722 I St., N.W., local, 1-800-827-1000)

Vet Center:
Washington, D.C. 20011 (1250 Taylor St., N.W., 202-726-5212)

FLORIDA

VA Medical centers:
Bay Pines 33744 (10000 Bay Pines Blvd., P.O. Box 5005, Bay Pines, FL

33744, 727-398-6661/888-820-0230)

Gainesville 32608-1197 (1601 S.W. Archer Rd., 352-376-1611 or 800-324-8387)

Lake City 32025-5808 (619 S. Marion Avenue, 386-755-3016 or 800-308-8387)

Miami 33125 (1201 N.W. 16th St., 305-575-7000 or 888-276-1785)

Orlando 32803 (5201 Raymond St., 407-629-1599 or 800-922-7521)

Tampa 33612 (13000 Bruce B. Downs Blvd., 813-972-2000 or 888-716-7787)

West Palm Beach 33410-6400 (7305 N. Military Trail, 561-422-8262 or 800-972-8262)

Clinics:

Boca Raton 33433 (901 Meadows Rd., 561-416-8995)

Bradenton 34208 (5530 S.R. 64, 941-721-0649)

Brooksville 34613 (14540 Cortez Blvd., Suite 200, 352-597-8287)

Clermont 34711 (805 Oakley Seaver Drive, 352-536-8200)Coral Springs 33065 (9900 West Sample Road, Suite 100, 954-575-4940)

Daytona Beach 32114 (551 National Health Care Dr., 386-323-7500)

Deerfeld Beach 33442 (2100 S.W. 10th St., 954-570-5572)

Delray Beach 33445 (4800 Linton Blvd., Suite 300E, 561-495-1973)

Eglin AFB 32542 (100 Veterans Way, 850-609-2600/866-520-7359)

Fort Myers 33916 (3033 Winkler Extension, 239-939-3939)

Ft. Pierce 34950 (71901 S. 25th Street Suite 101, 772-595-5150)

Hollywood 33021 (3702 Washington St., Suite 201, 954-986-1811)

Hollywood 33024 (Pembroke Pines, 7369 W. Sheridan St., Suite 102, 954-894-1668)

Homestead 33030 (950 Krome Avenue, Suite 401, 305-248-0874)

Jacksonville 32206 (1833 Boulevard, 904-232-2751)

Key Largo 33037 (105662 Overseas Highway, 305-451-0164)

Key West 33040 (1300 Douglas Circle, Building L-15, 305-293-4609)

Kissimmee 34741 (2285 North Central Avenue, 407-518-5004)

Lakeland 33811 (4237 South Pipkin Road , 863-701-2470)Lecanto 34461 (2804 W. Marc Knighton Ct., Suite A, 352-746-8000)

Leesburg 34748 (711 W. Main St., 352-435-4000)

Marianna 32446 (4970 Highway 90, 850-718-5620)

Miami 33135 (Healthcare for Homeless Veterans, 1492 West Flagler St., 305-541-5864)

Miami 33135 (Substance Abuse Clinic, 1492 West Flagler St., Suite 101, 305-541-8435)

Naples 34104 (2685 Horseshoe Drive - Suite 101, 239-659-9188)

New Port Richey 34654 (9912 Little Road, 727-869-4100)

Ocala 34470 (1515 Silver Springs Blvd., 352-369-3320)

Okeechobee 34972 (1201 N. Parrot Avenue, 863-824-3232)

Orange City 32763 (2583 South Volusia Ave., Ste 300, 386-456-2080)

Palm Harbor (35209 US Highway 19 North 727-734-5276)

Panama City Mental Health 32407 (4408 Delwood Ln, 850-636-7000 or 888-231-5047)

Panama City 32407 (Naval Support Activity-Panama City, 101 Vernon Ave Building 387, 850-636-7000 or 888-231-5047)

Pembroke Pines (Pembroke Pines, 7369 W. Sheridan St., Suite 102, 954-894-1668)

Pensacola 32507 (Joint Ambulatory Care Center, 790 Veterans Way, 850-912-2000/866-927-1420)

St. Petersburg (840 Dr. MLK Street North 727-502-1700)

Port Charlotte 33952 (4161 Tamiami Trail, 941-235-2710)

Port St. Lucie County PTSD Clinic 34986 (126 SW Chambers Court 772878-7876 Expanded Clinic 772-344-9288)

Sarasota 34233 (5682 Bee Ridge Rd., Suite 100, 941-371-3349)

Sebring 33870 (3760 U.S. Highway 27 South, 863-471-6227,)

St. Aug. ine 32086 (1955 U.S. 1 South, Suite 200, 904-829-0814 or 866-401-8387)

Stuart 34997 (3501 S E Willoughby Boulevard, 772-288-0304)

Sunrise 33351 (9800 W Commercial St., 954-475-5500)

Tallahassee 32308 (1607 St. James Ct., 850-878-0191)

The Villages 32162 (Laurel Lake Professional Park, 1950 Laurel Manor Drive, Building 240, 352-205-8900)

Vero Beach 32960 (372 17th Street, 772-299-4623)

Viera 32940 (2900 Veterans Way 321-637-3788)

Zephyrhills 33541 (6937 Medical View Ln., 813-780-2550)

Regional Offce:
St. Petersburg 33708 (mailing address: P.O. Box 1437, 33731; physical address: 9500 Bay Pines Blvd., statewide 1-800-827-1000)

Benefts Offces:
Fort Lauderdale 33301 (VR&E-28S, 9800 W. Commercial Blvd., Sunrise, FL 33351 1-800-827-1000)

Jacksonville 32256 (VR&E, 7825 Baymeadows Way, Suite 120-B, 1-800-827-1000)

Orlando 32801 (1000 Legion Pl., VRE-Suite 1500, C&P-Suite 1550, 1-800-827-1000)

Pensacola 32503-7492 (C&P, 312 Kenmore Rd., Rm. 1G250, 1-800-827-1000)

West Palm Beach 33410 (C&P, 7305 North Military Tr., Suite 1A-167, 1-800-827-1000)

Vet Centers:
Bay County 32408 (4408 Delwood Ln., 850-522-6102)

Clearwater 33761 (29259 US Highway 19N. 727-549-3600)

Clermont 34711 (1655 East Highway 50, Suite 502; 352-536-6701)

Daytona Beach 32117 (703 Avenue A, Bldg. 703, 386-366-6600)

Ft. Lauderdale 33304 (713 N.E. 3rd Ave., 954-356-7926)
Fort Myers 33916 (4110 Center Pointe Drive, Unit 204, 239-479-4401)
Gainesville 32607 (105 NW 75th St., Suite 2, 352-331-1408)
Jacksonville 32202 (300 East State St., 904-232-3621)
Jupiter 33458 (6650 W, Indiantown Road, Suite 120, 561-422-1220)
Melbourne 32935 (2098 Sarno Rd., 321-254-3410)
Miami 33122 (8280 NW 27th St., Suite 511, 305-718-3712)
Naples 34104 (2705 S. Horseshoe Dr., Unit 203, 239-313-9577)
Ocala 34471 (612 SW 1st Ave., 352-260-7183)
Odessa 33556 (4111 Land O'Lakes Blvd, 352-536-6701)
Okaloosa 32579 (Shalimar Centre II, 6 11th Ave, Ste G1-3, 850-651-1000)
Orlando 32822 (5575 S. Semoran Blvd., Suite 36, 407-857-2800)
Palm Beach 33461 (4996 10th Ave North Suite 6; 561-422-1201)
Pensacola 32501 (4504 Twin Oaks Dr., 850-456-5886)
Polk County 33542 (4237 S Pipkin Rd., 863-701-2470)
Pompano Beach 33073 (2300 West Sample Road, 954-357-5555)
Sarasota 34231 (4801 Swift Rd., 941-927-8285)
St. Petersburg 33710 (6798 Crosswinds Drive, Building A, 727-549-3633)
Tallahassee 32303 (548 Bradford Rd., 850-942-8810)
Tampa 33614 (4747 W. Waters Avenue, Suite 600, 813-228-2621)

National Cemeteries:
Barrancas 32508-1054 (1 Cemetery Rd., Naval Air Station Pensacola, 850-453-4846)
Bay Pines 33504-0477 (10000 Bay Pines Blvd., Bay Pines, 727-398-9426)
Florida 33513 (6502 SW 102nd Ave., Bushnell, 352-793-7740)
Jacksonville 32218 (4083 Lannie Rd., 904-766-5222)
St. Aug. ine 32084 (104 Marine St., 352-793-7740)
Sarasota 34241 (9810 State Road 72, Sarasota, 941-922-7200)
South Florida 33467 (6501 South State Road 7, Lake Worth, 561-649-6489)

GEORGIA
VA Medical centers:
Aug. a 30904-6285 (1 Freedom Way, 706-733-0188 or 800-836-5561)
Decatur 30033 (1670 Clairmont Road, 404-321-6111 or 800-944-9726)
Dublin 31021 (1826 Veterans Blvd., 478-272-1210 or 800-595-5229)

Clinics:
Albany 31701 (526 West Broad Avenue 229-446-9000)
Athens 30601 (9249 Highway 29, 706-227-4534)
Brunswick 31525 (1111 Glynco Parkway, 912-261-2355)
Columbus 31906 (1310 13th St., 706-257-7200)
Decatur 30030 (755 Commerce Dr., 2nd Floor, 404-417-5200)
East Point 30344 (1513 Cleveland Ave., 404-321-6111 x2600)
Kathleen 31047 (2370 S. Houston Lake Rd., 478-224-1309)

Lawrenceville 30043 (1970 Riverside Pkwy, 404-417-1750)

Macon 31220 (5398 Thomaston Road, Suite B, 478-476-8868)

Milledgeville (A Wing 1st Florr Wheeler Bld., 2249 Carl Vinson Highway 478-414-4540)

Newnan 30265 (39-A Oak Hill, 404-321-6111 x 2222)

Oakwood 30566 (3931 Munday Mill Rd., 404-728-8212)

Perry Outreach 31047 (2370 S. Houston Lake Road, 478-224-1309)

Rome 30161 (30 Chateau Dr, SE, 706-235-6581)

Savannah 31406 (325 West Montgomery Crossroads, 912-920-0214)

,Austell 30106 (2041 Mesa Valley Way, 404-329-2222 or 404-321-6111)

St. Marys 31558 (205 Lake Shore Point, 912-510-3420)

Stockbridge 30281 (175 Medical Blvd., 404-329-2222)

Valdosta 31602 (2841 N. Patterson Street, 229-293-0132)

Regional Offce:
Decatur 30033 (1700 Clairmont Rd., statewide 1-800-827-1000)

Vet Centers:
Atlanta 30324 (1440 Dutch Valley Place, Suite 1100, 404-347-7264)

Aug. a 30904 (2050 Walton Way, 706-729-5762)

Columbus 31901 (1824 Victory Dr., 706-687-4977)

Lawrenceville 30043 (930 River Centre Place, 404-728-4195)

Macon 31201 (750 Riverside Dr., 478-477-3813)

Marietta 30060 (40 Dodd Street, Suite 700, 404-327-4954)

Savannah 31406 (321 Commercial Drive, 912-961-5800)

VHA Chief Business Offce
Health Eligibility Center: Atlanta, 30329-1647 (2957 Clairmont Rd, STE 200, 404-828-5200)

National Cemeteries:
Georgia 30114 (2025 Mt. Carmel Church Lane, Canton, 866-236-8159)

Marietta 30060 (500 Washington Ave., 866-236-8159)

GUAM

Clinic:
Agana Heights 96919 (U.S. Naval Hospital, Bldg-1, E-200, Box 7608, 671-344-9200)

Benefts Offce/Vet Center:
Hagatna 96910 (Refection Center, Suite 201, 222 Chalan Santo Papa St., 671-472-7161)

Vet Center:
Hagatna 96910 (222 Chalan Santo Papa, 671-472-7161)

HAWAII

Medical Center:
Honolulu 96819-1522 (459 Patterson Rd., E Wing) (Hawaii, Guam, Saipan, Rota and Tinian at 800-827-1000; from American Samoa at 877-899-4400)

Clinics:
Hilo 96720 (1285 Wainuenue Ave., Suite 211, 808-935-3781)
Honolulu PTSD 96819 (3375 Koapaka St.,Suite I-560, 808-566-1546)
Kauai; Lihue 96766 (4485 Pahe'e Street, Suite #150, 808-246-0497)Kona; Kailua-Kona 75-377 Hualalai Rd., Kailua-Kona 808-329-0774
Maui; Kahului 96732 (203 Ho'ohana St., Suite 303, 808-871-2454)

Regional Offce:
Honolulu 96819-1522 (459 Patterson Rd., E Wing. Mailing address: PO Box 29020, Honolulu, HI 96820) (toll-free from Hawaii, Guam, Saipan, Rota and Tinian, 1-800-827-1000; toll-free from American Samoa, 684-699-3730)

VR&E Benefts Offces:
Hilo 96720 (1285 Waianuenue, 2nd Floor, 808-935-6691)
Kahului 96732 (203 Ho'ohana St., 808-873-9426)

Vet Centers:
Hilo 96720 (126 Pu'uhonu,Way, Suite 2, Hilo 808-969-3833)
Honolulu 96814 (1680 Kapiolani Blvd., Suite F.3, 808-973-8387)
Kailua-Kona 96740 96740 (Hale Kui Plaza, Suite 207, 73-4976 Kamanu St., 808-329-0574)
Kapolei 96707 (885 Kamokila Blvd., 808-421-8796)
Lihue 96766 (3367 Kuhio Hwy., Suite 101, 808-246-1163)
Wailuku 96793 (35 Lunalilo, Suite 101, 808-242-8557)

National Cemetery:
Nat. Mem. Cem. of the Pacifc 96813-1729 (2177 Puowaina Dr., Honolulu, 808-532-3720)

IDAHO

Medical Center:
Boise 83702 (500 W. Fort St., 208-422-1000)

Clinics:
Caldwell 83605 (4521 Thomas Jefferson Drive, 208-454-4820)
Coeur d'Alene 83815 (2177 Ironwood Center Dr.,. 208-665-1700)
Grangeville 83850 (711 W. North St., 208-983-4671)
Idaho Falls (3544 E. 17th St., Suite 104 208-522-2922)
Lewiston 83501 (1630 23rd Ave., Bldg. 2, Suites 301 & 401, 208-746-7784)

Pocatello 83201 (444 Hospital Way, Suite 801, 208-232-6214)
Salmon 83467 (705 Lena St., #203, 208-756-8515)
Twin Falls 83301 (260 2nd Ave, E., 208-732-0959)

Regional Offce:
Boise 83702 (444 W. Fort St., statewide, 1-800-827-1000)

Vet Centers:
Boise 83705 (2424 Bank Drive, 208-342-3612)
Pocatello 83201 (1800 Garrett Way, 208-232-0316)

ILLINOIS
VA Medical centers:
Chicago 60612 (820 South Damen Ave., 312-569-8387)
Danville 61832-5198 (1900 East Main Street, 217-554-3000 or 800-320-8387)
Hines 60141 (5000 S 5th Ave., 708-202-8387)
Marion 62959 (2401 West Main, 618-997-5311)
North Chicago 60064 (Captain James A. Lovell Federal Health Care Center, 3001 Green Bay Road, 847-688-1900 or 800-393-0865)

Clinics:
Aurora 60542 (161 S. Lincoln Way Suite 120, 630-859-2504)
Belleville 62223 (6500 W Main St., 314-286-6988)
Carbondale (1130 East Walnut St., 618-351-1031)
Chicago 60620 (7731 S Halsted St., 773-962-3700)
Chicago 60611 (211 E. Ontario, 312-569-8387)
Chicago Heights 60411 (30 E. 15th Street, Suite 314, 708-756-5454)
Decatur 62526-9381 (3035 East Mound Road, 217-875-2670)
Effngham 62401 (1901 S 4th St Suite 21, 217-347-7600)
Elgin 60120 (450 Dundee Rd., 847-742-5920)
Evanston 60202 (1942 Dempster St., 847-869-6315)
Freeport 61032 (1301 Kiwanis Dr., 815-235-4881)
Galesburg 61401 (387 East Grove, 309-343-0311)
Harrisburg (608 Rollie Moore Dr., 618-252-6150
Joliet 60435 (1201 Eagle St. 815-740-8100)
LaSalle 61354 (4461 N Progress Blvd. 815-223-9678)
Kankakee County 60914 (581 William Latham Dr. Suite 301, 815-932-3823)
Kenosha (8207 22nd Avenue, Suite 150)
Mattoon (501 Lake Land Blvd. 217-258-3370)
McHenry 60050 (620 South Route 31, 815-759-2306)
Mt. Vernon 62864 (4105 N. Water Tower Place 618-246-2910)
Oak Lawn 60453 (10201 S. Cicero Ave., 708-499-3675)
Oak Park 60302 (149 S. Oak Park Ave., 708-386-3008)
Orland Park 60462 (8651 W. 159th Street, 708-444-0561)

Peoria 61605-2400 (7717 N Orange Prairie Rd. 309-589-6800)
Quincy 62301 (721 Broadway, 217-224-3366)
Rockford 61107 (816 Featherstone Rd., 815-227-0081)
Springfeld 62702 (1227 S.Ninth St., 217-492-4955)

Regional Offce:
Chicago 60612 (2122 W. Taylor St., statewide 1-800-827-1000)

Benefts Offce:
North Chicago 60064 (3001 Green Bay Rd.,

Vet Centers:
Aurora 60504 (750 Shoreline Drive, Suite 150, 630-585-1853)
Chicago 60620 (7731 S. Halsted St., Suite 200, 773-962-3740)
Chicago Heights 60411 (1600 S. Halsted St., 708-754-0340)
East St. Louis 62203 (1265 N. 89th St., Suite 5, 618-397-6602)
Evanston 60202 (565 Howard St., 847-332-1019)
Moline 61265 (1529 46th Ave., 6, 309-762-6955)
Orland Park 60462 (8651 W. 159th Street, Suite 1, 708-444-0561)
Oak Park 60302 (155 S. Oak Park Blvd., 708-383-3225)
Peoria 61603 (8305 N. Allen Rd., 309-689-9708)
Rockford 61107 (7015 Rote Rd., 815-395-1276)
Springfeld 62702 (1227 S.Ninth St., 217-492-4955)
Sterling 61801 (406) Ave. C., 815-632-6200)

National Cemeteries:
Abraham Lincoln 60421 (20953 W. Hoff Rd., Elwood, 815-423-9958)
Alton 62003 (600 Pearl St., 314-845-8320)
Camp Butler 62707 (5063 Camp Butler Rd., Springfeld, 217-492-4070)
Danville 61832 (1900 East Main St., 217-554-4550)
Mound City 62963 (Highways 37 & 51, 314-845-8320)
Quincy 62301 (36th and Maine St., 309-782-2094)
Rock Island 61299-7090 (Rock Island Arsenal, Bldg. 118, 309-782-2094)

INDIANA
VA Medical centers:
Fort Wayne 46805 (2121 Lake Ave., 260-426-5431 or 800-360-8387)
Indianapolis 46202 (1481 W. 10th St., 317-554-0000 or 888-878-6889)
Marion 46953-4589 (1700 East 38th St., 765-674-3321 or 800-360-8387)
Muncie 47303-5263 (2600 W. White River Blvd., 765-284-6822)

Clinics:
Bloomington 47403 (455 South Landmark Avenue, 812-336-5723, or toll
   free 877-683-0865)

Crown Point 46307 (9301 Madison Street 219-662-5000)
Evansville 47715 (6211 E. Waterford Blvd. 812-465-6202)
Goshen 46526 (2014 Lincolnway East Ste. #3, 574-534-6108)
Indy West 46245 (3850 Shore Dr., Suite # 203, 317-988-1102 or 317-988-1139)
Lawrenceburg (600 Flossie Drive, 812-539-2313)
Martinsville CBOC 46151 (2200 John R. Wooden Drive, 317-988-2949)
Muncie 47303-5263 (2600 W. White River Blvd., 765-284-6822)
New Albany 47150 (811 Northgate Blvd, 502-287-4100)
Peru 46970-1027 (750 N. Broadway, 765-472-8900)
Richmond 47374 (4351 South A St., 765-973-6915)
Scottsburg 47170 (1467 N. Scott Valley Drive, 502-287-6900)
South Bend 46614-9668 (5735 S. Ironwood Road, 574-299-4847)
Terre Haute 47802 (110 W Honeycreek Pkwy, 812-232-2890)
Vincennes 47591 (1813 Willow St. Ste. 6A, 812-882-0894)
West Lafayette 47906 (3851 N. River Road, 765-464-2280)

Vet Centers:
Crown Point 46307 (107 E. 93rd, St., 219-736-5633)
Evansville 47711 (311 N. Weinbach Ave., 812-473-5993)
Fort Wayne 46807 (5800 Fairfeld Avenue, Suite 265, 260-460-1456)
Indianapolis 46208 (8330 Naab Rd., Suite 103, 317-998-1600)
South Bend 46614 (4727 Miami Street,St, 574-231-8480)

Regional Offce:
Indianapolis 46204 (575 North Pennsylvania St. statewide 800-827-1000)

National Cemeteries:
Crown Hill 46208 (700 W. 38th St., Indianapolis, 765-674-0284)
Marion 46952 (1700 E. 38th St., 765-674-0284)
New Albany 47150 (1943 Ekin Ave., 502-893-3852)

IOWA
VA Medical centers:
Des Moines 50310-5774 (3600 30th St., 515-699-5999 or 800-294-8387)
Iowa City 52246-2208 (601 Highway 6 West, 319-338-0581 or 800-637-0128)
Knoxville 50138 (1515 W. Pleasant Street, 641-842-3101 or 800-816-8878)

Clinics:
Bettendorf 52722 (2979 Victoria St., 563-332-8528)
Carroll 51401 (311 S. Clark Street, 712-794-6780) Opening Feb. 2011
Cedar Rapids 52404 (2230 Wiley Blvd., SW., 319-369-4340)
Decorah 52101 (915 Short St., 563-387-5840)
Dubuque 52001 (Mercy Health Center, 200 Mercy Drive., 563-588-5520)

Fort Dodge 50501 (2419 2nd Avenue N, 515-576-2235)
Marshalltown 50158 (101 Iowa Avenue West, 877-424-4404, 641-754-6700)
Mason City 50401 (520 S. Pierce, Suite 150, 641-421-8077)
Ottumwa 52501 (1009 East Pennsylvania Ave., 641-683-4300
Shenandoah 51601 (512 S. Fremont St, 712-246-0092)
Sioux City 51104 (1551 Indian Hills Drive, Suite 206, 712-258-4700)
Spirit Lake 51360 (1310 Lake St., 712-336-6400)
Waterloo 50701 (1015 S Hackett Rd., 319-235-1230)

Regional Offce:
Des Moines 50309 (210 Walnut St., Rm. 1063, statewide 1-800-827-1000)

Vet Centers:
Cedar Rapids 52402 (1642 42nd St. N.E., 319-378-0016)
Des Moines 50310 (2600 Martin Luther King Jr. Pkwy., 515-284-4929)
Sioux City 51104 (1551 Indian Hills Dr., Suite 214, 712-255-3808)

National Cemetery:
Keokuk 52632 (1701 J St., 309-782-2094)
National Cemetery:
Keokuk 52632 (1701 J St., 309-782-2094)

National Cemetery:
Keokuk 52632 (1701 J St., 309-782-2094)

KANSAS
VA Medical centers:
Leavenworth 66048-5055 (4101 S. 4th Street Traffcway, 913-682-2000 or 800-952-8387)
Topeka 66622 (2200 SW, Gage Boulevard, 785-350-3111 or 800-574-8387)
Wichita 67218 (5500 E. Kellogg, 316-685-2221 or 888-878-6881)

Clinics:
Chanute 66720 (629 South Plummer, 1-800-574-8387 Ext. 54750)
Emporia 66801 (Newman Hospital, 919 W. 12th Avenue, Suite D, 1-800-574-8387 Ext. 54750)
Ft. Dodge 67801 (300 Custer, 1-888-878-6881 x41040)
Ft. Scott 66701 (902 Horton St., 800-574-8387 Ext 54750)
Garnett 66032 (Anderson County Hospital: 421 South Maple, 800-574-8387 Ext 54750)
Hays 67601 (Hays Clinic: 207-B East Seventh, 1-888-878-6881 x41000)

Hutchinson 67502 (1625 E. 30th Ave., 888-878-6881 x41100)
Junction City 66441 (715 Southwind Dr., 800-574-8387 ext. 54670)
Kansas City 66102 21 N 12th Street, Bethany Medical Building, Suite 110,

1-800-952-8387 ext. 56990)

Lawrence 66049 (2200 Harvard Road, 800-574-8387 ext. 54650)

Liberal 67901 (Liberal Clinic: 2 Rock Island Road, Suite 200, 620-626-5574)

Paola 66071 (510 South Hospital Drive, 816-922-2160)

Manhattan Vet Center, 205 S. 4th St. Suite 1B, Manhattan, KS 66502

Parsons 67357 (1907 Harding Drive, 1-888-878-6881 x41060)

Russell 67665 (Regional Hospital Medical Arts Building: 200 South Main St., 785-483-3131 ext. 155)

Salina 67401 (1410 E. Iron, Suite 1, 1-888-878-6881 x41020)

Seneca 66538 (Nemaha Valley Community Hospital: 1600 Community Dr., 1-800-574-8387 EXT 54650)

Regional Offce:
Wichita 67208 (Wichita Regional Offce, P.O. Box 21318, 1-800-827-1000)

Benefts Offces:
Leavenworth 66048 (150 Muncie Rd.,)

Ft. Riley 66442 (VA Military Services Coordinators Offce)

Vet Center:
Manhattan 66502 (205 S. 4th Street, Suite B, 785-350-4920)

Wichita 67202 (251 N. Water, 316-265-0889)

National Cemeteries:
Fort Leavenworth 66027 (395 Biddle Blvd., 913-758-4105)

Fort Scott 66701 (900 East National Ave., 620-223-2840)

Leavenworth 66048 (150 Muncie Rd., 913-758-4105)

KENTUCKY

VA Medical centers:
Lexington-Cooper Division 40502 (1101 Veterans Dr., 859-233-4511 or 888-824-3577)

Lexington-Leestown Division 40511 (2250 Leestown Rd., 859-233-4511 or 888-824-3577)

Louisville 40206 (800 Zorn Avenue, 502-287-4000 or 800-376-8387)

Clinics:
Bellevue 41073 (103 Landmark Dr. 3rd foor, 859-392-3840)

Berea 40403 (209 Pauline Drive 859-986-1259)

Bowling Green 42103 (Hartland Medical Plaza, 1110 Wilkinson Trace Cir., 270-796-3590)

Carrollton 41008 (309 Eleventh St., 502-732-7146)

Carrollton 41008 (1911 US Highway 227, 502-287-6060)

Clarkson 42726 (619 W. Main St., 866-653-8232)

Florence 41042 (7711 Ewing Boulevard, 859-282-4480)

Ft. Campbell 42223 (Desert Storm Ave. Building 39, 270-798-4118)

Ft. Knox 40121 (Ireland Army Community Hospital 289 Ireland Avenue, 502-624-9396)

Hanson 42413 (926 Veterans Drive, 270-322-8019)

Hazard 41701 (210 Black Gold Blvd., 606-436-2350)

Hopkinsville (1102 South Virginia Drive 270-885-2106)

Louisville 40207 (4010 Dupont Circle,Suite 100 502-287-6986)

Louisville-Newburg 40218 (3430 Newburg Rd., 502-287-6223)

Louisville-Shively 40216 (3934 North Dixie Highway, Suite 210, 502-287-6000)

Louisville-Standiford Field 40213 (1101 Grade Ln., 502-413-4635)

Mayfeld 42066 (1253 Paris Rd Suite A, 270-247-2455)

Morehead (333 Beacon Hill Drive, Suite 100 (606) 784-3004)

Owensboro 42303 (3400 New Hartford Road, 270-684-5034)

Paducah 42001 (2620 Perkins Creek Dr., 270-444-8465)

Prestonsburg 41653 (5230 Kentucky. Route 321, Suite 8 606-886-1970)

Somerset 42503 (163 Tower Circle, MedPark West Medical Campus 606-676-0786)

Regional Offce:
Louisville 40202 (321 W. Main St., Ste., 390, statewide 1-800-827-1000)

Benefts Offce:
Ft. Knox 40121 (Building 1109-B Room 24, P.O. Box 937)

Vet Centers:
Lexington 40507 (301 E. Vine St., Suite C, 859-253-0717)

Louisville 40208 (1347 S. 3rd St., 502-634-1916)

National Cemeteries:
Camp Nelson 40356 (6980 Danville Rd., Nicholasville, 859-885-5727)

Cave Hill 40204 (701 Baxter Ave., Louisville, 502-893-3852)

Danville 40442 (277 N. First St., 859-885-5727)

Lebanon 40033 (20 Highway 208, 270-692-3390)

Lexington 40508 (833 W. Main St., 859-885-5727)

Mill Springs 42544 (9044 West Highway 80, Nancy, 859-885-5727)

Zachary Taylor 40207 (4701 Brownsboro Rd., Louisville, 502-893-3852)

LOUISIANA
VA Medical centers:
New Orleans 70113 (1601 Perdido Street.,800-935-8387)

Alexandria 71360 (2495 Hwy 71 N Shreveport Hwy Pineville, LA , 318-473-0010 or 800-375-8387)

Shreveport 71101-4295 (510 E. Stoner Ave., 318-221-8411 or 800-863-7441)

Clinics:
Baton Rouge 70809 (7968 Essen Park Ave., 225-761-3400)
Bogalusa 70427 (319 Memphis St., 800-935-8387)
Franklin 70538 (603 Haifeigh St., 337-828-9092)
Hammond 70403 (1131 South Morrison Blvd., 985-902-5100)
Houma 70360 (1750 Martin Luther King Jr Blvd Ste 107, 985-851-0188)
Jennings 70546 (1907 Johnson St., 337-824-1000)
Lafayette 70501 (2100 Jefferson St. Bldg B, 337-261-0734)
Monroe 71203 (250 De Siard Plaza Dr., 318-343-6100)
Natchitoches 71457 (740 Keyser Avenue, 318-357-3300)
New Orleans 70112 (1601 Perdido St., 800-935-8387)
Reserve 70084 (247 Veterans Blvd., 985-479-6770)
Slidell 70460 (60491 Doss Dr. Suite B, 985-690-2626)

Regional Offce:
New Orleans 70113 (1250 Poydras St., Suite 200., 1-800-827-1000)

Benefts Offces:
Fort Polk Intake Site 71459 (Bayne-Jones Army Community Hospital, 1585 3rd St. Rm 1221., 800-827-1000)
Shreveport 71101 (510 E. Stoner Ave.,)
Pineville 71360 (2495 Shreveport Highway, 71 North)

Vet Centers:
Alexandria, 70303 (5803 Coliseum Blvd, Suite D, 318-466-4327)
Baton Rouge 70809 (5207 Essen Lane, Suite 2, 225-761-3440)
New Orleans 70062 (2200 Veterans Memorial Blvd., Suite 114, 504-565-4977)
Kenner 70062 (2200 Veterans Blvd., Suite 114, 504-464-4743)
Shreveport 71104 (2800 Youree Dr., Bldg. 1, Suite 1, 318-861-1776)

National Cemeteries:
Alexandria 71360 (209 E. Shamrock St., Pineville, 601-445-4981)
Baton Rouge 70806 (220 N. 19th St., 225-654-3767)
Port Hudson 70791 (20978 Port Hickey Rd., Zachary, 225-654-3767)

MAINE
VA Medical Center:
Aug. a 04330 (1 VA Center, 207-623-8411 or 877-421-8263)

Clinics:
Bangor 04401(35 State Hospital Street., Suite 3B, 207-561-3600)
Calais 04619 (50 Union St., 207-904-3700)
Caribou 04736   (163 Van Buren Drive, Suite 6, 207-493-3800)
Lewiston 04240 (15 Challenger Drive, 207-623-8411 x4601)
Lincoln 04457 (99 River Road, 207-403-2000)
Portland 04101 144 Fore Street, 207-623-8411, X3500)

185

Rumford 04726 (431 Franklin St., 207-369-3200)
Saco 04072 (655 Main St., 207-294-3100)

Part-Time Access Points:
Bingham 04920 (241 Main Street, 866-961-9263)
Fort Kent 04743 (197 East Main Street, 207-834-1572)
Houlton 04730 (20 Hartford Street, 207-403-2000)

Regional Offce:
Togus 04330 (1 VA Center, Aug. a, statewide 1-800-827-1000; VR&E
   Division 207-623-8411 ext 4600)

Vet Centers:
Bangor 04401 (352 Harlow St., 207-947-3391)
Caribou 04619 (456 York St., York Street Complex, 207-496-3900)
Lewiston 04240 (Pkwy Complex, 29 Westminster St., 207-783-0068)
Portland 04103 (475 Stevens Ave., 207-780-3584)
Springvale 04083 (628 Main St., 207-490-1513)

National Cemetery:
Togus 04330 (1 VA Center; 508-563-7113/4)

MARYLAND
VA Medical centers:
Baltimore 21201 (10 North Greene St., 410-605-7000 or 800-463-6295)
Baltimore-Community Living & Rehabilitation Center 21218 (3900 Loch
Raven Boulevard, 410-605-7000 or 800-463-6295)
Perry Point 21902 (361 Boiler House Drive 410-642-2411 or 800 949-
1003)

Clinics:
Baltimore-Loch Raven Community Living & Rehabilitation Center 21218
(Baltimore-Loch Raven 21218 (3901 The Alameda,, 410-605-7650or 800-
463-6295)
Baltimore VA Annex 21201 (209 West Fayette Street, 410-637-1256 or
410-605-7000)
Cambridge 21613 (830 Chesapeake Dr., 410-228-6243 or 877-864-9611)
Charlotte Hall 20622 (State Veterans Home, 29431 Charlotte Hall Rd.,
301-884-7102)
Cumberland 21502 (200 Glenn St., 301-724-0061)
Fort Detrick 21702 (1433 Porter St., 301-624-1200)
Fort Howard 21052 (9600 North Point Rd., 410-477-1800 or 800-351-
8387)
Ft. Meade 20755 (2479 5th Street, 410-305-5300)
Glen Burnie 21061 (808 Landmark Dr., Suite 128, 410-590-4140)
Greenbelt 20770 (7525 Greenway Center Dr., Suite T-4, 301-345-2463)

Hagerstown 21742 (Hub Plaza Bldg, 1101 Opal Ct., 301-665-1462)
Pocomoke 21851 (1701 Pocomoke Marketplace, Unit 211)

Regional Offce:
Baltimore 21201 (31 Hopkins Plaza Federal Bldg., 1-800-827-1000)

Vet Centers:
Annapolis 21401 (100 Annapolis Street, Suite 102, 410-605-7826)
Baltimore 21208 (1777 Reisterstown Road, suite 199, 410-764-9400)
Cambridge 21613 (830 Chesapeake Drive, 410-228-6305)
Clinton 20735 (7905 Malcomb Rd., 301-856-7173)
Dundalk 21222 (1555 Merritt Blvd., 410-282-6144)
Elkton 21921 (103 Chesapeake Blvd., Suite A, 410-392-4485)
Silver Spring 20817 (10411 Motor City Dr., 240-395-1425)

National Cemeteries:
Annapolis 21401 (800 West St., 410-644-9696/7)
Baltimore 21228 (5501 Frederick Ave., 410-644-9696/7)
Loudon Park 21228 (3445 Frederick Ave., Baltimore, 410-644-9696/7)

MASSACHUSETTS
VA Medical centers:
Bedford 01730 (200 Springs Rd., 781-687-2000 or 800-422-1617)
Brockton 02301 (940 Belmont St., 508-583-4500)
Jamaica Plain 02130 (150 South Huntington Ave., 617-232-9500)
Leeds 01053-9764 (Northampton VA, 421 North Main St., 413-584-4040 or
    800-893-1522)
West Roxbury 02132 (1400 VFW Parkway, 617-323-7700)

Clinics:
Boston 02114 (251 Causeway St., 617-248-1000)
Dorchester 02121 (895 Blue Hill Ave, 617-822-7146)
Fitchburg 01420 (Health Alliance Burbank Hospital, 275 Nichols Rd., 800-
    893-1522)
Framingham 01702 (61 Lincoln St., Suite 112, 508-628-0205)
Gloucester 01930 (Addison Gilbert Hospital, 298 Washington St., 978-282-
    0676 ext. 1782)
Greenfeld 01301 (143 Munson St., 800-893-1522)
Haverhill 01830 (108 Merrimack St., 978-372-5207)
Hyannis 02601 (233 Stevens St., 508-771-3190)
Lowell 01852 (130 Marshall Rd., 978-671-9000)
Lynn 01904 (225 Boston Rd., 1st Floor, 781-595-9818)
Martha's Vineyard 02557 (Hospital Rd., 508-693-0410
Nantucket 02554 (Nantucket Cottage Hospital, 57 Prospect St., 508-825-
    8100)
New Bedford 02740 (175 Elm St., 508-994-0217)

Pittsfeld 01201 (73 Eagle St., 800-893-1522)
Plymouth (116 Long Pond Road 800-865-3384)
Quincy 02169 (Quincy Medical Center, 2nd foor, 114 Whitwell St., 617-376-2010)
Springfeld 01104 (25 Bond St., 800-893-1522)
Worcester 01605 (605 Lincoln St., 800-893-1522)

Regional Offce:

Boston 02203-0393 (JFK Federal Building, Room 1625, Government Center,
  statewide 1-800-827-1000) (Towns of Fall River & New Bedford, counties of Barnstable, Dukes, Nantucket, Bristol, part of Plymouth served by
  Providence, R.I., VA Regional Offce)

Vet Centers:

Boston 02215 (665 Beacon St., 617-424-0665)
Brockton 02401 (1041-L Pearl St., 508-580-2730)
Hyannis 02601 (474 West Main St., (508-778-0124)
Lowell 01852 (10 George Street, 978-453-1151)
New Bedford 02719 (73 Huttleston Avenue, 508-999-6920)
Springfeld 01103 (1985 Main St., Northgate Plaza, 413-737-5167)
Worcester 01605 (691 Grafton St., 508-753-7902)
National Cemetery:
Massachusetts NC 02532 (Connery Ave., Bourne, 508-563-7113/4)

National Cemetery:

Massachusetts 02532 (Connery Ave., Bourne, 508-563-7113/4)

MICHIGAN

VA Medical centers:

Ann Arbor 48105 (2215 Fuller Rd., 734-769-7100 or 800-361-8387)
Battle Creek 49037 (5500 Armstrong Rd., 269-966-5600 or 888-214-1247)
Detroit 48201 (4646 John R. St., 313-576-1000 or 800-511-8056)
Iron Mountain 49801 (325 East H St., 906-774-3300 or 800-215-8262)
Saginaw 48602 (1500 Weiss St., 989-497-2500 or 800-406-5143)

Clinics:

Alpena 49707 (180 North State Avenue, 989-356-8720)
Bad Axe 48413 (1142 S. Van Dyke Road, 989-269-7445)
Benton Harbor 49022 (115 Main St., 269-934-9123)
Clare 48617 (11775 N. Isabella Road, 989-386-3113)
Flint 48532 (G-2360 South Linden Rd., 810-720-2913)
Gaylord 49735 (806 S. Otsego, 989-732-7525)
Grand Rapids 49505 (3019 Coit St., NE, 616-365-9575)
Hancock 49930-1495 (787 Market St., Quincy Center Suite 9, 906-482-7762)

Ironwood 49938 (629 W. Cloverland Dr., Suite 1, 906-932-0032))
Jacksonr 49254 (Michigan Center 4328 Page Ave., 517-764-3609
Sault Ste. Marie 49788 (509 Osborn Blvd., 906-253-9383)
Lansing 48910 (2025 S. Washington Ave., 517-267-3925)
Marquette 49855 1414 W. Fair Ave. Suite 285, 906-226-4618)
Manistique 49854 (813 East Lakeshore Drive 906-341-3420)
Menominee 49858 (1110 10th Ave., Suite 101, 906-863-1286)
Muskegon 49442 (165 E. Apple Ave., Suite 201, 231-725-4105)
Oscoda 48750 (5671 Skeel Ave., Suite 4, 989-747-0026)
Pontiac 48341(44200 Woodward Avenue, Suite 208, 248-332-4540)
Saginaw 48603 (VA Healthcare Annex, 4241 Barnard Road, 989-497-2500
or 800-406-5143)
Traverse City 49684 (3271 Racquet Club Dr., 231-932-9720)
Yale 48097 (7470 Brockway Road, 810-387-3211)

Regional Offce:
Detroit 48226 (Patrick V. McNamara Federal Bldg., 477 Michigan Ave.,
Rm. 1280, 1-800-827-1000)

Vet Centers:
Dearborn 48124-3438 (2881 Monroe St., Suite 100, 313-277-1428)
Detroit 48201 (4161 Cass Ave., 313-831-6509)
Escanaba 49829 (3500 Ludington St. Suite 110, 906-233-0244)
Grand Rapids 49546 (2050 Breton Road, SE Grand Rapids, 616-285-
5795)
Pontiac 48341 (44200 Woodward Avenue, 248-874-1015)
Saginaw 48603 (4048 Bay Rd., 989-321-4650)

National Cemetery:
Fort Custer 49012 (15501 Dickman Rd., Aug. a, 269-731-4164)
Great Lakes 48442 (4200 Belford Rd., Holly,248-348-8603)

MINNESOTA
VA Medical centers:
Minneapolis 55417 (One Veterans Dr., 612-725-2000 or 866-414-5058)
St. Cloud 56303 (4801 Veterans Dr., 320-252-1670 or 800-247-1739

Clinics:
Alexandria, 56308 (515 22nd Ave. E., 320-759-2640)
Bemidji 56601 (705 5th St., NW, Suite B 218-755-6360)
Brainerd 56401 (722 NW 7th St., 218-855-1115)
Fergus Falls 56537 (1839 N. Park St., 218-739-1400)
Hibbing 55746 (1101 East 37th St., Suite 220, 218-263-9698)
Maplewood 55109 (2785 White Bear Ave., Suite 210, 651-290-3040)
Montevideo 56265 (1025 North 13th St., 320-269-2222)
Rochester 55901 (3900 55th St., NW, 507-252-0885)

St. James 56081 (1101 Moultin and Parsons Dr., 507-375-9670)

Regional Offce:
St. Paul 55111 (Bishop Henry Whipple Federal Bldg., 1 Federal Dr., Fort Snelling 1-800-827-1000)

(Counties of Becker, Beltrami, Clay, Clearwater, Kittson, Lake of the Woods,

Mahnomen, Marshall, Norman, Otter Tail, Pennington, Polk, Red Lake, Roseau, Wilkin served by Fargo, N.D., VA Regional Offce)

Vet Centers:
Brooklyn Park 55445 (7001 78th Avenue N, Suite 300, 763-503-2220
Duluth 55802 (405 E. Superior St., Suite 160 218-722-8654)
St. Paul 55112 (550 County Road D, Suite 10 New Brighton 651-644-4022

National Cemetery:
Fort Snelling NC 55450-1199 (7601 34th Ave. So., Minneapolis, 612-726-1127)

MISSISSIPPI
Medical centers:
Biloxi 39531 (400 Veterans Ave., 228-523-5000 or 800-296-8872)
Jackson 39216 (1500 E. Woodrow Wilson Dr., 601-362-4471 or 800-949-1009, in-state)

Clinics:
Byhalia 38611 (12 East Brunswick St., 662-838-2163)
Columbus 39702 (824 Alabama St., 662-244-0391)
Greenville 38703 (1502 S Colorado St., 662-332-9872)
Hattiesburg 39401 (231 Methodist Blvd., 601-296-3530)
Houlka 38850 (106 Walker St., 662-568-3316)
Kosciusko 39090 (332 Hwy 12W, 662-289-1800)
Meadville 39653 (595 Main Street East, 601-384-3650)
Meridian 39301 (13th St., 601-482-7154)
Natchez 39120 (105 Northgate Drive, Suite 2, 601-442-7141)
Smithville 38870 (63420 Highway 25 N., 662-651-4637)
Tremont, 38876 (10103 Highway 78 West, 662-652-3361)
Tupelo 38801 (499 Gloster Creek Village, Suite D1, 662-690-8007

Regional Offce:
Jackson 39216 (1600 E. Woodrow Wilson Ave., statewide 1-800-827-1000)

Vet Centers:
Biloxi 39531 (288 Veterans Ave., 228-388-9938)
Jackson 39216 (1755 Lelia Dr., Suite 104, 601-965-5727)

National Cemeteries:
Biloxi 39535-4968 (P.O. Box 4968, 400 Veterans Ave., 228-388-6668)
Corinth 38834 (1551 Horton St., 901-386-8311)
Natchez 39120 (41 Cemetery Rd., 601-445-4981)

MISSOURI
VA Medical centers:
Columbia 65201-5297 (800 Hospital Dr., 573-814-6000)
Kansas City 64128 (4801 Linwood Blvd., 816-861-4700 or 800-525-1483)
Poplar Bluff 63901 (1500 N. Westwood Blvd., 573-686-4151)
Saint Louis-Jefferson Barracks 63125-4101 (1 Jefferson Barracks Dr., 314-652-4100 or 800-228-5459)
Saint Louis-John Cochran Division 63106 (915 North Grand Blvd., 314-652-4100 or 800-228-5459)

Clinics:
Belton 64012 (17140 Bel-Ray Pl., 816-922-2161)
Branson 65616 (5571 Gretna Rd., 417-243-2300 or 866-951-8387)
Camdenton 65020 (940 Executive Drive, 573-302-7890)
Cameron 64429 (1111 Euclid Dr., 816-922-2500 ext. 54251)
Cape Girardeau 63701 (3051 Williams St, 573-339-0909)
Farmington 63640 (1580 W. Columbia St., 573-760-1365)
Kirksville 63501 (1510 North Crown Dr., 660-627-8387)
Jefferson City 65109 (2707 W. Edgewood, 573-635-0233)
McComb 39648 (1308 Harrison Ave., 601-250-0965

Mexico 65265 (Missouri Veterans Home, One Veterans Dr., 573-581-9630)
Mt Vernon 65712 (600 N Main, 417-466-4000 or 800-253-8387)
Nevada 64772 (322 South Prewitt, 417-448-8905)
North St. Louis 63033 (6854 Parker Road, 314-286-6988)
Osage Beach 65065 (Lake of the Ozarks Clinic, 940 Executive Dr., 573-302-7890)
Paola 66071 (501 S. Hospital Dr, 913-294-9628)
Salem 65560 (Hwy 72 North, 573-729-6626 or 1-888-557-8262)
Sedalia 65301 (3320 West 10th St., 660-826-3800)
St. Charles 63368 (844 Waterbury Falls Drive, 314-286-6988)
St. James 65559-1999 (Missouri Veterans Home, 620 N. Jefferson, St., 573-265-0448)
St. Joseph 64506 (3302 S. Belt Highway, Suite O., 800-952-8387 ext. 56925)
St. Louis 63136 (10600 Lewis and Clark Blvd, 314-286-6988)
Warrensburg 64093 (1300 Veterans Dr., (660-747-3864)
Waynesville 65583 (Ft. Leonard Wood 700 GW Lane St., 573-774-2285
West Plains 65775 (1211 Missouri Ave, 417-257-2454)
Regional Offce:
St. Louis 63103 (400 South 18th St., statewide 1-800-827-1000)

191

Benefts Offce:
Kansas City 64128 (VAMC 4801 Linwood Blvd., Bldg 2, 1st Floor, 816-753-1866)

Vet Centers:
Columbia 65202 (4040 N. Rangeline Dr., 573-814-6206)
Kansas City 64111 (4811 Main St., Suite 107, 916-753-1866)
Springfeld 65807 (3616 S. Campbell, 417-881-4197)
St. Louis 63103 (2901 Olive St., 314-531-5355)

National Cemeteries:
Jefferson Barracks 63125 (2900 Sheridan Rd., St. Louis, 314-845-8320)
Jefferson City 65101 (1024 E. McCarty St., 314-845-8320)
Springfeld 65804 (1702 E. Seminole St., 417-881-9499)

MONTANA
VA Medical centers:
Fort Harrison 59636-1500 (3687 Veterans Drive, P.O. Box 1500, 406-442-6410 or 877-468-8387)

Clinics:
Anaconda 59711 (118 East 7th St., 406-496-3000)
Billings 59102 (1775 Spring Creek Ln., 406-373-3500)
Bozeman 59715 (300 N. Wilson, Suite 703G, 406-582-5300)
Cut Bank 59427 (#8 2nd Ave SE, 406-873-9047)
Glasgow 59230 (630 2nd Ave., South, Suite A, 406-228-4101)
Glendive 59330 (2000 Montana Ave., 406-377-4755)
Great Falls 59405 (1417-9th St., South, Suite 200/300, 406-791-3200)
Hamilton 59840 (299 Fairgrounds Suite A, 406-363-3352) Primary Care
   Telehealth Outreach Clinic
Havre 59501, (130 13th Street, Suite 1) (406-265-4304)
Kalispell 59901 (31 Three Mile Dr Ste 102, 406-758-2700)
Lewistown, MT 59457 (629 NE Main St. (Hwy 87) Ste. 1, 406-535-4790)
Miles City 59301 (Clinic / Living Center, 210 S. Winchester, 406-874-5600)
Missoula 59808 (2687 Palmer St., Suite C, 406-493-3700)
Plentywood 59254 (Sheridan Memorial Hospital, 440 West Laurel Avenue,
   406-765-3718) Primary Care Telehealth Outreach Clinic

Regional Offce:
Fort Harrison 59636-0188 (3633 Veterans Dr., PO Box 188, 1-800-827-1000)

Vet Centers:
Billings 59102 (2795 Enterprise Avenue, Suite 1, 406-657-6071)

Great Falls 59401 (615 2nd Avenue North, 406-452-9048)
Kalispell 59901 (690 North Meridian Road, Suite 101, 406-257-7308)
Missoula 59802 (500 N. Higgins Ave., 406-721-4918)

NEBRASKA

VA Medical centers:
Omaha 68105 (4101 Woolworth Ave., 402-346-8800/800-451-5796)

Clinics:
Alliance 69301 (524 Box Butte Ave., 605-745-2000 ext. 2474)
Bellevue 68113 (2501 Capehart Rd, 402-591-4500)
Gordon 69343 (807 N Ash St. 305-282-1442)
Grand Island 68803-2196 (2201, No. Broadwell Ave., 308-382-3660/866-580-1810 - also includes a community living center)
Holdrege 68949 (1118 Burlington St., 308-995-3760; 866-580-1810)
Lincoln 68510 (600 South 70th St., 402-489-3802/866-851-6052)
Norfolk 68701 (710 S. 13th St, Suite 1200 402-370-4570)
North Platte 69101 (600 East Francis, Suite 3, 308-532-6906; 866-580-1810)
O'Neill 68763 (555 E. John St., 402-336-2982
Scottsbluff 69361 (1720 E Portal Place, 308-220-3930)
Sidney 69162 (1116 10th Ave., 308-254-6085)

Regional Offce:
Lincoln 68501 (3800 Village Drive, PO Box 85816 5631 S. 48th St.statewide 1-800-827-1000)

Vet Centers:
Lincoln 68510 (3119 O St., Suite A, 402-476-9736)
Omaha 68131 (2428 Cuming St., 402-346-6735)
National Cemetery:
Fort McPherson NC 69151-1031 (12004 S. Spur 56A, Maxwell, 888-737-2800)

National Cemetery:
Fort McPherson 69151-1031 (12004 S. Spur 56A, Maxwell, 888-737-2800)

NEVADA

VA Medical centers:
Las Vegas 89106 (901 Rancho Lane, Mailing Address: P.O. Box 360001, North Las Vegas, NV 89036, 702-636-3000/888-633-7554)
Reno 89502 (1000 Locust Street, 775-786-7200 or 888-838-6256)

Clinics:
Elko 89801 (Gateway Center, Building 1, 2715 Argent Avenue 1-800-613-

4012 ext. 2575)

Ely 89301 (William B. Ririe Hospital, 6 Steptoe Circle, 775-289-3612)

Fallon 89406 (Lahontan Valley Outpatient Clinic: 345 West A St., 775-428-6161 or 866-504-0490)

Henderson 89014 (2920 N. Greenvalley Pkwy. Suite 215, 702-636-6363)

Las Vegas 89106 (Center for Homeless Veterans, 916 West Owens Ave., 702-636-6380)

Las Vegas 89130 (Northwest Clinic) 3968 North Rancho Dr. 702-791-9020

Las Vegas 89113 (Southwest Clinic) 7235 S. Buffalo Dr. 702-791-9040

Las Vegas 89106 (West Clinic, 630 S. Rancho Rd., 702-636-6355)

Minden 89423 (Carson Valley Clinic, 925 Ironwood Dr., Suite 2102, 888-838-6256 x4000)

Pahrump 89048 (2100 E. Calvada Blvd., 775-727-7535)

Winnemucca 89445 (3298 Traders Way, 877-320-4990 or 775-623-9575)

Regional Offce:
Reno 89511 (5460 Reno Corporate Dr., statewide 1-800-827-1000)

Benefts Offce:
Las Vegas 89107 (4800 Alpine Pl., Suite 12, 1-800-827-1000)

Vet Centers:
Henderson 89014 (400 Stephanie Street, Suite 180, 702-791-9100)

Las Vegas 89146 (1919 So. Jones Blvd., Suite A., 702-251-7873)

Reno 89503 (5580 Mill St. Suite 600, 775-323-1294)

NEW HAMPSHIRE
VA Medical Center:
Manchester 03104 (718 Smyth Road, 603-624-4366 or 800-892-8384)

Clinics:
Conway 03818 (71 Hobbs Street, or 800-892-8384 ext. 3199)

Littleton 03561 (685 Meadow Street Suite 4, 603-444-1323)

Portsmouth 03803 (302 Newmarket St. Building 15, 603-624-4366 ext. 3199)

Somersworth 03878 (200 Route 108 N, 603-624-4366, Ext. 3199)

Tilton 03104 (NH Veterans Home, 630 West Main St., 603-624-4366 ext.3199)

Regional Offce:
Manchester 03101 (Norris Cotton Federal Bldg., 275 Chestnut St., 1-800-827-1000)

Vet Center:
Manchester 03104 (103 Liberty St., 603-668-7060/61)

Berlin 03581 (515 Main Street, 603-752-2571)

NEW JERSEY

VA Medical centers:
East Orange 07018 (385 Tremont Avenue, 973-676-1000)
Lyons 07939 (151 Knollcroft Road, 908-647-0180)

Clinics:
Brick 08724 (970 Rt. 70, 732-206-8900)
Camden 08104 (300 Broadway, Suite 103, 877-232-5240 or 215-823-5240)
Cape May 08204 (1 Monroe Ave., 609-898-8700)
Elizabeth 07206 (654 East Jersey Street, Suite 2A, 908-994-0120)
Ft. Dix 08640 (Marshall Hall, 8th and Alabama, 609-562-2999)
Hackensack 07601 (385 Prospect Avenue, 201-487-1390)
Hamilton 08619 (University Offce Plaza I, 3635 Quakerbridge Road, 609-570-6600)
Jersey City 07302 (115 Christopher Columbus Dr., 201-435-3055/3305)
Morristown 07960 (340 West Hanover Ave., 973-539-9791/9794)
Newark 07102 (20 Washington Place, 973-645-1441)
Paterson 07503 (275 Getty Avenue, Building 275, St. Joseph's Hospital & Medical Center, 973-247-1666)
Piscataway 08854 (14 Wills Way, Building 4, 732-981-8193)
Sewell 08080-2525 (211 County House Road, 215-823-5800)
Tinton Falls 07701 (55 Gilbert St. Bld. 4, Suite 4101, 732-842-4751)
Vineland 08360 (1051 West Sherman Ave. Bldg 3, Unit B, 302-994-2511, extension 6500)

Regional Offce:
Newark 07102 (20 Washington Pl., statewide 1-800-827-1000)
(Philadelphia,
PA Regional Offce serves counties of Atlantic, Burlington, Camden, Cape May,
Cumberland, Gloucester, Salem)

Vet Centers:
Bloomfeld 07003 (2 Broad St., Suite 703, 973-748-0980)
Ewing 08618 (934 Parkway Ave., 2nd Fl., 609-882-5744)
Lakewood 08701 (1255 Rt. 70, Parkway 70 Plaza, 908-607-6364)
Secaucus 07094 (110A Meadowlands Pkwy., Suite 102, 201-223-7787)
Ventnor 08406 (6601 Ventnor Ave., Suite 105, 609-487-8387)

National Cemeteries:
Beverly 08010 (916 Bridgeboro Rd., 215-504-5610)
Finn's Point 08079 (Box 542, R.F.D. 3, Fort Mott Rd., Salem, 215-504-5610)

NEW MEXICO
VA Medical Center:
Albuquerque 87108-5153 (1501 San Pedro Drive, SE, 505-265-1711 or 800-465-8262)

Clinics:
Alamogordo 88310 (3199 N White Sands Blvd, Suite D10 575-437-7000)
Artesia 88210-3712 (1700 W. Main St., 575-746-3531)
Clovis 88101 (921 East Llano Estacado, 575-763-4335)
Durango 81301 (1970 East Third Avenue, Suite 102, (970) 247-2214)
*Espanola 87532 (105 Coronado St., Suite B, 505-367-4213)
Farmington 87401-5638 (1001 W. Broadway, Suite C, 505-326-4383)
Gallup 87301 (320 Hwy 564, 505-722-7234)
Las Cruces 88001 (1635 Don Roser, 505-522-1241)
Hobbs 88240 (1601 N. Turner, 432-263-7361 or 800-472-1365)
*Las Vegas 87701 (624 University Ave., Las Vegas, 505-425-1910)
Raton 87740-2234 (1275 S. 2nd St., 575-445-2391)
Rio Rancho 87214 (1760 Grande Blvd., SE 505-896-7200)
Santa Fe 87505 (2213 Brothers Road, Suite 600, 505-986-8645)
Silver City 88601 (1302 32nd St., 575-538-2921)
Truth or Consequences 87901 (1960 North Date St., 575-894-7662)

Regional Offce:
Albuquerque 87102 (Dennis Chavez Federal Bldg., 500 Gold Ave., S.W., statewide 1-800-827-1000)

Vet Centers:
Albuquerque 87104 (1600 Mountain Rd. N.W., 505-346-6562)
Farmington 87402 (4251 E. Main, Suite C, 505-327-9684)
Las Cruces 88001 (230 S. Water St., 575-523-9826)
Santa Fe 87505 (2209 Brothers Rd., Suite 110, 505-988-6562)

National Cemeteries:
Fort Bayard 88036 (P.O. Box 189, 915-564-0201)
Santa Fe 87501 (501 N. Guadalupe St., 505-988-6400 or toll-free 877-353-6295)

NEW YORK
VA Medical centers:
Albany 12208 (113 Holland Ave., 518-626-5000)
Batavia 14020 (222 Richmond Ave., 585-297-1000 or 888-798-2302)
Bath 14810 (76 Veterans Ave., 607-664-4000 or 877-845-3247)
Bronx 10468 (130 West Kingsbridge Rd., 718-584-9000 or 800-877-6976)
Brooklyn 11209 (800 Poly Place, 718-836-6600)
Buffalo 14215 (3495 Bailey Ave., 716-834-9200 or 800-532-8387)
Canandaigua 14424 (400 Fort Hill Ave., 585-394-2000)

Castle Point 12511 (Route 9D, 845-831-2000)

Montrose 10548 (2094 Albany Post Rd., Route 9A, 914-737-4400)

New York 10010 (423 East 23rd Street, 212-686-7500)

Northport 11768 (79 Middleville Road, 631-261-4400 or 800-551-3996)

Syracuse 13210 (800 Irving Ave., 315-425-4400 or 800-792-4334)

Domicialiary:

Jamaica 11425 (St. Albans Primary & Extended Care Center, 179-00
Linden Blvd. & 179 St., 718-526-1000)

Montrose 10548 ((2094 Albany Post Rd., Route 9A, P.O. Box 100, 914-737-4400)

Clinics:

Auburn 13021 (17 Lansing St., 315-255-7002)

Bainbridge 13733 (109 North Main St., 607-967-8590)

Bay Shore 11706 (132 E. Main Street, 631-754-7978)

Binghamton 13901 (Garvin Building, 425 Robinson St., 607-772-9100)

Brooklyn 11201 (40 Flatbush Ave. Extension, 8th Fl., 718-439-4300)

Carmel 10512 (Provident Savings Bank, 2nd Fl, 1875 Rt 6, 845-228-5291)

Carthage 13619 (3 Bridge St., 315-493-4180)

Catskill 12414 (Columbia Greene Medical Arts Building, Suite A102, 159,
Jefferson Hgts, 518-943-7515

Clifton Park 12065 (1673 Route 9, 518-383-8506)

Cortland 13045 (1104 Commons Avenue, 607-662-1517)

Dunkirk 14048 (166 East 4th St., 800-310-5001)

Dunkirk 14048 (166 East 4th St., 716-203-6474)

East Meadow 11554 (2201 Hempstead Turnpike, Bld. Q 631-754-7978)

Elizabethtown 12932 (75 Park St., PO Box 277 518-873-6377)

Elmira 14901 (200 Madison Avenue Suite 2E, 877-845-3247

Fonda 12068 (2623 State Highway 30A, 518-853-1247)

Glens Falls 12801 (84 Broad St., 518-798-6066)

Goshen 10924 (30 Hatfeld Lane, Suite 204, 845-294-6927)

Ithaca 14850 (10 Arrowwood Drive, 607-274-4680)

Jamestown 14701 (608 W. 3rd St., 716-338-1511)

Kingston 12401 (63 Hurley Ave., 845-331-8322)

Lackawanna 14218 (OLV Family Care Center, 227 Ridge Rd., 716-822-5944)

Lockport 14094 (5883 Snyder Dr., 716-438-3890)

Malone 12953 (3372 State Route 11 Main Street, 518-483-1529)

Massena 13662 (Memorial Hospital, 1 Hospital Dr., 315-769-4253)

Monticello 12701 (55 Sturgis Road, 845 791-4936)

New City 10956 (345 North Main Street, 845-634-8942)

New York 10027 (55 West 125th St., 646-273-8125)

New York 10011   (Opiate Substitution Program, 437 W 16 St., 646-273-8100)

Niagara Falls 14301-2300 (2201 Pine Avenue, 716-862-8580

Olean 14760-2658 (465 North Union St., 716- 373-7709)

Oswego: 13126 (437 State Route 104 E, 315-207-0120)

Patchogue 11772 (4 Phyllis Drive, 631-475-6610 /PC 631-758-4419)

Pine Plains 12567 (2881 Church St., Rt. 199, 518-398-9240)

Plainview 11803 (1425 Old Country Rd.,)

Plattsburgh 12901 (80 Sharron Ave. 518-561-6247)

Port Jervis 12771 (150 Pike St., 845-856-5396)

Poughkeepsie 12603 (Rt. 55, 488 Freedom Plains Rd., Suite 120, 845-452-5151)

Riverhead 11901 (300 Centre Cr., 631-754-7978

Rochester 14620 (465 Westfall Rd., 585-463-2600)

Rome 13441 (125 Brookley Road, Building 510, 315-334-7100)

Schenectady 12308 (1322 Gerling Street, Sheridan Plaza, 518-346-3334)

Springville 14141 (27 Franklin Street, Suite 1 716 592-7400)

Staten Island 10314 (1150 South Ave, 3rd Floor – Suite 301, 718-761-2973)

Sunnyside 11104 (47-01 Queens Blvd., 718-741-4800)

Troy 12180 (295 River St., 518-274-7707)

Valley Stream 11580 (99 S. Central Ave., 631-754-7978)

Warsaw 14569 (Wyoming County Community Hospital, 400 North Main St., 585-786-8940x4960)

Wellsville 14895 (3458 Riverside Dr., Route 19, 1-877-845-3247)

White Plains 10601 (23 South Broadway, 914-421-1951)

Yonkers 10705 (124 New Main St., 914-375-8055)

Regional Offces:

Buffalo 14202 (Niagara Center, 130 S. Elmwood Ave., 1-800-827-1000)
     (Serves counties not served by New York City VA Regional Offce.)

New York City 10014 (245 W. Houston St., statewide 1-800-827-1000)
     (Serves counties of Albany, Bronx, Clinton, Columbia, Delaware, Dutchess,

Essex, Franklin, Fulton, Greene, Hamilton, Kings, Montgomery, Nassau, New York,

Orange, Otsego, Putnam, Queens, Rensselaer, Richmond, Rockland, Saratoga,

Schenectady, Schoharie, Suffolk, Sullivan, Ulster, Warren, Washington, Westchester.)

Benefts Offces:

Albany 12208 (113 Holland Ave., 1-800-827-1000)

Rochester 14620 (465 Westfall Rd., 1-800-827-1000)

Syracuse 13202 (344 W. Genesee St., 1-800-827-1000)

Vet Centers:

Albany 12205 (17 Computer Drive West., 518-626-5130)

Babylon 11702 (116 West Main St., 631-661-3930)

Binghamton 13901 (53 Chenango St,. 607-722-2393)

Bronx 10468 (2471 Morris Avenue, Suite 1A 718-367-3500)
Brooklyn 11201 (25 Chapel St., Suite 604, 718-624-2765)
Buffalo 14228 (2372 Sweet Home Road, 716-862-7350)
Middletown 10940 (726 East Main street Suite 203 845-342-9917)
New York 10004 (32 Broadway, Suite 200, 212-742-9591)
New York 10035 (2279 3rd Avenue, 212-426-2200)
Rochester 14620 (1867 Mt. Hope Ave., 585-232-5040)
Staten Island 10301 (150 Richmond Terrace, 718-816-4499)
Syracuse 13210 (716 E. Washington St., 315-478-7127)
White Plains 10601 (300 Hamilton Ave., 1st Fl., Suite C 914-682-6250)
Watertown 02601 (210 Court St., 315-782-0217
Woodhaven 11421 (75-10B 91st Ave., 718-296-2871)
Plainview 11803 (1425 Old Country Rd. 516-572-8455)

National Cemeteries:
Bath 14810 (76 Veterans Ave., San Juan Ave., 607-664-4853/4806)
Calverton 11933-1031 (210 Princeton Blvd., 631-727-5410/5770)
Cypress Hills 11208 (625 Jamaica Ave., Brooklyn, 631-454-4949)
Long Island 11735-1211 (2040 Wellwood Ave., Farmingdale, 631-454-
    4949)
Saratoga 12871-1721 (200 Duell Rd., Schuylerville, 518-581-9128)
Woodlawn 14901 (1825 Davis St., Elmira, 607-732-5411)

NORTH CAROLINA
VA Medical centers:
Asheville 28805 (1100 Tunnel Road, 828-298-7911 or 800-932-6408)
Durham 27705 (508 Fulton St., 919-286-0411)
Fayetteville 28301 (2300 Ramsey St., 910-488-2120 or 800-771-6106)
Salisbury 28144 (1601 Brenner Avenue, 704-638-9000 or 800-469-8262)

Clinics:
Charlotte 28213 (8601 University East Drive, 704-597-3500)
Durham 27705 (1824 Hillandale Road, 919-383-6107)
Fayetteville 28304 (1991 Fordham Drive, 910-822-7998)
Franklin 28734 (647 Wayah St., 828-369-1781)
Greenville 27858 (800 Moye Blvd., 252-830-2149)
Hamlet 28345 (100 Jefferson St., 910-582-3536)
Hickory 28602 (2440 Century Place, SE, 828-431-5600)
Midway Park 28544 241 Freedom Way, Suite 1 910-353-6406
Morehead City 28557 (5420 Highway 70, 252-240-2349)
Pembroke 28372 (139 Three Hunts Drive, 910-521-8452)
Raleigh 27610 (3305 Sungate Blvd., 919-212-0129)
Raleigh 27603 (3040 Hammond Business Place, Suite 105, 919-899-6259)
Raleigh/Brier Creek 28617 (8081 Arco Corporate Drive, Suite 130, 919-
286-5220)

Rutherford 28139 (374 Charlotte Road 828-288-2780
Wilmington 28401 (736 Medical Center Drive, Suite 102, 910-763-5979)
Winston-Salem 27103 (190 Kimel Park Dr., 336-768-3296)
Winston-Salem Annex 27127 (2101 Peters Creek Parkway, 336-761-5300)

Regional Offce:
Winston-Salem 27155 (Federal Bldg., 251 N. Main St., statewide 1-800-827-1000,
Benefts Delivery at Discharge Offce Winston-Salem 27101 (Attn: BDD, 100 N. Main St., Ste 1700)
Quick Start Offce Winston-Salem 27101 (Attn: Quick Start, Federal Bldg, 100 N. Main Street. Suite 1900
Nationwide Loan Guaranty Certifcate of Eligibility Center 1-888-244-6711

Vet Centers:
Charlotte 282602 (2114 Ben Craig Drive, Suite 300, 704-549-8025)
Fayetteville 28311 (4140 Ramsey St., Suite 110, 910-488-6252)
Greensboro 27406 (2009 S. Elm-Eugene St., 336-333-5366)
Greenville 27834 (1021 WH Smith Blvd., Suite 100, 252-355-7920)
Jacksonville 28540 (110A Branchwood Drive, Dr., 919-672-0814)
Raleigh 27604 (1649 Old Louisburg Rd., 919-856-4616)

National Cemeteries:
New Bern 28560 (1711 National Ave., 252-637-2912)
Raleigh 27610-3335 (501 Rock Quarry Rd., 252-637-2912)
Salisbury 28144 (501 Statesville Blvd., 704-636-2661/4621)
Wilmington 28403 (2011 Market St., 252-637-2912)

NORTH DAKOTA
VA Medical Center:
Fargo 58102 (2101 Elm Street, 701-232-3241 or 800-410-9723)

Clinics:
Bismarck 58503 (2700 State Street, 701-221-9152)
Dickinson 58601 (33 9th Street, 701-483-6017)
Grafton 58237 (Developmental Center Health Service Building, West Sixth Street, 701-352-4059)
Grand Forks 3221- (32nd Ave. S. Grand Forks, ND 58201 701-335-4380)
Jamestown 58401 (2430 20th St. SW, Suite 8 701-952-4787)
Minot 58705 (10 Missile Avenue, 701-727-9800)
Williston 58801 (205 Main Street, Williston ND 58801   701-572-2470)

Regional Offce:
Fargo 58102 (2101 Elm St., statewide 1-800-827-1000)

Vet Centers:
Bismarck 58501 (1684 Capital Way, 701-224-9751)
Fargo 58103 (3310 Fiechtner Dr., Suite 100, 701-237-0942)
Minot 58701 (1400 20th Avenue SW, Suite 22041 3rd St. N.W., 701-852-0177)

OHIO

VA Medical centers:
Chillicothe 45601 (17273 State Route 104, 740-773-1141 or 800-358-8262)
Cincinnati 45220 (3200 Vine Street, 513-861-3100 or 888-267-78730)
Cleveland 44106 (10701 East Blvd., 216-791-3800)
Columbus 43209 (420 N. James Road, 614-257-5200 or 888-615-9448)
Dayton 45428 (4100 W. 3rd Street, 937-268-6511 or 800-368-8262)

Clinics:
Akron 44319 (55 W. Waterloo 330-724-7715)
Ashtabula 44004 (1230 Lake Avenue, 866-463-0912)
Athens 45701 (510 West Union Street 740-593-7314)
Cambridge 43727 (2146 Southgate Pkwy., 740-432-1963)
Canton 44702 (733 Market Avenue South, 330-489-4600)
Cincinnati 45245 (4355 Ferguson Drive, Suite 270, 513-943-3680)
Cleveland 44113 (4242 Loraine Ave., 216-939-0699)
Clermont County 45244 (4600 Beechwood Road)
East Liverpool 43920 (15655 St Rt. 170, 330-386-4303)
Gallipolis 45631 (323A Upper River Road, 740-446-3934)
Georgetown 45121 (4903 State Route 125, 937-378-3414)
Grove City 43123 (1955 Ohio Drive, 614-257-5800)
Hamilton 45011 (1750 South Erie Highway, (513) 870-9444)
Lancaster 43130 (1703 N. Memorial Dr. 740-653-6145)
Lima 45804 (1303 Bellefontaine Ave., 419-222-5788)
Lorain 44052 (205 West 20th Street, 440-244-3833
Mansfeld 44906 (1456 Park Avenue West, 419-529-4602)
Marietta 45750 (418 Colegate Drive, 740-568-0412)
Marion 43302 (1203 Delaware Avenue, Corporate Center #2, 740-223-8089)
Middletown 45042 (4337 N. Union Road, 513-423-8387)
New Philadelphia 44663 (1260 Monroe Ave., Suite 1A, New 330) 602-5339)
Newark 43055 (1912 Tamarck Rd., 740-788-8329)
Painesville 44077 (7 West Jackson Street, 440-357-6740)
Portsmouth 45622 (840 Gallia St., 740-353-3236)
Ravenna 44266 (6751 N. Chestnut St., 330-296-3641)
Sandusky 44870 (3416 Columbus Avenue, 419-625-7350)
Springfeld 45505 (512 South Burnett Road, 937-328-3385
St. Clairsville 43950 (103 Plaza Dr., Suite A, 740-695-9321 or 740-695-

3721)
Toledo 43614 1200 S. Detroit Ave.,, 419-259-2000)
Warren 44485 (1400 Tod Ave. (NW), 330-392-0311)
Wilmington 45177 (448 West Main Street, 937-382-3949)
Youngstown 44505 (2031 Belmont Avenue, 330-740-9200)
Zanesville 43701 (2800 Maple Avenue, 740-453-7725)

Regional Offce:
Cleveland 44199 (Anthony J. Celebrezze Fed. Bldg., 1240 E. 9th St.,
   1-800-827-1000)

Benefts Offces:
Cincinnati 45202 (36 E. Seventh St., Suite 210, 1-800-827-1000)
Columbus 43219 (420 N. James Road, 1-800-827-1000)

Vet Centers:
Cincinnati 45203 (801-B W. 8th Street., Suite 126, 513-763-3500)
Cleveland 44137-1915 (5310-1/2 Warrensville Center Road, 216-707-
7901)
Columbus 43215 (30 Spruce St., 614-257-5550)
Columbus 43215 (30 Spruce St., 614-257-5550)
Dayton ,45417 (627 E. Medical Plaza, 6th Floor, Edwin C. Moses Blvd.,
937-461-9150)
Maple Heights 44137 (5310 1/2 Warrensville Center Road, 216-707-7901)
(Previously Cleveland Heights)
Parma 44129 (5700 Pearl Rd., Suite 102, 440-845-5023)
Toledo 43614 (1565 S. Byrne Rd., Suite 104, 419-213-7533)

National Cemeteries:
Dayton 45428-1088 (4100 W. Third St., 937-262-2115)
Ohio Western Reserve 44270 (10175 Rawiga Rd. PO Box 8 Rittman, 330-
   335-3069)

OKLAHOMA
VA Medical centers:
Muskogee 74401 (1011 Honor Heights Drive, 918-577-3000 or 888-397-
   8387)
Oklahoma City 73104 (921 NE 13th Street, 405-456-1000)

Clinics:
Ada (301 N. Monte Vista, 580-436-2262)
Altus 73521 (201 S. Park Lane. 580-482-9020)
Ardmore: 73401 (2002 12th Ave. NW, Suite E, 580-226-4580)
Enid 73701 (915 E. Garriott, Suite G., 580-242-5100)
Fort Sill 73503 (4303 Pittman and Thomas Bldg. 580-585-5600)

Jay (1569 North Main Street 918-253-1900 or 888-424-8387)
Hartshorne 74547 (1429 Pennsylvania Ave., 888-878-1598)
Stillwater 74074 (320 N. Perkins Ave., 405-624-0334)
Tulsa 74145 (9322 East 41st St., 918-628-2500)
Ponca City/Blackwell 74631 (1009 W. Ferguson Ave, 580-363-0052)
Vinita 74301 (269 S. 7th St. 918-713-5400)
Wichita Falls 76301 (1800 7th Street, 940-723-2373)
Oklahoma City Satellite Clinic "North May Clinic" 73120 (2915 Pine Ridge Road, 405-752-6500)

Regional Offce:
Muskogee 74401 (Federal Bldg., 125 S. Main St., Compensation & Pension: 1-800-827-1000, Education National Call Center: 1-888-442-4551, National Direct Deposit: 1-877-838-2778)

Benefts Offce:
Oklahoma City 73102 (Federal Campus, 301 NW 6th St., Suite 113, 1-800-827-1000)
Tulsa 74145 (Ernest Childers Outpatient Clinic, 9322 East 41 St, Room 220, 1-800-827-1000)

Vet Centers:
Lawton 73501 (1016 SW, C Avenue **Suite** B, 580-585-5885)
Oklahoma City 73118 (1024 N.W. 47th, 405-270-5184)
Tulsa 74134- (14002 E. 21st Street, Suite 200, 918-628-2760)

National Cemeteries:
Fort Gibson 74434 (1423 Cemetery Rd., 918-478-2334)
Fort Sill 73538 (2648 NE Jake Dunn Rd., 580-492-3200)

OREGON
VA Medical centers:
Portland 97239 (3710 SW U.S. Veterans Hospital Rd., 503-220-8262 or outside Portland area 800-949-1004)
Roseburg 97470 (913 NW Garden Valley Blvd., 541-440-1000 or 800-549-8387)
Southern Oregon Rehabilitation Center and Clinics (97503, 8495 Crater Hwy, 541-826-2111)

Clinics:
Bandon 97411 (1010 1st Street, SE, Suite 100, 541-347-4736)
Bend 97701 (2650NE Courtney Dr., 503-220-8262 or outside Portland area 800-949-1004)
Boardman Telehealth 97818 (2 Marine Dr., Ste 103, 541-481-2255)
Brookings 97415 (555 Fifth Street, 541-412-1152)
Burns-Hines Outreach Clinic 97720 (271 N. Egan Burns, OR 541-573-

8869)

Community Resource and Referral Center (308 SW 1st Ave. 503–808-1256 or toll free at 1-800-949-1004 Ext. 51256)

Enterprise Telehealth 97828 (401 NE 1st St., 541-526-0219)

Eugene 97404 (100 River Ave., 541-607-0897)

Grants Pass 97525 (520 SW Ramsey Ave., Suite 102, 541-955-5551)

Hillsboro 97006 (1925 Amber Glen Parkway Ste #300, 503-906-5000 or outside Portland area 800-949-1004)

Klamath Falls 97601 (2819 Dahlia St., 541-273-6206)

La Grande 97850 (202 12th St., 541-963-0627)

Lakeview 97630 (1130 North 4th St., 541-273-6206)

Newport Outreach Clinic (1010 SW Coast Highway, Newport 541-265-4182 or outside Portland area 800-949-1004)

Eat Portland 97220 (10535 NE Glisan St., Gateway Medical Bldg., 2nd Fl., 503-220-8262, or outside Portland area 800-949-1004

Salem 97301 (1660 Oak Street SE, 503-220-8262 or outside Portland area 800-949-1004)

Salem 97301 (1660 Oak Street SE Ste #100, 503-220-8262, or outside Portland area 800-949-1004)

Warrenton 97146 (91400 Rilea Neacoxie St., Building 7315, 503-220-8262, or outside Portland area 800-949-1004)

White City 97503 Rehab & Clinics (8495 Crater Lake Hwy., 541-826-2111)

Regional Offce:
Portland 97204 (100 SW Main St. FL2., 1-800-827-1000)

Vet Centers:
Eugene 97403 (1255 Pearl St., 541-465-6918)

Grants Pass 97526 (211 S.E. 10th St., 541-479-6912)

Portland 97220 (8383 N.E. Sandy Blvd., Suite 110, 503-273-5370)

Salem 97301 (12645 Portland road, NE., Suite 250

National Cemeteries:
Eagle Point 97524 (2763 Riley Rd., 541-826-2511)

Roseburg 97470 (1770 Harvard Blvd, 541-826-2511)

Willamette 97266-6937 (11800 S.E. Mt. Scott Blvd., Portland, 503-273-5250)

PENNSYLVANIA
VA Medical centers:
Altoona 16602 (2907 Pleasant Valley Boulevard, 814-943-8164)

Butler 16001 (325 New Castle Road, 724-287-4781 or 800-362-8262)

Coatesville 19320 (1400 Black Horse Hill Road, 610-384-7711 ext. 4239)

Erie 16504 (135 East 38 Street, 814-868-8661 or 800-274-8387)

Lebanon 17042 (1700 South Lincoln Avenue, 717-272-6621 or 800-409-8771)

Philadelphia 19104 (3900 Woodland Avenue, 800-949-1001 or 215-823-5800)

Pittsburgh 15260 (H. John Heinz Progressive Health Center, 1010 Delafeld Road, 866-482-7488 or 412-822-2222)

Pittsburgh 15240 (University Drive Division: University Drive, 412-688-6000 or 1-866-482-7488)

Wilkes-Barre 18711 (1111 East End Blvd., 570-824-3521

Clinics:

Allentown 18103 (3110 Hamilton Boulevard, 610-776-4304 or 866-249-6472)

Bangor 18013 (701 Slate Belt Boulevard, 610-599-0127)

Bradford 16701 (23 Kennedy Street, Suite 101, 814-368-3019)

Berwick 18603 (301 W. Third Street, 570-759-0351)

Camp Hill 17011 (25 N. 32nd Street, 717-730-9782)

Camp Hill 17011 (25 N. 32nd Street, 717-730-9782)

Cranberry Township 16066 (Freedom Square, 1183 Freedom Road, Suite A101, 724-741-3131)DuBois 15801 (190 West Park Avenue, Suite 8, 814-375-6817)

Ellwood City 16117 (Ellwood City Hospital, Medical Arts Building, Suite 201, 304 Evans Drive 724-285-2203)

Foxburg 16036 (ACV Medical Center, 855 Route 58, Suite 1, 724-659-5601)

Ford City 16226 (Klingensmith Building, 313 Ford City, Suite 2B, 724-763-4090) Frackville 17931 (10 East Spruce St., 570-874-4289)

Franklin 16323 (Venango County Clinic, Pennwood Center, 464 Allegheny Boulevard, 866-962-3260

Greensburg 15601 (5274 Route 30 East, Suite 10, 724-216-0317)

Hermitage 16148 (295 N. Kerrwood Dr., Suite 110, 724-346-1569)

Horsham 19044 (433 Caredean Dr., 215-823-6050)

Johnstown 15904 (1425 Scalp Ave., Suite 29, 814-266-8696)

Kittanning 16201 (Armstrong Memorial Hospital 1 Nolte Dr., 724-543-8711)

Lancaster 17605 (1861 Charter Lane, Green Field Corporate Center, Suite 121, 717-290-6900)

Meadville 16335 (16954 Conneaut Lake Road, 866-962-3210)

Monaca 15061 (90 Wagner Rd., 724-709-6005)

New Castle 16101 (Ridgewood Professional Centre, 1750 New Butler Road, 724-598-6080)

Northampton Clinic & Rehab Ctr (701 Slate Belt Boulevard Bangor 610-597-0127)

Parker 16049 (ACV Medical Center, 855 Route 58, Suite 1, 724-659-5601)

Pottsville 17901 (Good Samaritan Medical Mall, 700 Schuylkill Manor Road, Suite 6, 570-621-4115)

Reading 19601 (St. Joseph's Community Center, 145 N. 6th St., 610-208-4717)

Sayre 18840 (1537 Elmira St., 570-888-6803)

Schuylkill 17972 (6 South Greenview Rd., 570-621-4115)

Spring City 19475 (11 Independence Drive 610-384-7711 ext. 4239)

Springfeld 19064 (Crozer Keystone Healthplex, 194 W. Sproul, Road, Suite 105, 610-384-7711 ext. 4239)

State College 16801 (3048 Enterprise Drive, 814-867-5415)

Tobyhanna 18466 (Tobyhanna Army Depot Building 220, 570-615-8341)

Uniontown 15401 (635 Pittsburg Rd., Suite 520, 724-439-4990)

Warren 16365 (3 Farm Colony Dr., 866-682-3250)

Washington 15301 (Washington Crown Center Mall, Room 450, 1500 West Chestnut St, 724-250-7790)

Wilkes-Barre 18711 (1111 East End Boulevard, 570-824-3521)

Williamsport 17701 (1705 Warren Avenue, Werner Building – 3rd Floor, Suite 304, 570-322-4791)

York 17402 (2251 Eastern Boulevard, 717-840-2730 or 717-854-2322)

Benefts Offce:

Wilkes-Barre 18702 (1123 East End Blvd., Bldg. 35, Suite 11, 1-800-827-1000)

Regional Offce:

Philadelphia 19101 (P.O. Box 8079, 5000 Wisssahickon Avenue, statewide 1-800-827-1000) - Serves counties in Pennsylvania: Adams, Berks, Bradford,

Bucks, Cameron, Carbon, Centre, Chester, Clinton, Columbia, Dauphin, Delaware, Franklin, Juniata, Lackawanna, Lancaster, Lebanon, Lehigh, Luzerne, Lycoming, Miffin, Monroe, Montgomery, Montour, Northampton, Northumberland, Perry, Philadelphia, Pike, Potter, Schuylkill, Snyder, Sullivan, Susquehanna, Tioga, Union, Wayne, Wyoming, York. Serves counties in New Jersey: Atlantic, Burlington, Camden, Cape May, Cumberland, Gloucester, Salem).

Pittsburgh 15222 (William S. Moorehead Federal Building, 1000 Liberty Ave. stateside 1-800-827-1000) - Serves counties in Pennsylvania: Allegheny, Armstrong, Beaver, Bedford, Blair, Butler, Cambria, Clarion, Clearfeld, Crawford, Elk, Erie, Fayette, Forest, Fulton, Greene, Huntington, Indiana, Jefferson, Lawrence, McKean, Mercer, Somerset, Venango, Warren, Washington, and Westmoreland. Serves counties in West Virginia: Brooke, Hancock. Marshall, and Ohio)

Vet Centers:

Bristol 19007 (2 Canal's End Plaza, Suite 201B, 215-823-4590)

Erie 16501 (1000 State St., Suite 1&2, 814-453-7955)

Dubois 15801 (100 Meadow Lane, Suite 8, 814-372-2095)

Harrisburg 17102 (1500 N. 2nd St., Suite 2, 717-782-3954)

McKeesport 15131 (2001 Lincoln Way, 412-678-7704)

Norristown 19401 (314 E. Johnson Highway, Suite 201, 215-823-5245)

Philadelphia 19107 (801 Arch St., Suite 102, 215-627-0238)

Philadelphia 19120 (101 E. Olney Ave., 215-924-4670)
Pittsburgh 15205 (2500 Baldwick Rd., Suite 15, 412-920-1765)
Scranton 18505 (1002 Pittston Ave., 570-344-2676)
Williamsport 17701 (49 E. Fourth Street, Suite 104, 570-327-5281)

National Cemeteries:
Indiantown Gap 17003-9618 (R.R. 2, P.O. Box 484, Indiantown Gap Rd., Annville, 717-865-5254/5)
Nat. Cem. of the Alleghenies 15017 (1158 Morgan Rd., Bridgeville, 724-746-4363)
Philadelphia 19138 (Haines St. & Limekiln Pike, 215-504-5610)
Washington Crossing 18940 (830 Highland Rd., Newtown, 215-504-5610)

PHILIPPINES

Clinics:
1302 Pasay City (1501 Roxas Boulevard, 011-632-318-8387, International Mailing Address: DPO
AP 96515)

Regional Offce:
1302 Pasay City (1501 Roxas Boulevard, 011-632-550-3888, International Mailing Address: DPO
AP 96515)

PUERTO RICO

Medical Center:
San Juan 00921-3201 (10 Casia Street, 787-641-7582 or 800-449-8729)

Clinics:
Arecibo 00612 (Victor Rojas II / Zona Industrial Carr. 129, 787-816-1818)
Guayama 00784 (FISA Bldg 1st Floor, Paseo Del Pueblo, km 0.3, lote no 6, 787-866-8766)
Mayagüez 00680-1507 (Avenida Hostos #345, 787-265-8805)
Ponce 00716-2001(Paseo Del Veterano #1010, 787-12-3030)

Regional Offce:
San Juan 00968-8024 (50 Carretera 165 Adjacent to El Nuevo Dia Building), Guaynabo. Serving all Puerto Rico and the Virgin Islands, 1-800-827-1000)

Benefts Offces:
Mayaguez 00680-1507 (Ave. Hostos 345, Carretera 2, Frente al Centro Medico, 1-800-827-1000)
Ponce 00731 (Paseo del Veterano #1010, 1-800-827-1000)
Arecibo 00612 (Victor Rojas II/ Zona Industrial Carr. 129, 1-800-827-1000)

Benefts Offces:
Mayaguez 00680-1507 (Ave. Hostos 345, Carretera 2, Frente al Centro Medico, 1-800-827-1000)
Ponce 00731 (10 Paseo del Veterano, 1-800-827-1000)
Arecibo 00612 (Gonzalo Marin 50, 1-800-827-1000)

Vet Centers:
Arecibo 00612-4702 (52 Gonzalo Marin St., 787-879-4510/4581)
Ponce 00731 (35 Mayo St., 787-841-3260)
San Juan 00921 (Condominio Med. Ctr. Plaza, Suite LC8A11, La Riviera, 787-749-4409)
National Cemetery:
Puerto Rico 00961 (Ave. Cementerio Nacional 50, Barrio Hato Tejas, Bayamon, 787-798-8400)

RHODE ISLAND
VA Medical Center:
Providence 02908 (830 Chalkstone Avenue, 401-273-7100 or 866-590-2976)

Clinic:
Middletown 02842 (One Corporate Place, 401-847-6239)

Regional Offce:
Providence 02903 (380 Westminster St.; statewide, 1-800-827-1000)

Vet Center:
Warwick 02889 (2038 Warwick Ave., 401-739-0167)

SOUTH CAROLINA
Regional Offce:
Columbia 29209 (6437 Garners Ferry Rd., statewide 1-800-827-1000)

VA Medical centers:
Charleston 29401 (109 Bee Street, 843-577-5011 or 888-878-6884)
Columbia 29209 (6439 Garners Ferry Road, 803-776-4000)

Clinics:
Aiken 29803 (951 Millbrook Ave., 803-643-9016)
Anderson 29621 (1702 E. Greenville Street, 864-224-5450)
Beaufort 29902 (Pickney Road, 843-770-0444)
Florence 29505 (1822 Sally Hill Farms Blvd. 843-292-8383)
Greenville 29605 (3510 Aug. a Rd., 864-299-1600)
Goose Creek 29445 (2418 NNPTC Circle, 843-577-5011 or 888-878-6884)
Myrtle Beach 29577 (3381 Phillis Blvd., 843-477-0177)

North Charleston 29406 (9237 University Blvd, 843-789-6400)
Orangeburg 29118 (1767 Villagepark Drive, 803-533-1335)
Rock Hill 29730 (205 Piedmont Blvd, 803-366-4848)
Spartanburg 29303 (279 North Grove Medical Park Drive, 864-582-7025)
Sumter 29150 (407 North Salem Avenue, 803-938-9901)
Nursing Home:
Walterboro 29488 (2461 Sidneys Road, Veterans Victory House, 843-538-3000)
Nursing Home:
Walterboro 29488 (2461 Sidneys Road, Veterans Victory House, 843-538-3000)

Regional Offce:
Columbia 29209 (6437 Garners Ferry Rd 1-800-827-1000)

Vet Centers:
Charleston 29406 (5603-A Rivers Avenue, 843-789-7000)
Columbia 29201 (11710-A Richland Street, 803-765-9944)
Greenville 29601 (14 Lavinia Ave., 864-271-2711)
North Charleston 29406 (5603-A Rivers Ave., 843-747-8387)

National Cemeteries:
Beaufort 29902-3947 (1601 Boundary St., 843-524-3925)
Florence 29501 (803 E. National Cemetery Rd., 843-669-8783)
Fort Jackson 29229 (4170 Percival Rd., Columbia, 803-699-2246)

SOUTH DAKOTA
VA Medical centers:
Fort Meade 57741 (113 Comanche Road, 605-347-2511 or 800-743-1070)
Hot Springs 57747 (500 North 5th Street, 605-745-2000 or 800-764-5370)
Sioux Falls 57105 (2501 W. 22nd Street, 605-336-3230 or 800-316-8387)

Clinics:
Aberdeen 57201 (2301 8th Ave. NE., Suite 225, 605-629-3500)
Eagle Butte 57625 (15 Main Street, 605-9672644)
McLaughlin, SD 57642 (302A Sale Barn Rd., 605-823-4574)
Mission 57555 (153 Main Street, 605-856-2295)
Pierre 57501 (1601 North Harrison, Suite 6, 605-945-1710)
Pine Ridge (605-718-1905)
Rapid City 57701 (3525 5th Street, 605-718-1095)
Wagner 57380 (400 W. Hwy. 46-50, 605-384-2340)
Watertown 57201 (917 29th St. SE, 605-884-2420)
Winner 57580 (1436 E. 10th St., 605-842-2443)

Regional Offce:
Sioux Falls 57105 (2501 W. 22nd St., statewide 1-800-827-1000)

Vet Centers:
Martin 57551 (105 East Hwy 18, 605-685-1300)
Rapid City 57701 (621 6th St., Suite 101, 605-348-0077)
Sioux Falls 57104 (601 S. Cliff Ave., Suite C, 605-330-4552)

National Cemeteries:
Black Hills 57785 (20901 Pleasant Valley Dr., Sturgis, 605-347-3830)
Fort Meade 57785 (P.O. Box 640, Old Stone Rd., Sturgis, 605-347-3830)
Hot Springs 57747 (500 N 5th St., 605-347-3830)

TENNESSEE
VA Medical centers:
Memphis 38104 (1030 Jefferson Avenue, 901-523-8990 or 800-636-8262)
Mountain Home 37684 (Corner of Lamont and Sydney Streets, P.O. Box
    4000, 423-926-1171 or 877-573-3529)
Murfreesboro 37129 (3400 Lebanon Pike, 615-867-6000 or 800-876-7093)
Nashville 37212 (1310 24th Avenue South, 615-327-4751 or 800-228-
    4973)

Clinics:
Bristol 24202 (2426 Lee Highway, Preston Square, 276-645-4520)
Chattanooga 37411 (150 Debra Rd., Suite 5200, Bldg. 6200, 423-893-
    6500)
Clarksville 37043 (1832 memorial St, 931-645-3552
Cookeville 38501 (851 S. Willow Avenue, Suite 108, 931-284-4060)
Covington 38127 (N. Memphis, 3461 Austin Peay Highway, 901-261-4500)
Dover 37058 (1021 Spring Street, 931-232-5329)
Dyersburg 38024 (433 East Parkview Street, 731-287-7289)
Jackson 38305 (180 Old Hickory Blvd, 731-661-2750)
Maury County (833 Nashville Highway 931-981-6930)
McMinnville (1014 S. Chancery Street, 931-474-7700)
Meharry (1818 Albion Street, Nashville, TN 615-873-6700)
Memphis 38116 (1056 East Raines Rd., 901-271-4900)
Morristown 37813 (925 E. Morris Blvd., 423-586-9100)
Nashville (Women's Clinic, 1919 Charlotte Ave 615-873-8000)
Norton 24273 (654 Highway 58 East, Virginia/KY Regional Center, 276-
    679-8010)
Knoxville 37923 (8033 Ray Mears Blvd. 865-545-4592)
Rogersville 37857 (401 Scenic Drive, 423-235-1471)
Savannah 38372 (765-A Florence Rd, 731-925-2300)
Tullahoma 37389 (225 First Street, 931-454-6134)

210

Regional Offce:
Nashville 37203 (110 9th Ave., South, statewide 1-800-827-1000)

Vet Centers:
Chattanooga 37411 (951 Eastgate Loop Rd., Bldg. 5700, Suite 300, 423-855-6570)

Johnson City 37604 (2203 McKinley Road, Suite 254, 423-928-8387)

Knoxville 37914 (2817 E. Magnolia Ave., 865-545-4680)

Memphis 38104 (1407 Union Ave., Suite 410, 901-544-0173)

Nashville 37217 (1420 Donelson Pike, Suite A-5, 615-366-1220)

National Cemeteries:
Chattanooga 37404 (1200 Bailey Ave., 423-855-6590)

Knoxville 37917 (939 Tyson St., N.W., 423-855-6590)

Memphis 38122 (3568 Townes Ave., 901-386-8311)

Mountain Home 37684 (P.O. Box 8, VAMC, Bldg. 117, 423-979-3535)

Nashville 37115-4619 (1420 Gallatin Rd. S., Madison, 615-860-0086)

TEXAS

VA Medical centers:
Amarillo 79106 (6010 Amarillo Boulevard West 806-355-9703 or 800-687-8262)

Big Spring 79720 (300 Veterans Blvd., 432-263-7361 or 800-472-1365)

Bonham 75418 (1201 E. 9th Street, 903-583-2111 or 800-924-8387)

Dallas 75216 (4500 South Lancaster Road, 214-742-8387 or 800-849-3597)

El Paso 79930 (5001 North Piedras Street, 915-564-6100 or 800-672-3782)

Harlingen 78550 (Health Care Center at Harlingen, 2601 Veterans Drive, 956-291-9000)

Houston 77030 (2002 Holcombe Blvd., 713-791-1414 or 800-553-2278)

Kerrville 78028 (3600 Memorial Blvd, 830-896-2020)

San Antonio 78229 (7400 Merton Minter Blvd., 210-617-5300 or 877-469-5300

Temple 76504 (1901 Veterans Memorial Drive, 254-778-4811 or 800-423-2111)

Waco 76711 (4800 Memorial Drive, 254-752-6581 or 800-423-2111)

Clinics:
Abilene 79602 (3850 Ridgemont Dr., 432-263-7361 or 800-472-1365)

Austin 78741 (7901 Montopolis Drive (relocating to, 512-389-1010 or 800-423-2111)

Beaumont 77707 (3420 Veterans Circle, 409-981-8550 or 1-800-833-7734)

Beeville 78102 (302 S. Hillside Dr., 361-358-9912 or 210-617-5300)

Bridgeport 76426 (806 Woodrow Wilson Ray Cir., 940-683-2538)

Brownwood 76801 (2600 Memorial Park Drive, 325-641-0568 or 800-423-

211

2111)

Bryan/College Station 77845 (1652 Rock Prairie Road, Suite 100, 979-680-0361)

Cedar Park 78613 (701 E. Whitestone Boulevard. 512-260-1368 or 800-423-2111)

Conroe 77304 (800 Riverwood Ct., Ste. 100, 936-522-4000 or 800-553-2278, ext. 1949)

Corpus Christi 78405 (5283 Old Brownsville Road, 361-806-5600)

Del Rio 78840 (1801 Bedell, 830-775-1166)

Denton 76205 (2223 Colorado Blvd., 940-891-6350)

El Paso 79936 (2400 Trawood Dr., Suite 200, 915-564-7880)

Fort Worth 76119 (2201 SE LOOP 820, 817-335-2202 or 800-443-9672)

Fort Stockton 79735 (2071 North Main St., 432-263-7361 or 800-472-1365)

Galveston 77550 (3828 Ave N, 409-761-3200 or 800-553-2278, ext. 12600)

Granbury 76049 (601 Fall Creek Hwy., 817-326-3902)

Greenville 75407 (4006 Wellington Rd., Ste. 100, 903-450-4788)

Harlingen 78550 (2106 Treasure Hills Blvd, 956-366-4500)

Katy (750 Westgreen Blvd opens in May 2013)

Kingsville 78363 (415 S. 6th Street, 361-592-3237)

La Grange 78945 (890 E. Travis Street 979-968-5878 or 800-423-2111)

Lake Jackson 77566 (208 Oak Drive South Lake Jackson 979-230-4852)

Laredo 78041 (6551 Star Court, 956-523-7850, reflls: 1-800-209-7377)

Longview 75601 (1005 North Eastman Road, 903-247-8262 or 800-957-8262)

Lubbock 79412 (6104 Avenue Q South Drive, 806-472-3400)

Lufkin 75904 (2206 North John Redditt Drive, 936-671-4300 or 1-800-209-3120)

McAllen 78503 (2101 S. Colonel Rowe Blvd, 956-618-7100 or 866-622-5536)

New Braunfels 78130 (189 E. Austin, Suite 106, 830-629-3614)

Northeast 78217 (2391 NE Loop 410 Suite 101, 210-590-0247)

Northwest 78228 (4318 Woodcock, Suite 120, 210-736-4051)

Odessa 79762 (4241 N. Tanglewood, Suite 201, 432-263-7361 or 800-472-1365)

Palestine 75801 (2000 So. Loop 256, Suite 124, 903-723-9006)

Paris 75460 (635 Stone Ave., 903-785-9900)

Pecan Valley 78222 (4243 E. Southcross, Suite 206, 210-337-4316)

Richmond 77469 (22001 Southwest Freeway, Ste. 200, 832-595-7700 or 1-800-553-2278, ext. 12800)

San Antonio 78240 (Frank M, Tejeda OPC, 5788 Eckhert Road, 210-699-2100)

San Antonio Dental Clinic 78299 (8410 Data Point, 210-949-8900)

San Angelo 76905 (2018 Pulliam, 432-263-7361)

San Antonio 78226 (1831 S. General McMullen, 210-434-4742)

Seguin 78155 (526 E. Court Street, 830-629-3614)
Sherman 75090 (3811 US 75N., 903-487-0477)
Stamford 79553 (1601 Columbia Street, 432-263-7361 or 800-472-1365)
SW Military 78221 (1714 SW Military, 210-923-1166 ext. 0777)
Temple 76502 (4501 S. General Bruce Dr., Suite 75, 254-771-9400 or 800-423-2111)
Texas City 77591 (9300 Emmett F. Lowry Expressway, Ste. 206, 1-800-553-2278 or 409-986-2900)
Tyler 75708 (3414 Golden Rd, 903-590-3050)
Tyler (Second location beginning in June:1827 Troop Hwy., Ste. 1827, Tyler, TX 75701)
Victoria 77901 (1908 North Laurent Street, Suite 150, 361-582-7700 or 800-209-7377)
Wichita Falls 76301 (1800 7th St., 940-723-2373)

Regional Offces:
Houston 77030 (6900 Almeda Rd., statewide, 713-383-1999 or 1-800-827-1000. Serves counties of Angelina, Aransas, Atacosa, Austin, Bandera, Bee, Bexar, Blanco, Brazoria, Brewster, Brooks, Caldwell, Calhoun, Cameron, Chambers, Colorado, Comal, Crockett, DeWitt, Dimitt, Duval, Edwards, Fort Bend, Frio, Galveston, Gillespie, Goliad, Gonzales, Grimes, Guadeloupe, Hardin, Harris, Hays, Hidalgo, Houston, Jackson, Jasper, Jefferson, Jim Hogg, Jim Wells, Karnes, Kendall, Kennedy, Kerr, Kimble, Kinney, Kleberg, LaSalle, Lavaca, Liberty, Live Oak, McCulloch, McMullen, Mason, Matagorda, Maverlck, Medina, Menard, Montgomery, Nacogdoches, Newton, Nueces, Orange, Pecos, Polk, Real, Refugio, Sabine, San Aug. ine, San Jacinto, San Patricio, Schleicher, Shelby, Starr, Sutton, Terrell, Trinity, Tyler, Uvalde, Val Verde, Victoria, Walker, Waller, Washington, Webb, Wharton, Willacy, Wilson, Zapata, Zavala)
Waco 76799 (One Veterans Plaza, 701 Clay Ave; statewide, 1-800-827-1000; serves the rest of the state. In Bowie County, the City of Texarkana is served by Little Rock, AR, VA Regional Offce, 1-800-827-1000.)

Benefts Offces:
Abilene 79602 (Taylor County Plaza Bldg., Suite 103, 400 Oak St., 1-800-827-1000)
Amarillo 79106 (6010 Amarillo Blvd. W., 1-800-827-1000)
Austin 78741 (2901 Montopolis Dr., Room 108, 1-800-827-1000)
Camp Mabry in Austin 78763 (Bldg. 10, Room 217, 1-800-827-1000)
Corpus Christi 78405 (4646 Corona Dr., Suite 150, 1-800-827-1000)
Dallas 75216 (4500 S. Lancaster Rd., 1-800-827-1000)
El Paso 79930 (5001 Piedras Dr., 1-800-827-1000)
Fort Hood 76544 (Bldg. 18010, Room A-308, 1-800-827-1000)
Ft. Worth 76119 (2201 SE Loop 820., 1-800-827-1000)
Lubbock 79410 (6104 Ave. Q S Drive, Rm. 132, 1-800-827-1000)

McAllen 78503 (109 Toronto Ave., 1-800-827-1000)
San Antonio 78240 (5788 Eckert Rd., 1-800-827-1000)
Temple 76504 (1901 Veterans Memorial Dr., Room 5G38 [BRB], 1-800-827-1000) (MWF 9:00-3:30)
Tyler 75701 (1700 SSE Loop 323, Suite 310, 1-800-827-1000)

Vet Centers:
Abilene 79602 (400 Oak St., 325-674-1328)
Amarillo 79109 (3414 Olsen Blvd., Suite E., 806-354-9779)
Austin 78741 (2015 S I.H. 35, Suite 101, 512-416-1314)
Corpus Christi 78411 (4646 Corona, Suite 250, 361-854-9961)
Dallas 75231 (10501 N. Central Expressway, Suite 213, 214-361-5896)
El Paso 79925 (1155 Westmoreland, Suite 121, 915-772-0013)
Fort Worth 76104 (1305 W. Magnolia, Suite B, 817-921-9095)
Harris County 77014 (14300 Cornerstone Village Dr., #110, 713-578-4002)
Houston 77098 (2990 Richmond Ave., Suite 325, 713-523-0884)
Houston 77024 (701 N. Post Oak Rd., Suite 102, 713-682-2288)
Jefferson County 77702, (990 IH 10 N, Suite 147, 409-981-8576)
Killeen Heights 76548 (302 Millers Crossing, Suite #4, 254-953-7100)
Laredo 78041 (6999 McPherson Rd.,102, 956-723-4680)
Lubbock 79410 (3106 50th St., 806-792-9782)
McAllen 78504 (801 W Nolana Loop, Suite 140, 956-631-2147)
Mesquite 75149 (502 West Kearney, Suite 300,972-288-8030)
Midland 79705 (2817 W. Loop 250N Suite E, 432-697-8222)
San Antonio NW 78254 (9910 W. Loop 1604 North, Suite 126, 210-688-0606)
Tarrant County 76013 (3337 W Pioneer Pkwy, 817-274-0981)

National Cemeteries:
Dallas-Fort Worth 75211 (2000 Mountain Creek Parkway, 214-467-3374)
Fort Bliss 79906 (Box 6342, 5200 Fred Wilson Rd., 915-564-0201)
Fort Sam Houston 78209 (1520 Harry Wurzbach Rd., San Antonio, 210-820-3891/3894)
Houston 77038 (10410 Veterans Memorial Dr., 281-447-8686)
Kerrville 78028 (VAMC, 3600 Memorial Blvd., 210-820-3891/3894)
San Antonio 78202 (517 Paso Hondo St., 210-820-3891/3894)

UTAH
VA Medical Center:
Salt Lake City 84148 (500 Foothill Drive, 801-582-1565 or 800-613-4012)

Clinics:
Ogden 84403 (982 Chambers Street, 801-479-4105)

Orem 84057 (1443 W. 800 North, Suite 302, 801-235-0953)
Price 84501 (189 South 600 West, Suite B, 435-613-0342)
Roosevelt 84066 (245 W. 200 N., 435-725-1050)
St. George 84770 (1067 East Tabernacle, Suite 7, 435-634-7608)
West Valley City 84120 (2750 South 5600 West, 801-582-1565)

Regional Offce:
Salt Lake City 84158 (P.O. Box 581900, 550 Foothill Dr., statewide 1-800-
  827-1000)

Vet Centers:
Provo 84604 (1807 No. 1120 West, 801-377-1117)
Salt Lake City 84106 (1354 East 3300 South, 801-584-1294)
Washington County 84770 (1664 S Dixie Dr, Suite C-105, 435-673-4494)

VERMONT
VA Medical Center:
White River Junction 05009 (215 North Main Street, 802-295-9363 or 866-
  687-8387)

Clinics:
Bennington 05201 (186 North Street, 802-447-6913)
Brattleboro 05301 (71 GSP Drive, 802-251-2200)
Colchester 05446 (162 Hegeman Ave., Unit 100, 802-655-1356)
Keene 03431 (640 Marlboro Road, Rte 101 603-358-4900)
Littleton, NH 03561 (685 Meadow St., Suite 4, 603-444-1323)
Newport 05855 (189 Prouty Drive, 802-334-4131)
Rutland 05701 (215 Stratton Road, 802-770-6713)

Rgional Offce:
White River Junction Junction 05009 (215 N. Main St., 1-800-827-1000)

Vet Centers:
Gorham, NH 03581 (515 Main St., 603-752-2571)
South Burlington 05403 (359 Dorset St., 802-862-1806)
White River Junction 05001 (222 Holiday Inn Dr., #2 Gilman Offce
  Complex, 802-295-2908 or 1-800-649-6603)

VIRGINIA
VA Medical centers:
Hampton 23667 (100 Emancipation Drive, 757-722-9961)
Richmond 23249 (1201 Broad Rock Boulevard, 804-675-5000 or 800-784-
  8381)
Salem 24153 (1970 Roanoke Boulevard, 540-982-2463 or 888-982-2463)

Clinics:

Alexandria 22310 (6940 South Kings Highway Suite #208, 703-313-0694)
Bristol 24202 (Preston Square, 2426 Lee Highway, Suite 200, 276-645-4520)
Charlottesville 22911 (650 Peter Jefferson Pkwy., Suite 160, 434-293-3890)
Covington 24426 (VFW Post #1033, 710 E. Dolly Anne Drive, 540-982-2463)
Danville 24540 (705 Piney Forest Rd., 434-710-4210)
Emporia 23847 (1746 East Atlantic Street, 434-348-1055)
Fredericksburg 22401 (1965 Jefferson Davis Hwy., Suite 100, 540-370-4468)
Harrisonburg 22801 (1755 S. High St., 540-442-1773)
Fort Belvoir (9300 DeWtt Loop 571-231-2408
Lynchburg 24501 (1600 Lakeside Drive, 434-316-5000)
Kernstown 22602 (170 Prosperity Drive, 540-869-0600)
Norton 24273 (654 Hwy 58 East, 276-679-8010)
Tazewell 24651 (123 Ben Bolt Ave., 276-988-2526)
Staunton 24401 (102 Business Way, 540-886-5777)
Stuarts Draft 24477 (3251 Stuarts Draft Hwy, VFW Post #9339, 540-982-2463)
Virginia Beach 23462 (244 Clearfeld Ave., 722-9961 ext 1900)
Winchester (170 Prosperity Drive 540-869-0600)
Wytheville 24382 (100 Peppers Ferry Road, 276-223-5400)

Regional Offce:

Roanoke 24016-1928 (116 North Jefferson Street, , statewide 1-800-827-1000)

Benefts Offces:

Hampton 23605 (5200 West Mercury Blvd., Suite 295)
Norfolk 23513 (2551 Eltham Avenue, Suite E)

Vet Centers:

Alexandria 22310 (86940 South Kings Highway, Suite 204, 703-360-8633)
Norfolk 23504 (1711 Church Street, Suite A & B, 757-623-7584)
Richmond 23230 (4902 Fitzhugh Ave., 804-353-8958)
Roanoke 24016 (350 Albemarle Ave., SW, 540-342-9726)
Virginia Beach 23452 (324 South Port Circle, Suite 102)

National Cemeteries:

Alexandria 22314 (1450 Wilkes St., 703-221-2183/2184)
Balls Bluff 22075 (Rte. 7, Leesburg, 540-825-0027)
City Point 23860 (10th Ave. & Davis St., Hopewell, 804-795-2031)
Cold Harbor 23111 (6038 Cold Harbor Rd., Mechanicsville, 804-795-2031)
Culpeper 22701 (305 U.S. Ave., 540-825-0027)

Danville 24541 (721 Lee St., 704-636-2661)
Fort Harrison 23231 (8620 Varina Rd., Richmond, 804-795-2031)
Glendale 23231 (8301 Willis Church Rd., Richmond, 804-795-2031)
Hampton 23667 (Cemetery Rd. at Marshall Ave., 757-723-7104)
Hampton 23669 (VAMC, Emancipation Dr., 757-723-7104)
Quantico 22172 (P.O. Box 10, 18424 Joplin Rd. (Rte. 619), Triangle 703-221-2183/2184)
Richmond 23231 (1701 Williamsburg Rd., 804-795-2031)
Seven Pines 23150 (400 E. Williamsburg Rd., Sandston, 804-795 2031/2278)
Staunton, 24401 (901 Richmond Ave., 540-825-0027)
Winchester 22601 (401 National Ave., 540-825-0027)

VIRGIN ISLANDS

Clinics:
St. Croix 00850-4701 (Village Mall, 16, Box 10553 RR02, Kingshill, 340-778-5553)
St. Croix (TMedical Foundation Bldg., Suite 1010, 50 Estate Thomas), Suite 304 & 310,
St. Thomas Medical Foundation, 340- 774-6674

Benefts:
Served by San Juan, Puerto Rico, VA Regional Offce, 1-800-827-1000

Vet Centers:
St. Croix 00850-4701 (Village Mall, 16, Box 10553 RR02, Kingshill, 340-778-5553)
St. Croix 00802 (St Thomas CBOC VI Medical Foundation 50 Estate Thomas, Suite 101) 340-774-6674

WASHINGTON

VA Medical centers:
American Lake 98493 (9600 Veterans Drive, Tacoma, 800-329-8387 or 253-582-8440)
Seattle 98108 (1660 S. Columbian Way, 800-329-8387 or 206-762-1010)
Spokane 99205 (4815 N. Assembly Street, 509-434-7000 or 800-325-7940)
Tacoma 98493 (9600 Veterans Dr., 253-582-8440 or 800-329-8387)
Vancouver 98661 (1601 E. 4th Plain Blvd, 360-696-4061 or 800-949-1004)
Walla Walla 99362 (77 Wainwright Drive, 509-525-5200 or 888-687-8863)

Clinics:
Bellevue 98005 (13033 Bel-Red Road, Suite 210, 425-214-1055)
Bremerton 98312 (925 Adele Avenue, 360-782-0129)
Federal Way 98003 (34617 11th Place South, 253-336-4142)
Mount Vernon 98274 (307 S. 13th Street, Suite 200, 360-848-8500)

Port Angeles 98362 (1005 Georgianna St., 360-565-9330)
Richland 99352 (Richland Federal Bldg., 825 Jadwin Ave., Ste. 250, 509-946-1020)
Seattle 98125 (12360 Lake City Way NE, Suite 200, 206-384-4382)
South Sound 98532 (151 NE Hampe Way Suite B2-6, Chehalis, 360-748-3049)
Wenatchee 98801 (2530 Chester-Kimm Road, 509-663-7615)
Yakima 98902 (717 Fruitvale Blvd., 509-966-0199)
Yakima Mental Health Clinic 98902 (2119 W. Lincoln Ave, 509-457-2736

Regional Offce:
Seattle 98174 (Fed. Bldg., 915 2nd Ave., statewide 1-800-827-1000)
Benefts Offces:
Fort Lewis 98433 (Waller Hall Rm. 700, P.O. Box 331153, 253-967-7106)
Bremerton 98337 (W. Sound Pre-Separation Center, 262 Burwell St., 360-782-9900)

Benefts Offces:
Joint Base Lewis McChord 98433 (Waller Hall Bldg 2140 Rm. 700 Mail Stop 62, P.O. Box 339500, 253-967-7106)
Bremerton 98337 (W. Sound Pre-Separation Center, 264 Burwell St., 360-782-9900)

Vet Centers:
Bellingham 98226 (3800 Byron Ave., Suite 124, 360-733-9226)
Everett 98201 (3311 Wetmore Ave., Everett, WA, 425-252-9701)
Seattle 98121 (2030 9th Ave., Suite 210, 206-553-2706)
South King County 98032 (32020 32nd Ave. S, Suite 110, 253-838-3090)
Spokane 99206 (100 N. Mullan Rd., Suite 102, 509-444-8387)
Tacoma 98409 (4916 Center St., Suite E, 253-535-7038)
Walla Walla 99362 (1104 Poplar St., 509-526-8387)
Yakima 98902 (2119 W. Lincoln Ave., 509-457-2736)

WEST VIRGINIA
VA Medical centers:
Beckley 25801 (200 Veterans Avenue, 304-255-2121 or 877-902-5142)
Clarksburg 26301 (One Medical Center Drive, 304-623-3461 or 800-733-0512)
Huntington 25704 (1540 Spring Valley Drive, 304-429-6741 or 800-827-8244)
Martinsburg 25405 (510 Butler Avenue, 304-263-0811 or 800-817-3807)

Clinics:
Charleston 25302 (104 Alex Ln., 304-926-6001)
Franklin 26807 (314 Pine Street, 304-358-2355)
Logan 25601 (403 Justice Avenue., 304-752-8355

218

Maxwelton 24957 (804 Industrial Park Road, 304-497-3900 or 1-877-902-5142)
Parkersburg 26101 (2311 Ohio Avenue, Suite A, 304-422-5114)
Parsons 26287 (206 Veterans Lane, 304-478-2219)
Petersburg 26847 (Grant Memorial Hospital, 117 Hospital Dr.,304-257-5817)
Sutton 26601 (93 Skidmore Lane, 304-765-3480)
Westover 26501 (40 Commerce Drive, Suite 101, 304-292-7535)

Regional Offce:
Huntington 25701 (640 Fourth Ave., statewide 1-800-827-1000; counties of Brooke, Hancock, Marshall, Ohio, served by Pittsburgh, Pa., VA Regional Offce)

Vet Centers:
Beckley 25801 (1000 Johnstown Rd. 304-252-8220)
Charleston 25302 (521 Central Ave., 304-343-3825)
Huntington 25701 (3135 16th St. Rd., Suite 11, 304-523-8387)
Martinsburg 25401 (900 Winchester Ave., 304-263-6776)
Morgantown 26501-3434 (34 Commerce Drive, Suite 101, 304-291-4303)
Princeton 24740 (905 Mercer St., 304-425-5653)
Wheeling 26003 (1054 Bethlehem Blvd.,304-232-0587)

National Cemeteries:
Grafton 26354 (431 Walnut St., 304-265-2044)
West Virginia 26354 (42 Veterans Memorial Ln, Grafton, 304-265-2044)

WISCONSIN

VA Medical centers:
Madison 53705 (2500 Overlook Terrace, 608-256-1901)
Milwaukee 53295 (5000 West National Avenue, 888-469-6614 or 414-384-2000)
Tomah 54660 (500 E. Veterans Street, 608-372-3971 or 800-872-8662)

Clinics:
Appleton 54914 (10 Tri-Park Way, 920-831-0070)
Baraboo 53913 (1670 South Boulevard, 608-356-9318)
Beaver Dam 53916 (215 Corporate Drive, Suite B, 920-356-9415)
Chippewa Falls 54729 ((2503 County Hwy, I , 715-720-3780)
Cleveland 53015 (1205 North Avenue, 920-693-5600)
Green Bay 54303 (141 Siegler Street, 920-497-3126)
Hayward 54843 (,15954 River's Edge Dr, Suite 103 715-934-5454)
Janesville 53545 (2419 Morse St. Suite 120 ,, 608-758-9300)
Kenosha 53140 (800 55th Street, 262-653-9286)

La Crosse 54601 (2600 State Road, Phone: 608-784-3886)
Owen 54460 (8 Johnson Street, 715-229-4701)
Rhinelander 54501 (639 West Kemp Street, 715-362-4080)
Rice Lake 54868 (2700A College Drive, 715-236-3355)
Superior 54880 (3520 Tower Avenue, 715-392-9711)
Union Grove 53182 (21425 Spring Street, 262-878-7001)
Wausau 54401 (515 South 32nd Avenue, 715-842-2834)
Wisconsin Rapids 53545 (555 W. Grand Ave, 715-424-4682)

Regional Offce:
Milwaukee 53214 (5400 W. National Ave., statewide 1-800-827-1000)

Vet Centers:
Madison 53703 (706 Williamson St., 608-264-5342)
Green Bay 54304 (1600 S. Ashland Avenue, 920-435-5650)
La Crosse 54601 (20 Copeland Ave, 608-782-4403)
Milwaukee 53218 (5401 N. 76th St., Suite 100 414-536-1301)

National Cemetery:
Wood 53295-4000 (5000 W. National Ave., Bldg. 1301, Milwaukee, 414-382-5300)

WYOMING
VA Medical centers:
Cheyenne 82001 (2360 E. Pershing Blvd., 307-778-7550 or 888-483-9127)
Sheridan (1898 Fort Road, 307-672-3473 or 866-822-6714)

Clinics:
Afton Outreach Clinic 83110 (125 S. Washington 307-886-5266)
Casper 82601 (4140 S. Poplar St., 307-235-4143 or 1-866-338-5168)
Evanston 82930 (Evanston Valley Business Park, 1565 S Highway 150 # E, 877-733-6128)
Gillette 82718 (604 Express Drive, 307-685-0676)
Newcastle 82701 (1124 Washington Blvd., 307-746-4491)
Powell 82435 (777 Avenue H, 307-754-7257 or 1-888-284-9308)
Riverton 82501 (2300 Rose Lane, 307-857-1211 or 1-866-338-2609)
Rock Springs 82901 (1401 Gateway Blvd., 307-362-6641 or 866-381-2830)
Worland 82401 (510 South 15th Suite D., 307-347-2808 or 877-483-0370)

Primary Care Telehealth Outreach Clinics:
Afton Outreach Clinic 83110 (125 S. Washington 307-886-5266)
Evanston 82930 (Evanston Valley Business Park, 1565 S Highway 150 #

E, 877-733-6128)
Rawlins PCTOC (1809 East Daley St. 307-324-5578)
Worland PCTOC (510 S 15th Street, Suite D 307-347-2808 or 877-483-0370

Mobile Telehealth Clinics:
307-778-7550 ext. 3816
Sterling, CO (Every Tuesday, 10:00 AM—5:00PM., American Legion, Post # 20, 1602 Hwy. 6)
Laramie, WY (Every Friday, 10:00 AM—3:00PM. WY Army Guard Armory, 2901 Armory Road)
Torrington, WY (Every Thursday, 10:00 AM—5:00PM. VFW Post 2908, 2908 West 25th Ave)
Wheatland, WY (Every Wednesday, 10:00 AM—3:00PM. Fire Dep't. Training Facility, 759 East Cole St.) Worland 82401 (1415 Howell Avenue, 877-483-0370)

Benefts Offce:
Cheyenne 82001 (2360 E. Pershing Blvd., statewide 1-800-827-1000)

Vet Centers: Casper 82601 (1030 North Poplar, Suite B, 307-261-5355)
Cheyenne 82001 (3219 East Pershing Blvd., 307-778-7370)

Index

About the Author
Judge Hal Moroz

~ ~ ~ ~ ~

"A wise man will hear, and will increase learning;
and a man of understanding shall attain unto wise counsels:
To understand a proverb, and the interpretation;
the words of the wise, and their dark sayings."
~~~ *Proverbs 1:5-6*

~ ~ ~ ~ ~

Hal Moroz is an Attorney & Counselor at Law, as well as a former Judge. He served as both a county Judge and a city Chief Judge in the State of Georgia. Judge Moroz is also a retired U.S. Army airborne Infantry officer, and longtime veterans advocate. In fact, for more than a decade Judge Moroz has trained lawyers on veterans law matters at legal seminars for the State Bar of Georgia, and represented U.S. military veterans around the world and before the U.S. Court of Appeals for Veterans Claims and the United States Supreme Court.

Judge Moroz is the founder of the Veterans Law Center, Inc., a non-profit, 501(c)(3) charitable organization that serves the interests of America's 24 million military veterans. Located on the internet at VeteransLawCenter.org, the Veterans Law Center provides support and counsel to America's honorably discharged veterans, wherever they may be, and they do this free of charge to them.

~ ~ ~ ~ ~

Hal Moroz can be reached through an internet search or through his email at the Veterans Law Center at moroz@veteranslawcenter.org or hal@morozlaw.com or his website: MorozLaw.com

~~~~~~~~~~

"With all the creative energy at our command, let us begin an era of national renewal. Let us renew our determination, our courage, and our strength. Let us renew our faith and our hope. We have every right to dream heroic dreams."
~~~ President Ronald Reagan
First Inaugural Address, January 20, 1981

"Whether therefore ye eat, or drink, or whatsoever ye do, do all to the glory of God."
~~~ Psalm 37:23

Postscript
Acknowledgements

~ ~ ~ ~ ~

"In every thing give thanks:
for this is the will of God in Christ Jesus concerning you."
~~~ 1 Thessalonians 5:18

~ ~ ~ ~ ~

I am thankful for all things! And, in particular, I am thankful for the encouragement of many friends, and I do mean friends, without whom this work would not have been possible.

Let me also take this opportunity to acknowledge the support and contributions of the State Bar of Georgia, particularly the *Georgia Bar Journal*, the U.S. Department of Veterans Affairs, the Veterans Law Center, and those fellow-military veterans who thought this work important enough to publish as a book.

And last, but not least, I am thankful for the legions of young American men and women, who, throughout our history, answered their country's call, and moved toward the sound of the cannon fire to secure this last best hope for man on earth. It will always be a source of pride and inspiration to me, that at a time in our world when men of courage and honor were few and hard to find, I stood amongst such giants in the U.S. Army Airborne Infantry!

~~~~~~~~~~

"Greater love hath no man than this,
that a man lay down his life for his friends."
~~~ John 15:13